Child Psychotherapy

Child Psychotherapy

S. R. SLAVSON

COLUMBIA UNIVERSITY PRESS

New York · 1952

MANUFACTURED IN THE UNITED STATES OF AMERICA

This volume is affectionately dedicated to
the memory of

JOHANN H. W. VAN OPHUIJSEN, M.D.

healer, teacher, and humanitarian

Preface

THE PRESENT VOLUME is an attempt to reflect the growing conviction of many who are working with people in various fields of endeavor that the individual cannot be viewed apart from the total setting in which he grows and lives. Economists, some of the more progressive sociologists, and cultural anthropologists have brought to bear their findings to buttress the age-long recognition of this fact. The more enlightened among the social scientists are accepting this ecological relationship of the individual to his total environment: physical, economic, familial, social, the total culture, and the values of the world in which he lives. These insights have penetrated the practices of law, medicine, and psychiatry, as well as all other formal and informal social services. I was among those who had the privilege some decades ago of pointing out this integrated relationship of the individual and his society.

While this book is primarily intended as a clinical study with special emphasis upon the treatment process of the emotionally disturbed and socially maladjusted child under twelve years of age, I found it advisable to point out other elements as well. Among them are the basic bio-psychological drives that actuate a human being toward making an effort for physical and psychological survival and self-realization and his need for inner and outer equilibria. To lay a sound foundation for clinical efforts, it seemed necessary to point up the various and multifarious forces and influences that shape the human personality in its dynamic movement toward health, as well as those that interfere with the trend toward wholeness.

These positive and negative forces emanate from the person of the individual, but are shaped and conditioned by environment. The most potent single patterning force is the family. But the family incorporates and reflects the physical, material, economic, and cultural climate of the wider world. The character of the family and the interpersonal relations in it determine the formation and malformation of the child's character and personality. It is against this backdrop of climate and events that the clinician must view the patients who come to him for corrective help. Only when the patient is understood in the total setting of his economic level, family, and culture can he be helped.

In view of these considerations, I have divided this book into three main parts: Development, Pathogenesis, and Psychotherapy. The first two are designed to place briefly before the reader the pertinent facts and information concerning the primary and basic life forces operating in the individual and the interferences with them, some of which are inherent in our particular civilization. Those deprivations, noxious entities, and pathogenic irritants to which he is subjected as a result of parental and other problems are evaluated, and the resulting syndromes are described. The third part attempts to delineate, in a fairly detailed manner, what corrective efforts are suitable to the particular personality problems that result from these interferences with healthy growth with which the psychotherapist has to deal.

No open-minded psychotherapist who has had experience with patients of various ages, social levels, and a variety of clinical entities can vouch for the universal effectiveness of any one technique. Experience and reflection cannot but lead to the inevitable conclusion that therapeutic measures must be suited to the nature and needs of the patient, as well as to the facilities, equipment, personality, and preferences of the psychotherapist himself. It is with this broad view and with what one may describe as "intellectual hospitality" that this book was conceived and executed.

No one can practice or write effectively on psychotherapy without recognizing that his roots go down to the sound bedrock of Freudian psychology and the gigantic formulations of that genius and father of all sound psychiatry and psychotherapy. This work is no exception to that rule. It is, however, equally inevitable that anyone with a broad view of his profession, who has worked within the framework of our dynamic and variegated society, should recognize the need for modifying practices to meet special needs even when fundamental concepts remain intact. This is even more true of work with children.

As the reader will find in the body of this volume, there are many and indisputable reasons why this is the case. The child's basic personality structure and ego organization are such that Freudian techniques, which were derived from experience with adult psychoneurotics, have to be vastly modified in child psychotherapy. This is in no way a repudiation of this master's work and his creation. I believe that it is rather a compliment to a master to acknowledge that his work permits flexibility and readaptation. In a personal conversation Freud himself stated: "I have dug the tunnel. Others will have to let in the light." Such is the attitude of real greatness, for only the great are secure enough to permit flexibility in their thinking; initiative on the part of others is no threat to them.

This volume is an outcome of four decades of work with people in many relationships and settings; the majority were children and adolescents. It also reflects almost twenty years of clinical experience that favored learning, experimentation, and reflection.

I am indebted to many writers and coworkers whose ideas I have either consciously adopted or unconsciously absorbed, but I hope that I have reevaluated and assimilated them in the context of my own thinking and convictions. I offer the final product of this protracted effort to the reader.

I am aware that many of the ideas contained in this volume may not be new, but it is hoped that new vigor and meaning is given them by a fresh restatement in a different context, in new relations, and in the integrative approach to the bio-psycho-social entity that is MAN. It has always been my conviction that an accumulation of facts without adequate knowledge for applying them may cause a form of intellectual and cultural indigestion that often proves to be a great disadvantage. Here an effort has been made to instrumentalize discrete facts by establishing their organic relation in the life of the individual and society and in the clinical work with children, as well as with adults.

I wish particularly to acknowledge my indebtedness to Dr. André Glaz for reading several portions of this book and for his valuable suggestions. However, I solely am responsible for all statements and conclusions.

S. R. Slavson

New York
June, 1952

Contents

PART THREE: PSYCHOTHERAPY

PART ONE

Development

I

Normal Needs in Child Development

SURVIVAL AS A MAJOR URGE

IN THE INTEREST OF CLARITY it is necessary to make some assumptions about the nature of man to serve as a frame of reference for the discussions in this volume. The lack of a common basis for understanding man, his nature, his urges, and his behavior, would inevitably lead to confusion. Lester F. Ward [1] has pointed out that there are distinct "modalities" in the various realms of nature, such as chemism, bathmism, zoism, and psychism (to which may also be added groupism). Actually, a basic characteristic of all living tissues and organisms (bathmism and zoism) is the urge to live and to survive. Furthermore, while this urge is observable in the behavior of individuals, its ultimate aim, which is also the prime intent of nature, is to assure the survival of the species. The death urge, or the urge to cease being, may or may not exist; at best it is subsidiary to the urge to live.[2] Consciously each organism struggles to continue its existence intact, and the urge to die cannot be conceived except as a perversion of the life urge, or Eros. In whatever form the drive to survive may manifest itself, in lower animals and humans this primary and major drive, namely, to conserve the individual and the species, constitutes the basis for understanding and evaluating human behavior in its complex and multifarious manifestations.

THE FOUR LIFE-PRESERVING FUNCTIONS

The physiological processes through which the survival of individual and species is secured involve three orifices: the mouth,

[1] Lester F. Ward, *Pure Sociology*, New York, Macmillan, 1911, p. 101.

[2] Freud's concept of Thanatos as opposed to Eros corresponds to the Hindu concept of the urge to return to Nirvana, or to become one with the infinite, from which, it is supposed, each entity had originally been separated.

the rectum, and the genitals. It is upon these orifices that life actually depends. The intake of food is achieved through the mouth, and the disposal of wastes through the rectum provides room for further intake of food. These processes are essential for the generation of the energies which sustain life in the individual. Sexual activity is the means provided by nature for the survival of the species.

To insure these three life-preserving functions, upon which survival of the individual and the species depend, both the activities and the organs (orifices) involved are cathexized, that is, they are endowed with intense pleasure. The pain of hunger and the pleasures concomitant to eating assure the organism's intake of food. Hunger and thirst set up physical tensions and psychological anxiety that activate the organism toward behavior leading to the intake of food. The assuaging of such tensions, on the other hand, yields pleasure and a sense of well-being. Delay in evacuation produces distress, while ejection of waste is accompanied by pleasure and a feeling of relief. Sexual activity is charged with intense pleasure, and delay or the absence of it gives rise to organic tensions and various psychological disturbances.

A fourth mechanism of survival, less discernible, is organ activity. Orderly and balanced activity of the internal organs of the body produces a kinesthetic equilibrium that results in a state of well-being. Similarly, adequate exertion of the muscles is essential to physical and emotional health. The use of the neuromuscular system yields pleasure and aids growth; inactivity or overexertion produces discomfort and tension and stunts growth. These four major activities are essential to all animals, but for man they involve in addition important psychological concomitants.

The infant's random, purposeless, and aimless jerky movements of arms and legs are known as "kyrokinesis." Often when a high pitch of such uncontrollable activity sets in, the infant's face grows red with tenseness and an expression akin to anxiety is registered. He is unable to stop the movements voluntarily, and it may become necessary for the mother or the nurse to prevent these movements and help the baby recover a state of quietus by gently holding down his arms and legs. Physiologically these kyrokinetic movements are a result of unsheathed nerves, which allow impulses to radiate within the nervous system rather than be canalized toward specific muscles. This canalization is established later in the child's organic development and appears as selective, inhibitory, and controlling mechanisms.

Kyrokinesis is followed by a more prolonged period of "microkinesis." This period is characterized by the comparatively purposeful and aim-directed movements and activity of the infant and child during which he is able to handle small objects only. It is the period of "small-muscle activity." Later these microkinetic activities are succeeded by "macrokinesis," or large-muscle activity, such as walking, running, and handling small objects. These various phases of instinctual motility are essential for the growing and evolving personality, for through them not only is growth of the organism aided but the child also acquires power to deal with and control his environment.

Activity has long been accepted by enlightened parents and teachers as the most sound means of education. It has also been recognized, though more recently, as essential to the treatment of mental and emotional disorders.[3] It is especially effective in treating children, who can communicate better by action than by language. Play therapy is based on activity, during which its patterns are carefully noted and their meaning interpreted. In group therapy with children, as well, activity is utilized. The use of activity in therapy is based on the well-established fact that not only is children's behavior significant but also under specific conditions it serves to strengthen the ego and redistribute the libido.

Most, if not all, of man's psyche is organized around the activities in the four areas described, and interference with them produces not only organic deficiency but also psychological tensions. Dr. Ribble[4] has shown, for example, that the sucking associated with food intake—hence with survival—is in itself a

[3] See S. R. Slavson and others, "Children's Activity in Casework Therapy," *Journal of Social Casework*, April, 1949.

[4] Margaret Ribble, *The Rights of Infants*, New York, Columbia University Press, 1943.

primary instinct and needs gratifications dissociated from ingestion of food. Sucking is an end in itself. The sucking reflex is independent of its aim. She has further shown that frustration of the sucking activity of an infant presages anxiety and other personality disturbances later in life. These and similar phenomena are important. It is with them that we must deal if we are to understand the formation and malformation of the human personality.

NURTURE, DISCIPLINE, AND EDUCATION

In our society the infant and the child experience three stages as related to their treatment by adults, which, though quite distinct, in many respects exist contemporaneously and even coalesce. These are nurture, discipline, and education.

The period of nurture occurs in early infancy, when the child lives a parasitic life, largely an extension of intra-uterine existence. During this period all his needs and wants are more or less instantaneously satisfied. His peremptory demands, conveyed by crying and screaming, are immediately met. At this period the child, though a completely dependent entity, is at the same time autonomous. He does not submit to external discipline or routines, nor does he conform to the will of others. His life energies are centered around and focused on his wants, his needs, his impulses; and these are unconditionally gratified. His behavior is imperious, autocratic, and entirely self-centered.

As he grows older and becomes ready for them, limitations are placed upon this autistic and socially unreasonable behavior. Usually the first changes made are in the eating process, in which easy ingestion by sucking is replaced by other forms of feeding that require effort on his part, such as taking food from a spoon and a cup and later biting and masticating it. These new feeding methods involve effort on the child's part. He is no longer completely indulged, but is expected to exert himself in order to gain oral and gastrointestinal gratifications and to sustain himself.

These new experiences make the child aware of other persons, apart from himself. This, perhaps, is the point at which the earliest identifications with other persons and object relations have their beginnings.

The transition from complete autonomy and self-centeredness to partial submission to routines and the need to exert effort ushers in the period of discipline. Habit training, which is first concerned with food intake, progresses later to training in anal and urethal activity. The child finds the latter controls in some ways even more difficult to accept, because then he gives up part of himself (urine or feces) to the will of another person, the nurse or the mother. Though he rebelled against giving up the nipple and eating from a spoon, this deprivation was easier for him to accept, for he was *receiving* (food). In toilet training he *gives up* part of himself (feces) and his autonomy at the bidding of another person. The struggles that ensue and the manner in which they are dealt with by his mother or the nurse determine in large part the self-organization of the child and his personality when he reaches adulthood.

Discipline is essential. Its value lies in the fact that it strengthens the ego so that a person can deal adequately and independently with his urges and with outer pressures. It prevents one from becoming a victim of anarchic impulses, narcissistic self-indulgence, and false feelings of omnipotence. Discipline by parents and teachers, therefore, is necessary, but it must be employed in a manner that will lead to self-discipline—that is, inner strength and the desire to inhibit impulses without destructive emotional consequences. This type of self-discipline is engendered, not by repressing and punishing, but rather by inducing the identification and willing acceptance of the world's values which results from the child's love and acceptance of the parent, nurse, and teacher who personify these vlaues.

Education, the third stage, starts later in life—in our culture around the ages of five or six years, when a definite regimen of acquiring skills, learning facts, and training in social behavior is introduced. Actually this limited and false, though prevalent, view of education is inimical to the healthy development of a balanced personality. *Educo* means to "draw out," and the closer home and school education follow that concept, the more salutary are the results. Education's true aim should be to provide the child with opportunities and encouragement for testing his slowly growing powers, for expressing his emerging talents, finding adequate identifications and ego ideals, and establishing controls as well as channels for sublimation of inherent aggressive urges and drives.[5]

DEVELOPMENTAL PHASES AND ACTIVITY PATTERNS

Among the many basic needs of the child is the orderly and sound development of his dynamic drives for action, achievement, and reality control. They appear in a definite sequence and in relation to the growth of physical and psychological powers, and reveal themselves as interest. Numerous students of "child development" have described a large variety of phases and stages and their sequences in the onward progress of maturation. For our present purpose and in order to lay a foundation for our specific thesis we shall attempt to formulate the dynamic (activity) drives, their nature, manifestations, and implications for adaptive patterns in five different, though obviously related, categories, as follows: (1) play activity phase, (2) utility phase, (3) reflective phase, (4) social phase, and (5) communal phase. Each of these phases gives rise to a corresponding *activity pattern:* (1) manipulative-exploratory, (2) mechanistic-practical, (3) epistemonic-intellectual, (4) group association, and (5) community participation.

The activity phase, in which manipulative-exploratory patterns predominate, is marked by play and little organized activity. It is characterized by the absence of, or only vaguely defined, aims or objectives. The purpose is rather to discharge excess energies generated by the body and the psychological need to experiment with and investigate the environment so as to achieve security and establish control over it. Play and experimentation

[5] I have suggested elsewhere the differentiation between "schooling" and "education." What passes now for education is really schooling, for in most important respects present-day schools are not educational.

in their multifarious forms predominate in this phase. What is commonly known as curiosity also appears at this stage, but differs from the curiosity of a later phase, the reflective. Here the aim is, not to relate causes to results, manifestations to reason, but rather to effect and experience the phenomena themselves.[6] The pattern of behavior during this phase is, as already stated, manipulative-exploratory. To utilize his growing powers and to gain security and control the child manipulates objects in his environment as freely as he is permitted. While physiologically this acting is probably caused by excess energy due to growth, at the same time the child develops psychologically as he explores and becomes acquainted with his environment and gains power over it. This in turn begets security. Play is the most common form of activity at this phase.

When adults prohibit the child's indulgence in what to them seems random and purposeless actions, his growing powers become stunted. At the same time the foundations for future feelings of weakness and inadequacy are laid. Freedom in play is of utmost importance at this phase of development as a basis for wholesome personality. But it must be recognized that such play-activity should be carried on only in a properly planned and suitable setting designed for this purpose. It must afford no danger to the child or annoyance to adults. This fact was vaguely recognized when nurseries and play and rumpus rooms were introduced into homes. Arranging a suitable environment for the different stages in the child's development I have described as *graded reality;* this principle should be more widely applied in homes, schools, recreational, and other settings where children of different ages play, work, and learn, as well as in psychotherapy. Among the many materials suitable for this phase are toys, dolls, blocks, wagons, engines, clay, plasticene, finger paints, crayons, water colors, mud, sand, water, fire, and means of locomotion such as cycles and wagons.

The utility phase appears at about seven or eight years of age,

[6] I have suggested that the "drive to be the cause" is part of man's psyche. See my *Science in the New Education,* New York, Prentice-Hall, 1934, p. 137. This drive toward being a *machina dei* may be a sublimation of the aggressive instinct or, perhaps, is inherent to the human psyche as an independent characteristic.

that is, after the period of the Oedipal conflict, and its nature and content are to a large extent determined by the degree of resolution of that conflict. When this has been adequately accomplished, the child has been freed to move outward centrifugally and to utilize his environment for his evolving powers and needs. During this period the child is interested in making things of utilitarian value, playing with chemicals, electricity, dynamos, and similar objects. But it must be understood that at this stage the child is still not too interested in sources or reasons, and he should not be urged into such intellectual pursuits. His interest rather is to test his power and to exert his strength against materials in his environment and to make things that are of value and significance to him and others near him.[7]

During this phase, with its corresponding mechanistic-practical pattern, materials are required out of which definite objects can be fashioned. In this phase the child not only makes objects which are practical but also takes them apart, reassembles them, and seeks to produce something new and original. Some of the objects usually made by boys are boats, bread boards, rolling pins, hat racks, shelves, boxes, pictures, and book shelves. They become interested in arts and crafts, in various forms of woodwork, and in playing with science materials. Girls grow interested in cooking, needlework, dolls, and the assumption of various roles in their play in which they become more acquainted with reality and prepare themselves for the parts they are to take in subsequent phases of their development. We can discern in all these activities, whether of boys or of girls, the fact that sexual libido is transmuted into nonsexual libido, which is characteristic of the latency period in development.

At this period one of the major difficulties for the child is school. In our culture schooling corresponds in point of time to the practical-inventive phase, and overemphasis on intellectuality in the curriculum rather than upon experience with actual situations is definitely harmful. In addition to other undesirable results, it affects negatively the development of the sense of reality.

At twelve or thirteen the *reflective* or *epistemonic* interests

[7] See p. 16.

appear. Because of the newly awakened sexual impulses, the youngster becomes interested in understanding his own bodily processes, and as a reflection of this also the outside world. He now desires to understand the causations of phenomena, the reasons for much that occurs in and around him, and seeks explanations for them. It is at this stage that book learning and school subjects, if properly selected, can be valuable and effective.

Later in this stage, and as a direct result of his inquiring propensities, the *social* phase sets in, although during the practical phase also group associations outside the home have been growing in importance. At first these are loose groups with weak ties or friendships. However, as the youngster passes from puberty into early adolescence friendships with individuals and ties to groups become even more important. Because of the stages in libido development, these attachments and associations are invested in persons of the same sex, which later change to heterosexual interests. The former are both a testing out and a protective device. The youngster tests himself first with persons who constitute less of a threat before venturing out into more hazardous precincts. Boys and girls therefore form separate groups and friendships, but these lines of demarcation are soon broken down. Association between members of both sexes replaces the earlier same-sex relations. During this period coeducation should be very helpful, although in my opinion it is not so desirable during latency and puberty. In adolescence coeducation follows the natural psycho-organic development of the individual.

We shall not discuss the *communal* phase in development, because this appears at an age outside the limits set by this volume, which is twelve years. Interest in community affairs is at best rudimentary at this age, and therefore we can omit it from our discussions. Such interests appear in early adolescence. They stem from the reawakened sexual drives and serve as a preparation for parenthood.

Table 1 illustrates the relation of the various phases, patterns, and activity types.

TABLE 1

PHASES, PATTERNS, AND ACTIVITY TYPES [a]

Phase	*Approximate Age*	*Pattern*	*Activity Type*
Activity	Up to 7 or 8	Manipulative-exploratory	Play
Utility	8–13	Mechanistic-practical	Arts and crafts, science interests, folk-lore
Reflective	From 12	Epistemonic intellectual	Research, subject matter, efforts and intellectual understanding
Social	From 14	Group association	Clubs, group activities, individual and group associations
Communal	From 16	Group participation and individual inquiry	Participation and interest in larger communal and world affairs

[a] We must again emphasize that the phases and types of activity do not always follow the indicated order, nor are they sharply demarcated. Individual differences and environmental influences affect the order and nature of these developmental phenomena.

INTERESTS AND THEIR ROLE IN CHILD DEVELOPMENT

In helping the child to develop physical health, emotional maturity, and a sense of reality, it is essential to foster and encourage his genuine interests. Whenever parents or teachers either block or retard the natural cadence of interests or seek to accelerate it, nothing but serious malformation of personality can result. Not only is orderly development seriously interfered with but also resentment and hostility are mobilized against the interfering agents—parents, teachers, other adults, and society in general. Interference with the normal and spontaneous growth of the organism and its corresponding psychological development produces tension, anxiety, and mental unhealth. Sequence and cadence are entirely individual. No two children develop in the same order or at the same rate, nor are they possessed of precisely the same abilities and interests.

We suggest that for convenience interests be classified as organic, induced, forced, temporary, transitory, phasial, cyclical, focal, peripheral, and permanent.

Organic interests are those to which we have already referred indirectly in the discussion of phases and activity patterns. They are the interests that arise from maturational readiness and are an outcome of the organ's cumulative potential powers seeking expression in kinetic action. The transmutation of potential energy to kinetic energy is a dynamic process present in the organism as well as in the psyche.

However, children develop interests because of the various interactions with adults and other children in their environment, the examples set, and the cultural pattern. Social hunger, the need to please adults and be accepted by his peers, and his ready imitations and identifications cause the child to adopt interests that are not at all or only partially suited to his maturation and growth. Thus, a child may make an effort to learn to read and write at an age unsuitable for this effort. Many persons undertake occupations and professions for similar reasons. Such interests, which are innumerable, we designate as *induced interests.* Induced interests may be divided into two distinct categories: those that are voluntarily adopted through imitation and those deliberately induced by adults, initiated by precept, instruction, and indoctrination. Thus, in order to please an adult a child may undertake to study, join groups, or participate in activities that are too difficult and advanced. Such occupations are not as harmful as the latter interests which counteract organic development more than do the voluntary type, because the self-selective process does not operate here to the same extent. Both the organic and the voluntary-induced interests result from the child's having made his own selection on the basis of physical and psychological readiness. When interests are deliberately induced by an adult, they may not fit the direction or the rate of spontaneous development and may damage the personality.[8]

[8] It is inevitable that in life there should be precept and indoctrination. These are part of the living and socializing processes in a society and are essential for

The greatest damage results from the *forced interests,* if these can at all be dignified by the term "interests." They are directly imposed upon the child, who must submit to and participate in directed activities and learnings. The most universal of these is school attendance; religious observances are usually also in this category. In the home, as well, many "interests" are forced upon children, as when they are forced to participate in or to perform acts alien to their inclinations or organic and psychological readiness.[9] The harm is caused by the fact that the child is forced into occupations and learnings for which he is only too often physically, intellectually, or psychologically unprepared.

Even organic and voluntarily induced interests may be temporary, because of growth sequence of specific organs or neurological or glandular maturation at a particular time. Thus, *temporary interests* are playing with mud or water, music, singing, and painting, which may be soon discontinued. These interests should be encouraged to find expression when they appear and then allowed to wane. In addition to self-fulfillment and personality enrichment, this procedure aids reality testing, as a consequence of which the ego is strengthened. For when the child is forced to continue temporary interests, his progressive development may be blocked or restricted. Temporary interests are sometimes referred to also as *transitory. Transitory interests,* however, are of much shorter duration and may not always result from psychological growth or physcial development, but rather from accidental discoveries peripheral to some major interest.

Phasial interests correspond to the phase of physical and psychological development and last longer than the transitory. The most common manifestations of phasial interests in a child are running and climbing when his leg and arm muscles are at a period of most rapid growth. Later interests include activities

---

the survival of any culture or group. The only factors to be considered are timing and "dosing." Certainly in later puberty or adolescence social induction is inescapable, as it is also to a lesser extent during school years (latency) and even in early childhood (discipline). What is essential to consider is that the content, manner, degree and suitability be adjusted to the age and characteristics of the individual.

[9] The most harmful among these are sudden and peremptory changes in feeding patterns and toilet training. Another is enforced study of music.

that involve small muscles, because of their most rapid development at that particular time. Another common phase is that of accelerated curiosity during and immediately following the Oedipal period. The constant questioning by the child, which adults frequently find annoying, connotes his desire for genital enlightenment and is a transformation of the latter craving. Numerous phasial interests appear at various periods that correspond to developmental phases. Meeting the child's phasial interests is a basic requirement for his fullest development and for mental health. Interference with them retards growth, prevents emotional integration, and mobilizes hostility.

Interests also occur in *cycles*. The desire to sing, dance, and draw may occur at one stage of a child's development, vanish, and then reappear later. Playing with dolls, for example, may be resorted to at a later period in a child's life, as well as other, supposedly "regressive" interests and occupations. This *cyclical* manifestation of interest may be of organic origin, or it may be an indication of psychologic regression in times of stress.

Focal and *peripheral* interests refer to the fact that some coeval interests are of major importance, while others are secondary, or peripheral. To anyone who has the opportunity to observe the growth of children the relation between their focal and peripheral interests is evident. At different times manual work, intellectual attainments, schoolwork, or earning a parent's love may take precedence over other values. Some time later, having playmates and friends may assume greatest significance, even at the expense of other preoccupations that not long before were endowed with special importance.

This hegemony is present also in relation to school, hobbies, and recreation. A child may at one time become absorbed in the school's football team and may neglect not only his studies but even his health, his parents, and his friends. Others become so interested in subjects such as biology and in preparing and mounting collections and exhibits that other activities are relegated to the background. As is to be expected, in the adult focal and peripheral interests are more stabilized; they remain more or less in the same relationship. Thus, to the adult, stamp collecting always plays a role subordinate to earning a living. In the young child, because his personality is as yet unformed, focal and peripheral interests are less well defined and shift from one category to another. What is important one day may become of secondary value the following day.

Some interests remain *permanent.* These interests emanate from special hereditary dispositions, specific organic constitution or talent, strong identifications, or some other equally powerful determinant. There are scientifically or artistically inclined persons, idealists, and people of a practical turn of mind as a result of constitutional predispositions, as well as psychologically conditional preferences. Even constitutionally determined predilections may be intensified, weakened, or eliminated by social and psychologic conditioning and emotional attitudes toward parents, siblings, or other persons of importance to the individual. Permanent interests, however, are more or less the warp and the woof out of which human activities are woven. Each person must be given full opportunity to discover them through a free and variagated home and school education and helped to bring them to full fruition. It must be kept in mind that because of the labile nature of childhood [10] the most common interests in children are the temporary and the transitory. Permanent interests are usually recognizable after stabilization of the total personality is achieved.

EGO ORGANIZATION AND THE "REGULATIVE PRINCIPLE"

A liberal education aims to establish in individuals a selective capacity or judgment as to appropriate responses, qualitatively and quantitatively. We know that in a state of insanity, as an extreme case, the individual is incapable of appropriate responses. The psychotic's reactions are either over-controlled or devoid of the inhibitive restraints of the ego. While the selective capacity, which is a chief characteristic of a balanced personality, is minimal in the psychotic, it may also be defective or inadequate in adults who have other types of personality disorders. As can be expected, it is almost absent in the young child, since

[10] Pages 143 *et seq.*

it has first to be established through guided interaction with reality, a process that takes considerable time.

The capacities for selection, inhibition, and direction are predominantly determined by the dynamic relations in the family group. It is generally accepted that superego development occurs through relations with parents or their surrogates. However, the executive powers of the individual that make up his ego are derived from the same source. The relationships with and the examples set by parents and other important persons in the family have a permanent influence upon the future of the child's emotional development, the quality of his responses, and his self-discipline. Calm, capable, and self-controlled adults engender in children a tendency toward effective regulative powers and control. Example, however, is not the only factor. Direct impediment, prohibition, even infrequent mild punishment, and encouragement help the child to internalize the regulative powers of his elders. The child's inner authority is derived from external authority which he absorbs or internalizes (superego). But for this purpose teaching and discipline must be applied without violence or the evocation of resentment and defiance.

The earliest behavior of the child stems from the *id,* or the instinctive impulse drives. As impulses and uncontrolled acting out come under scrutiny and direct or indirect control by other persons, a system of regulative mechanisms are gradually evolved which in the adult, ideally at least, reach full organization. The acquisition of self-inhibition and control is usually attributed to direct outer discipline. This is, however, only partially true. Discipline may augment inhibitive and self-regulative processes, but if it is the sole source of control, various compensatory and reactive responses of a negative character are generated. A more sound system of regulative mechanisms results from identification with and internalization of the patterns of reaction and behavior of persons important in the life of the child, whom he accepts, likes and later respects.

The totality of the regulative, inhibitive, and integrative systems in the personality constitute what Freud has termed the "ego." I have already pointed out that of the three interrelated psychic factors—id, ego, and superego—the ego is the most complex.[11] In terms of structure and function, it is also the most important in children. Charged as it is with the responsibility of serving as the intermediary between the id and the superego—in itself a strenuous task—it has a number of other functions almost as difficult. One of these is holding in check the anarchic impulses of the id; another is to mediate between them and the demands, pressures, and mores of the outside world; still another is to integrate the total personality resources as they relate to one another and to the world. Thus, the major, though not the sole, function of the ego is to deal with inner and outer realities and to integrate and harmonize them.

We have become accustomed to accepting the fact, first annunciated by Freud, that the parents, particularly the father, are the sources of superego formation. According to this well-authenticated theory, the child internalizes their values and precepts of right and wrong, good and bad, permissions and prohibitions.[12] These eventually become structured in the unconscious and act as censors, the ego acting as the integrative, administrative, or executive agent. It is less universally recognized that the ego, as well, is derived from the parents. Parents demonstrate to the child patterns of reaction, control, and methods of dealing with inner and outer realities. Both excessive indulgence and overstrict discipline weaken the ego; in one instance, because narcissism is encouraged and self-regulative powers underdeveloped, in the other, because submission and obedience prevent autonomy and self-control. Similarly, when parents are weak and devoid of self-control the child also fails in those respects because of imitation, identification, and ideal formation.

11 S. R. Slavson, *Analytic Group Psychotherapy*, New York, Columbia University Press, 1949, p. 68.

12 I have already suggested that the parent-derived superego does not remain unmodified by later experience. The concepts of right and wrong (conscience), as well as the unconscious part of the superego, are influenced and modified by interpersonal experiences later in life, especially by significant group associations. The total culture as well as the necessities of one's life alter the original superego formation. I have suggested the term "group superego" for this phenomenon. See my *Introduction to Group Therapy*, New York, International Universities Press, 1943, pp. 229 *et seq.*

Obviously, adequate ego development and ego strength are not determined by example alone. Reality testing and the necessity of dealing with actual situations also strengthen the ego. The main source of a strong ego, however, is the security of love and protection and a sense of belonging and status in the family. The developmental view of ego is that its foundations are laid in infancy; that it is formed by a long and continuous process extending throughout the formative years and probably throughout life. In senility it begins to break down, that is, regressive ego functioning occurs. It must be noted in this connection that strength of the ego is not measured by its capacity to bear up under unusual conditions and crises, but rather by its functioning under ordinary daily circumstances.

It is clear that the strength of the ego and its executive powers cannot be evoked by verbal communication or by the teaching of principles. Power is engendered through active, dynamic interaction and through actual experience with things and people. Effective human environment includes emotions, ideas, values, principles, and people, as well as objects and materials. The "psychological disposition to inhibit instinctive impulses" (Roback) is derived from experiences in the home, the school, and with playmates as well as in the larger world and through contacts with persons who for one reason or another influence the developing personality of the child and the adult. The regulative principle (ego), therefore, emerges from the summation of the planned and incidental experiences and interactions to which the individual is subjected throughout his life.

ORGANIC FOUNDATIONS OF THE EGO

The psychogenic sources of personality must needs be the concern of the educator and the psychotherapist. But if they desire a full perspective of their work and recognize the inevitable limits upon their efforts, its biologic foundations must come under their scrutiny as well. Hereditary and constitutional predispositions and optimum capacities are the foundations upon which all work with persons has to be based. Despite the dearth of instrumentalities for objective determination of many of them, weight must be given to systemic factors, even if some of them have to be deduced or assumed.

These brief remarks upon a very important subject will suffice as an introduction to the suggestion that the ego has a biological base. Education and developmental opportunities may strengthen or weaken the ego, but its foundations are in the organism. The degree of native sensitivity and neurological and glandular balance and adequate functioning of the vital organs and physiologic harmony—all affect the individual's capacity to bear up under stress and strain. Inherent temperament and disposition are often major determinants in this regard, and efforts to "strengthen" the ego beyond these specific limits must be doomed to failure.

These and other limitations have only academic interest for the psychotherapist, because none of his patients has reached maximal development in any area of his personality. But it is important that the therapist, as well as the teacher, shall recognize maximal potentials for each and not attempt achievements beyond these limits. Organic and constitutional states also explain why some individuals present serious problems for treatment although their home environment has had a comparatively low pathoplastic content, while others, in whose homes there has been intense pathology, are comparatively free from serious malformations. This may be explained on the ground that the first had inherently low capacity for withstanding stress, while the other's capacity for it was of a higher level.

One must not, however, be too rash in making such assumptions. For a thorough study of the history of a case may reveal that despite the apparent pathology in the home there may have been present *supportive persons,* such as a grandparent, an uncle, or a much older sibling, who compensated for the parents' rejection, offered substitute gratifications, and supplied the *primary relations* essential for integrating and balancing psychic forces.

THE NEED FOR SECURITY AND GROWTH

In view of the fact that the urge to survive is so strongly cathexized, we can readily understand why all functions associated with it are endowed with intense pleasure, the striving for which is an integral part of the individual's primary endowments. An analysis of these drives as they are related to the child's personal survival shows that they belong in two categories: the *need for security* and the *need for growth.*

Security, which is of paramount importance, is derived from primary oral gratifications, absence of threat or danger from the external environment, and the perceptions that the individual is wanted and protected. The manner in which a child is fed, toilet trained, and exposed to the impact of the outside world and people (graded reality) lays the foundation for the final personality that will emerge from the totality of these experiences. If sucking, feeding, and evacuation are painful experiences, or the child is threatened or assailed, however slightly, anxiety and the feeling of inferiority will pursue him throughout his life. Even pressure from a rough sheet or blanket or inadequate support when he is lifted make the infant feel insecure and anxious. Hunger pangs, inevitable in scheduled feeding as against "demand feeding" (especially when the schedule is unsuitable for the individual child), threaten the awareness of survival security and cause fear and anger.

We have seen that growth of the child is made manifest by various types of motility, but motility is not solely a result of growth. Activity also stimulates growth, while frustration, in addition to setting up rage and tension, impedes growth. When frustrations to motility are applied violently, as is often the case, the child builds up feelings of resentment against the frustrating person, usually the parent. These feelings are later organized into specific attitudes, reactions, and behavior that extend to all persons and in all relations and form one's character.

Growth and security are closely connected dynamically. When one's security is threatened and anxiety sets in, the psychic energies are focused on the threatening situation. When energies are so occupied or tied down, they are automatically withdrawn from other areas. Growth in the latter is thus retarded, and imbalance results. Energies become fixed at the point of maximum anxiety. This is known as the *point of fixation.* Everyone is fixed at some point, endowed with various degrees of emotivity, which retarded his emotional development. Since the human organism functions as a unit, interference with the free flow of psychic energies also damages intellectual and physical development and social adaptations. Thus, restriction and insecurity beget inner distortions and outer maladjustment.

The earliest sources of security are the adults who take care of the infant and child. The growth and evolution of the total personality is in their hands. In the orderly development of the individual, he evolves "inner security," but this is always derived from the security represented by the protection and affection of adults. Because of his weakness the child cannot face the actualities of the world without help. He becomes capable of dealing with them because of the support he receives from these important adults, which should be gradually diminished so that in time he can become self-dependent. Such are the major avenues toward a developing sense of reality and of security.

Of greatest importance is the fact that when the child's security and growth needs are met, he feels wanted and loved. Denial, imprudent restrictions, frustration, and crude discipline make him feel that he is neither wanted nor loved, and doubt is created in his mind whether his parents have really begotten him. Furthermore, they foster anxiety, low self-esteem, the feeling of guilt, confused identity, and attitudes of dependence, submission, hostility, and aggression.

In the three major stages of development outlined on pages 6 to 8, few repressions or sublimations are demanded from the child in the stage of nurture. Here he can and does act out primary impulses. In later stages mild impediments are applied as the infant grows into childhood. It is when the child is placed in school that he experiences the full impact of frustrations to basic drives for neuro-muscular and vaso-motor activity. Here he is required to use extensively and concentratedly organs that are not sufficiently mature for such effort. At the same time, the use of other organs when they are growing rapidly and even at a maximal rate is limited or prohibited. A classical example of the former is learning to read at the age of six, which involves tension of the eye muscles and excessive effort in translating visual into ideational and then into vocal symbols; another is learning meaningless historical events. All of this results in frustration of the more urgent biological needs for play, free expression, exploration, and contact with actuality that lead to feelings of adequacy and security and ego development.

THE GENESIS OF HOSTILITY

It is understandable that because of the intense instinctual urges to survive, the infant would be strongly preoccupied with his sensations and their source, namely, with himself. The libido (life energies) is first focused on his own personality. Freud called this "ego-libido," or the stage when the ego and the libido are still united, which is characteristic of very young children as well as of adult psychotics. When, at about one year of age, the child discovers the separateness of the mother (or nurse) from himself, he becomes for the first time aware of his dependence, which, understandably, increases his anxieties, but at the same time his libido is directed toward them.

Up to this point the breast or bottle and all other services he received, such as being cleaned, bathed, and washed, were all achieved through his own will and power as reflected in his needs and demands. He was omnipotent. He now discovers that other persons are actually satisfying his needs and that he is dependent on them. This is the beginning of object relationships and the first rudimentary step toward detaching his libido from himself and attaching it to others. At least part of the child's libido now becomes "object-libido."

The child does not give up his feelings of self-importance without a struggle, however. He resists accepting his dependence. He makes demands upon the persons as if they were extensions of himself. The manner in which these are met during the nurture phase determines the intensity of this battle. Whether his imperious and seemingly unreasonable demands are dealt with gently and constructively or harshly and punitively determines whether the child's will is set against the world about him or not and defines the pattern of his subsequent feelings, attitudes, and behavior.

When the child realizes that he is unable to win in his struggle for autonomy, he invests is parents with the feelings of omnipotence and omniscience he has had about himself, for unless they are strong and powerful they are unable to protect and defend him. In doing this the child again follows through on his instinctual urges for survival, for these phantasies yield a sense of security. To protect him, the parents must be strong. When parents disappoint him in this respect, when they prove to be weak and inadequate, the child's security is threatened, and it becomes necessary for him to develop defense mechanisms that ultimately militate against satisfactory personal and social adaptations.[13]

The child's rebelliousness is further enhanced when the period of discipline is reached and he is trained in self-feeding and sphincter control and is faced with essential restriction to diffuse motility. Then negative feelings toward parents (or other persons directly involved) arise. Because he is restricted and controlled, he feels that he is no longer wanted or loved,[14] and he becomes either sad and depressed or negativistic and rebellious. But since the sources of his security at this stage are still the parents, he cannot permit himself to discharge his retalliatory hostility against them lest he lose their protection even more. Neither can he withhold it altogether. Therefore, he creates a phantom parental (father) image, upon which he displaces his hostile feelings and toward which he directs his hatred. Sometimes a child displaces this hostility upon himself by biting or hurting himself and by other self-destructive acts. By this strategy the child can discharge hostility without fear of being punished or abandoned. Later in life, individuals and symbols, particularly those representing authority, are fitted into this "father image," upon whom the repressed aggression originally felt toward parents is discharged. This phenomenon is of special importance in psychotherapy, for it is these primary hostile feelings with which we predominantly deal in treating emotionally disturbed persons.

[13] See case pp. 76–78.

[14] This is especially true when a sibling displaces him at this time.

The hostile feelings toward the parental image are usually displaced (or deflected) upon siblings, for every child feels that the love parents give to a sibling rightly belongs to him. But if the parent neglects or deprives one child in favor of another, or shows open preference, extreme forms of sibling rivalry may result.

The image upon which hostile feelings are projected becomes more important during the Oedipal conflict. We shall discuss this point more fully when the stages in libidinal development are described.[15] Freud has shown that at the Oedipal stage the pleasure-seeking sexual (not genital) urges of the child toward the parent of the opposite sex become crystallized. This occurs under normal conditions at about five years of age and continues for a year or two, though in disturbed persons this period may extend into adulthood or never occur at all. The sexual nature of the child's wishes toward his parent of the opposite sex are quite apparent, and since repressions have not been as yet established,[16] children at this age speak of their desire to have the parents all to themselves and marry them. But the parent of the same sex as the child stands in the way of attaining such wishes and becomes the object of even greater resentment and hostility. The child therefore has to struggle between two desires: the desire to possess one parent on the one hand, and the desire to avoid punishment by the second parent on the other.

The struggle for autonomy, freedom of expression, and self-determination which we have described in earlier parts of this chapter is usually bilateral; that is, it takes place between the child and one or both of the parents as individuals. During the Oedipal period, however, the child is in a struggle in which both parents and their relation to each other are involved. He is now pitted against not only each parent as an individual but also both of them as a couple. The first stage is known as pre-Oedipal, while the latter is designated as the "Oedipal conflict." The boy is interested in the mother, and the girl in the father. Each, however, is deterred because of the fear of the other parent. The boy wishes to have his mother as his sole object of love,

[15] See pp. 40–45.

[16] See pp. 78–82 and 143 *et seq.*

but if he does so, his father may punish him. This generates castration fears, and the manner in which the father deals with his son at this stage determines the course of the latter's character development. If the father treats him gently and prevents fear and submission, the Oedipal conflict will have a less damaging effect upon his character. However, if the father's behavior is harsh, cruel, or violent, the boy will develop a submissive character or become violently aggressive and disturbed.

The Oedipal conflict of the girl is considerably more complicated. Her mother, who has been the source of protection and security in the past, now becomes her enemy. That is, the girl has to turn against this source of security and the first object of her love. The boy continues in his loyalty to his original love-object, the mother. The girl turns against her and, therefore, becomes disloyal. This unfortunate situation permanently affects her personality and gives rise to feelings of guilt, vacillation, uncertainty, duplicity, dishonesty, and vindictiveness. Thus, we may expect that for psychological, as well as biological, reasons disturbances in women should be considerably more complex than in men.

Despite these unavoidable tensions and conflicts, a child's greatest security lies in the harmony and affection between his parents. Not only does a harmonious relation in the family as it is constituted today protect him against his own impulses, but it assures him also of protection and security and satisfies his needs for survival and attachment to a primary group. Strife between parents generates intense fear, anxiety, and confusion as to loyalties toward the contending parents. The child is frightened by manifestations of anger and discord. One of the reasons for this fear is that it threatens his security (survival). Another is that discord between parents creates doubts in his mind as to his being loved and wanted as well as feelings of guilt that he is the cause of the conflict.

AGGRESSION

In view of the fact that most children referred for psychological treatment manifest behavior disturbing to adults because it is "aggressive," special attention needs to be given aggression by the psychotherapist. However, one difficulty is that the term is used rather loosely. Within limits, aggression is normal and indispensable to life. Animals, and to a definite extent also plants, must be aggressive against their environment and each other in order to survive. Whether it concerns food-getting, safety, or procreation, aggression is the prevalent technique. Similarly, man acts aggressively against his environment and others to assure his status, security, and survival. In the realms of industry, business, science, art, and the other innumerable occupations and callings evolved by man aggression is fundamental.

But difficulty arises from the misunderstanding as to the distinction between normal and abnormal aggression. Normal aggression consists of directed acts leading to constructive survival and having socially-approved aims. It has purpose and direction. Abnormal aggression, on the other hand, is diffuse and is personally and socially valueless or injurious. It is subjectively determined, having as its purpose the release of inner stress and the discharge of hostile drives rather than a beneficial and acceptable personal or social objective.

Another source of confusion stems from the interchangeable use of the terms "aggression" and "hostility." Aggression manifests itself in acts, while hostility may be either active or passive. Hostility is rather an emotional state or disposition that colors acts and attitudes, but can be controlled or avoided.

Aggression and aggressive acts are inherent in the nature of childhood as it is also in all stages of development, but they should not be confused with hostility. The latter is intensified by frustration, rejection, insecurity, and other pathogenic experiences and relations. The child's random experimental and exploratory movements and acts, annoying as they may be, actually serve to discharge excess energy and help him become acquainted with reality and able to relate himself to it. So-called "aggression" of the child becomes more tolerable when understood in the light of the dynamism of his growth and development.

For the purpose of our present study aggression may be divided into four classifications: atavistic, phylogenic, ontogenic, and instrumental.

Atavistic aggression is tinged with or proceeds entirely from native cruelty. It is a survival from past evolutionary stages and may be a definite engram in the neurological structure of man. These hostile aggressive impulses were of value in the struggle for existence in primordial times in man's era and also in prehuman states. The practical value of such impulses has long since vanished, but the impulses themselves still persist. Popular enthusiasm for internecine, interracial, and international cruelty and warfare, the prejudices that lead to killing and torture (unless prohibited by law and restrained by force) attest to the existence of these hostile and cruel impulses in the unconscious of man. One of the tasks of civilization and education is to engender controls and provide sublimations for them.

Phylogenetic aggression consists of the set of aggressive, and sometimes even hostile trends, which have been evolved and approved by the race as part of its adaptive needs. At some points atavistic and phylogenic aggression seem to be similar. Actually there is a vast difference between the two. Atavistic aggression has as its cause the drive for biologic survival and is therefore ingrained in the constitution itself. Phylogenic aggression is not universal, for it is subject to cultural emphasis and is patterned by the experiences and needs of the race. Thus, we find that some types of behavior that are fully acceptable and approved at a given time or in one culture or society are abhorrent at other times or to other cultures. Aggression is as much a part of custom and mores as are other behavioral patterns and social values.

Ontogenetic aggression results from the experiences of an individual in his environment and the patterning of his behavior and attitudes by that environment. We have already seen that hostility is a result of interference with the child and the imposition of unnecessary and even necessary limitations. But restraint is determined by the immediate culture in which one lives—the family, the neighborhood, the nation, and the larger world values. Directness, indiscretion, boisterousness, disregard of others may be a part of one's emotional constellation resulting from a lack of sublimations and inadequate self-control (cultivation and "refinement").

Instrumental aggression is an integral part of living. Its aim is to secure the survival of the individual as a biologic and psychologic entity in a social setting. Under the best conditions it is controlled and directed and used consciously with definite aims in view and for results that fit into the life of the individual and the group of which he is a part. One of the aims of education and therapy is to transform or sublimate diffuse and purposeless aggression into instrumental aggression.

Some of the undesirable and sometimes veiled uses to which aggression is put to by children are prolonged infancy, attention getting, a desire to control the environment, to maintain infantile omnipotence, to achieve relief from organic tension, for grandeur phantasies, as defences against weakness and effeminacy, and strong hostility.[17] The question of aggression in its less desirable manifestations and methods of dealing with it in psychotherapy and child guidance are taken up in considerable detail in Chapter II.

THE SOCIAL BASES OF PERSONALITY DEVELOPMENT

After the subsiding of the Oedipal conflict, as well as the child's normal emotional preoccupation with other members of his immediate family, there sets in what can be described as *centrifugal libido development.* At the age of seven or eight the child displays increasing interest in others of his age, and what is characterized as "peer culture" grows more important. He becomes interested in friends, schoolmates, and playmates. Group association, first spontaneous and informal, later formal and organized, is a major need during latency, puberty, and adolescence. Thus, the libido changes its direction from its centripetal, ego-centered movement to out-reaching tendencies—

[17] For more detailed discussion of these and other topics see S. R. Slavson, "The Treatment of Aggression through Group Therapy," *American Journal of Orthopsychiatry,* Vol. XIII, No. 3, July, 1943.

first toward persons and objects in the immediate family environment, then to wider areas, including objects, other persons, groups, and later ideas and ideals.

Overlooking the group and culture as it affects psychosocial and psychosexual development of the individual is a serious defect in education and therapy. This oversight in home and school education is frequently at the root of personality maladjustment and of much social pathology. It is becoming increasingly apparent that the individual cannot be understood or treated apart from his cultural setting. All the conditions of his life, the biosphere, affect and mold him. In the broadest sense they are part and parcel of his personality. Even infants and young children are influenced by them via parents and nurses, as the latter are in turn affected by the social, economic, and psychological conditions of their own lives. Just as a plant cannot escape the effects of climate, man cannot escape the effects of his social environment. The kernel of a democratic society is the group. The capacity for group action and the individual's adaptation to group living are the foundations of the democratic life pattern, as well as signs of a wholesome personality development.

Association with groups must be recognized as an invaluable experience in the preparation for life in our culture. The capacity to work with and become part of a group indicates a well-balanced personality. One who isolates himself is as disturbed as one who pursues association too vehemently or one who consistently gets into difficulties with other people. Clusters, colonies, schools, flocks, herds, and groups are universal in nature. They are essential means for biologic survival in lower animals and in man. They are essential for the latter's psychologic and spiritual life also. As a social phenomenon, the group is not an invention of man; it has its roots in nature.[18] Man, however, consciously uses groups for enhancing his personality and for psychological survival. Every healthy person in our culture strives to be well thought of, respected, and wanted. Perhaps these cravings have their origin in the family, because of dependence on parents and their surrogates and sibling relations

[18] See W. C. Allee, *The Social Life of Animals*, New York, Norton, 1938.

and rivalries. They are probably further enhanced by our cultural values, such as grades in school and scores in recreation, and by community recognition.[19] Despite the many direct and tacit artifices for promoting social values, group life must be recognized as an extension of biologic life and as an integral part of nature. To this I have given the name "social hunger."

Whatever the *raison d'être,* an important fact to be recognized in dealing with people in education and therapy is that the craving for acceptance by, and association with, other persons is primary and instinctual. One of the universal complaints of a neurotic is that people do not like him, and he fears group association, which must result inevitably in pain or failure. Though the neurotic's disturbance is intrapsychic, it manifests itself as a maladjustment, and he ardently strives to overcome this handicap. But social maladaptation is not confined to the neurotic alone. Patients with other difficulties are similarly afflicted. Whether an individual falls within the clinical category of neurotic, psychotic, behavior or character disorder or the psychopathic personality, his difficulties are related to people. It is, therefore, understandable why an effort should be made to explore the possibilities of employing the group as a corrective tool.

In the orderly growth of an individual in our culture he comes in contact with eight types of group. While all of them contribute to ego building and social adaptation in similar ways, each makes, in addition, specific contributions to the formation of character. The groups, in the order in which they become important to the individual, are listed in Table 2. It should not be assumed that these groups are disparate. Most of them are coextensive, and the individual is under the influence of several of them at any given time.

Parents, teachers, and psychotherapists must keep in mind that the "socializing" process is very slow. It takes a long time for the child to perceive the world in terms other than of his cravings and needs, for being under the influence of his primitive impulses (id) and pleasure drives (libido) he considers it a part

19 We shall see presently that group acceptance also gives one a feeling of adequacy (p. 31).

TABLE 2

MAJOR CONTRIBUTIONS OF SUCCESSIVE GROUPS TO PERSONALITY DEVELOPMENT[a]

Order	*Group*	*Major Contribution*
1	Family	Acceptance; unconditional love
2	Nursery or play	Social experimentation (socialization)
3	School	Creative-dynamic expression
4	One sex	Identification (socialization); sexual reassurance
5	Heterosexual	Heterosexual adjustment
6	Occupational	Social adequacy; economic security
7	Adult voluntary	Social acceptance (socialization)
8	Family	Mating, parenthood, self-perpetuation

[a] For more detailed discussion of these groups see S. R. Slavson, *Character Education in a Democracy*, New York, Association Press, 1939, pp. 37–43; and "The Group in Development and in Therapy," in Proceedings of the National Conference of Social Work, 1938, pp. 339–43.

of himself. It is as though he incorporates it. This stage can be described as one of *oral incorporation*.[20] We have already indicated that the discovery of the existence of other persons as separate entities (tuum) first shocks and later annoys him. But supported by his physical growth and concomitant psychological development, the child ultimately accepts the separateness of his physical environment and of other persons. But to make this very difficult renunciation of his own powers, he needs help from persons nearest to him. He cannot easily abandon his feelings of omnipotence and adequately develop object relations without this help.

The result of detaching the environment from the child's personality and differentiating between himself and it we term *individuation*, that is, the individual's separateness from his environment and the separateness of the environment from him. While individuation at first threatens the child, it also lays the foundation for later healthy independence from objects and people.

At this stage the centrifugal movement of the object libido is

[20] At this stage the child incorporates the environment into himself. Freud described this stage as one in which narcissistic libido is predominant, and, as some have pointed out, it is the source of oral aggression.

reinforced. This is essential in wholesome development, for as a completely separate organism one cannot survive as a social or a biological entity. Interdependence is a basic law of life at all levels, and it is especially true of psychological (social) survival. Individuation alone, however, is not sufficient, though it is a necessary step. Satisfying and constructive object relations are products of the individual's return to his environment, but on a different basis. Instead of being submerged in it, as he has been before, he now merges in an equalitarian relation with it.

This stage can be characterized as *reintegration*, namely, the individual's reintegration into his environment, which is accomplished by acceptable identifications, sublimations, self-inhibition, and a growing sense of reality. These are some of the conditions under which a socialized self emerges, that is, the individual establishes workable and realistic "ego boundaries."

THE FEELINGS OF BELONGING, IDENTITY, AND ADEQUACY

A very important by-product of successful group association is an enhanced feeling of self-identity. The child's self-identity, or self-image, is derived from identification with persons important in his life and from belonging to and being accepted by them and later by others. An unwanted and rejected child does not have a feeling of belonging in the family group. In addition to the fact that he feels sad, lost, insecure, his sense of self-identity suffers. One is a person, an individual, only by virtue of his relation to others. The sense of self results from the awareness of these relations. A child who is treated cruelly by his parents questions the authenticity of his consanguinity with them; one who lacks family connections and does not feel that he belongs sees himself as in a void.

A boy of eight, whose parents were separated when he was young, lived in a number of homes of relatives and was boarded with strangers, until he wondered who he actually was. He once stopped before a mirror he was passing and asked himself aloud: "Who am I?" The lack of a continuous relation with his parents and a family group and the changing roles he was forced to assume in relation to the different personalities and group constellations in the various homes where he had lived, created confusion in his mind as to his own identity. His identity had become as fluid and amorphous as were his relations. Sound self-organization and the attitudes toward one's self are largely derived from the definiteness and solidity of continuous relations with important individuals and groups, of which the family is the first as well as the primary.

Another boy under treatment was described as much disturbed when any object that belonged to him was taken away. He acted "as though part of himself were removed." This boy had had very little security in his life. He had grown up with a rigid, rejecting mother and an indifferent father, and he had been greatly hampered by a lack of primary identifications. He therefore identified with substitute objects. Things became invested with special meaning that provided him security as well as objects for identification. This is also characteristic of the use of fetish toys.

The feeling that one belongs begets a feeling of security and adequacy. A child whose role in the family constellation and in other groups is definite and secure perceives himself as adequate and worthwhile. His sense of self-esteem is high, and his self-image is wholesome and positive. Studies of basic needs and cravings of individuals unmistakably show that adequacy is a primary and compelling motive in the psyche of individuals, a need derived from unavoidably comparing one's self with others. In a peer culture success is of utmost importance to the development of a wholesome self-image, and the criticism of schools because they threaten to undermine feelings of adequacy in children (and usually succeed in doing so) is quite justifiable.

While constructive and helpful attitudes of parents and others strengthen the ego and lay the foundations for a positive self-image, the very smallness of the child in a world of adults and larger children unavoidably induces feelings of weakness and inadequacy. These feelings are never quite eradicated. The more the child's physical and psychological weakness and inadequacy are emphasized, the more damaging they are and the greater are the impediments to future corrective experiences. One of the crises in this regard is the Oedipal conflict. Here the child is forced to admit his inadequacy when measured against the "giant" father or the "dragon" mother. Thus, the result of the Oedipal struggle, if not intelligently dealt with by the parents, not only creates anxiety, with a variety of reactions and neurotic formations, but also damages the feelings of adequacy and the image of self.

Similarly, the discovery of one's difference from others in the environment engenders feelings of inadequacy. One of the universal difficulties women experience in their adjustment as women and in assuming their role lies in their sudden discovery in childhood that they differ from their brothers and other boys. The recognition of this fact undermines their feelings of adequacy. A similar reaction results from differing racially, culturally, or religiously from others in the community, especially from those who are in the majority. A member of a minority group cannot but feel different and therefore inadequate and weak. His only source of strength is his group, through which his phantasies of potency are enhanced and his self-identity is established.[21]

[21] See also pp. 245–46, and my "Extrafamilial Influences in Pathogenesis," in *Social Science and Psychotherapy for Children*, ed. by Otto Pallak, Russell Sage Foundation. New York, 1952.

PART TWO

Psychopathology

II

Pathogenic Factors in Childhood

EFFECTS OF PRIMARY RELATIONS

WHENEVER NEEDS leading toward security and growth are properly met, the personality automatically tends to become integrated in structure and adequate in function. When these are interfered with in any way, a state of disorganization—illness—results. The major sources of personality disturbances are the earliest relations in the family circle—with parents, siblings, and other persons important to the child, that is, persons who are necessary for his security and growth. We propose to term these relations *primary relations.* The entire development of the child and the course of his later life depend upon and are determined by the nature of these relations during the stages of nurture, discipline, and education.

One of the common sources of psychologic difficulties is either that nurture—namely, the stage of dependence and need for protection—extended beyond a suitable period into the period when discipline should begin, or that discipline was begun too early—that is, it was substituted for nurture. Children in the first category—those for whom nurture is extended too long—are overprotected, infantilized, and pampered. They present problems of maladjustment because of weak egos; they are dependent, helpless, ineffectual, and usually develop into exploitive, demanding, and narcissistic persons. On the other hand, children whose parents or nurses control, discipline, and frustrate them and whose behavior was directed and restricted too early in life are likely to become provocative, hostile, and aggressive.

We have already seen that both growth and security depend upon primary relations and are, therefore, essential for biological as well as psychological survival. When these relations are inadequate and unsatisfying the child reacts with fear and depression, which may later become the dominant motifs of his life. Early fears, if they persist, are transformed into generalized anxiety and arrested development at the points of maximum anxiety.[1]

A full analysis of patients' *nuclear* [2] or central problems, if they do not stem from constitutional factors, always leads to the primary relations and traumatic experiences in their infancy and childhood. The plan of therapy for any given patient must, therefore, be based upon helping him to correct his feelings concerning these early relations, to resolve the fears, conflict, and guilt surrounding them, and to perceive or understand them in a new and more wholesome light.

DISTURBANCES IN LIBIDO ORGANIZATION

When the primary stages of nurture, discipline, and education have been dealt with inappropriately or their order has been reversed, there occurs a dislocation or distortion in the organization of the child's libido. The oral cravings for food, sucking, and the security of close physical contact must be properly met in the infant before he is ready for the next stage in libido development, namely, the anal stage. The disciplines involved in toilet training, for example, are as complex as they are difficult to both child and parent and must be applied with great understanding and care. Similarly, the slowly evolving sexual sensitivity (which must be differentiated from genitality) require well-guided and well-controlled supervision on the part of the parents.

Unwise treatment of the various stages in the libidinal development of the infant and child leads to fixations or overemphasis on one in relation to the others. Thus, an individual may be fixed at the oral or at the anal stage. We know that the obsessional-compulsive character (and neurosis) stems from libido fixation at the anal level, while manic-depressives are fixed at the oral level.

When food is withheld from an infant too long, as in poorly scheduled feeding, he becomes depressed, and when finally fed, he grows elated. This alternation between depression and ela-

[1] See p. 21. [2] See p. 229.

tion is characteristic of the cyclothymic (manic-depressive) personality. At the same time, because the child's preoccupation is with food, that is, oral deprivation, he associates organistically and psychologically all pleasure with oral activity. The significance and symbolic meaning of food pervade the entire personality when oral gratifications (nurture) have been inadequate, and later permeate all areas of the individual's life. Such persons are said to be fixed on the *oral level.* They derive all gratifications by way of the mouth, display anxiety about food, become voracious eaters, and the entire pattern of their personal and occupational activity is one of oral incorporation.[3] They are dependent, demanding, insatiable, and arbitrary. At the same time they display infantile traits. They are narcissistic, domineering, aggressive, and expect special consideration and munificence from others. Because of their basic oral characters, such people are loquatious and professionally they may become public speakers and singers. In their sexual adaptation, oralism may become the central or at least an important element.

Oral aggression, which is one of the concomitants of this stage of libido fixation, is the most difficult type of aggression to treat. Usually this is a form of disguised hostility and destructiveness. It is also a low level of primitivity in social behavior, and according to our experience it is probably untreatable in its severe or extreme forms. Giving and nurturing does not seem to quench psychological insatiability. To permit these children to act out their oral aggression in no way alters their need to impose upon people and to dominate them. They continue their imperious, querulous, gossipy practices.

Oral aggression, as here described, is seldom found among boys, and when it is, it exists only in a very mild form. In our culture aggressiveness in boys has other outlets; they can fight, physically attack the environment, and sublimate through various types of physical activity. Orally aggressive girls usually have special physical characteristics; they are plump, of good complexion, well-disposed, and voracious eaters.

Fixation of the libido can also occur on the *anal level* when

[3] See p. 32.

toilet training is attempted too early or is carried out too severely. We have seen that to the infant feces and urine are perceived as part and parcel of his body, and in toilet training he is asked to give up this part of himself under set conditions rather than at his own free will. Through such means as slapping the buttocks, a harsh threatening voice or being left alone on the toilet for prolonged periods the infant is finally forced to submit to his mother's demands. This experience forms the first link in an endless chain of submissions. Out of this grows the need, which persists throughout life, of submitting to and pleasing the mother and later others. When toilet training is imposed at too early an age, the infant's urge to please his mother causes him to exert himself to succeed and to receive his mother's praise and approval. Repetition of this compliance to his mother's will and the compelling need to get her approval becomes the motif of his life, and the anal-compulsive character emerges. Prompted by his mother's attitudes, feces become associated with dirt; hence his compulsive neatness and cleanliness. The prevalent code for life is being obliged to do (equated to "must") certain things in a specific way. This pattern grows into an obsession, and the resulting character structure is compulsive-obsessive and anal-sadistic. In this condition an excessive quantum of libido is fixed on the anal level, which becomes overconditioned.

In his struggle to retain (retension) and to avoid giving up (expulsion) a number of psychological concomitants arise in the child in addition to compulsive neatness and regularity. Among these are miserliness and stubbornness, which have a direct relation to the training in defecation. Here the stubborn desire to retain the feces lays the foundation for stubbornness and miserliness later in life.

The next stages in the libido development of the child are the *phallic* (pre-Oedipal) and the *genital* (Oedipal) phases, which occur at different times in the child's growth. The situation here is somewhat different; in these phases of child development, especially in its later stages, other people are the recipients of the child's pleasure drives. In the preceding two areas—the oral and the anal—the entire process is organ-centered, while in the area of sex, other persons, particularly the parents, are involved, and object relations are therefore facilitated. Societal taboos come into play here, and secrecy envelopes the entire subject. The parents' prohibitions against the manipulation of genitals, the shame thus evoked, the administering of punishment, and the parents' own embarassment—all serve to fix the child's interest in sex and to create mystery around sexual feelings and urges. Societal morals and ethics are much more concerned with the sexual development of the individual than they are with the oral or anal. In fact, the overconditioned anal person is considered a useful member of the group, because of his reliability, frugality, and his capacity to accumulate and hold worldly goods.

That interpersonal relationships are vastly more involved in the sexual development of the child than in other areas has become clear from the description of the Oedipal conflict. Some difficulties, however, arise earlier, in the pre-Oedipal and pregenital stages. The pleasure drives directed toward the mother usually receive a jolt, largely because of her own unresolved unconscious cravings, her unsuccessful repressions, her feelings of guilt and shame, and lastly, but most important, her own libidinal urges toward the child. These latent and inhibited feelings, which under the circumstances cannot be fully repressed, are unmistakably registered by the child and activate premature or accelerated sexual urges. This situation is aggravated in families where the relation between husband and wife is not fully satisfying and sexual incompatability is one of the problems. Under these circumstances the libidinal satisfactions normally derived from the marital partner is sought from the child, usually unconsciously, but sometimes consciously. Acceleration of sexual drives occurs also when both or either parent erotically overstimulate the offspring by excessive physical play, patting, and other forms of excitation. When the child sleeps with one or both parents in the same bed or in the same room, the difficulties are further increased.[4]

Congested living quarters add to the difficulties in developing wholesome sexuality, and therefore many children under treat-

[4] See p. 243.

ment who have lived in crowded quarters require special attention in this area.[5] Frequently, however, we are faced by a lack of appreciation on the part of parents of the seriousness of these involvements and by their reluctance to change sleeping arrangements.

One of the manifestations of the libido that needs to be taken into account is the interchangeability of the foci of libido manifestations. Although at first it was thought that erogenous zones were confined to the genitalia and surrounding areas, it has been shown since that they exist in many other parts of the body. Among these are the mouth and the rectum. They are responsive to excitation partly because they consist of mucus membrane, which is sensitive to stimuli, and partly because of the evolutionary background of man. Before the appearance of functional differentiation in the organism, a number of organs were coeval. The anus, urethra, and vagina, for example, converged into a common chamber, the cloaca, in most animals, and in the human male the urethra serves for the discharge of both urine and semen. The anus and the penis and the anus and the vagina are controlled by the same muscles and nerve endings. Erogenesis is, therefore, more widespread in the body than was supposed, which makes possible "polymorphous perversion," to which Freud has called attention.

With the onset of latency, important and definite structural and functional changes occur. In this connection it is necessary to keep in mind the fact that latency does not set in or end abruptly or at any specific time. Rather, it is a slowly emerging and equally slowly receding physical and psychological process. This process occurs through a gradual sloughing off of one type of strivings and characteristics, to be replaced in turn by others, which differ in nature and in aim. The transition may take several years, and the changes in personality are not clear-cut—they overlap—and among the situations with which one must deal in child psychotherapy is delayed, extended, or accelerated latency.

We saw how sexual development may be accelerated, but it

[5] See case reports on pp. 145 *et seq.*

may also be retarded. In addition to differences in individual rate and rhythm in development, normal libidinal strivings may be delayed beyond the age at which they should normally occur.[6] The Oedipal period is affected as to timing and character when the relation with parents is unfavorable.[7] Children whose growth is retarded generally are retarded also in this area. Where the child is overwhelmed by the father and is unable to resolve the conflict in a constructive manner, he may remain in the midst of it, as it were. The Oedipal conflict of some children is negative or inverted. This occurs under conditions in which the love of the child is directed toward the parent of the same rather than of the opposite sex; as a result, the roles of the two parents are reversed in the psychic development of the child.[8]

DISTURBANCES IN EGO DEVELOPMENT AND FUNCTION

Among the most important influences in character formation are the diminishing libido drives and the simultaneous increase in ego development during latency. This fact is especially important in psychotherapy with children, since at this stage of his development the ego predominates in the child.

Just as appropriate external controls strengthen the ego, rigid discipline and unquestioned submission, which are the two cardinal demands of home, school, and societal education, inevitably weaken ego organization. Similarly, the guilt and fear aroused in school and home serve further to weaken the ego and to retard emotional maturity. Because actuality is replaced by symbols in schools, which is essentially anxiety-evoking, the schools hamper the orderly development of the ego. We have seen that instead of freeing pupils to work with self-assertion and imagination and creative and purposeful effort, schools limit, control, punish, and inhibit them. Formal schooling results in frustrating the dynamic and progressive evolution of personality in all its areas, physical, aesthetic, creative, emotional, intellectual, and social. The effects of these frustrations are aggra-

[6] See p. 82.

[7] This and other facets of libido organization are discussed on pp. 78–82.

[8] See footnote 7, above.

vated further by the fear of failure and the resulting stigma and punishment. It is safe to assert that a very large proportion of the number of children requiring psychotherapy and guidance can be accounted for by the erroneous methods of schooling, for it does not ally itself with the child's growing ego. Formal education rather exerts its full authority to impose restrictions, controls, and frustrations. Even with unfriendly families and unfavorable homes children might still be able to carry their emotional burdens and achieve a reasonable equilibrium in their lives. But when also threatened by failure in their peer culture and in socially overestimated school achievement, they break down and are added to the rosters of child clinics and courts.

Well-organized, calm, and self-controlled parents demonstrate by their own behavior the strength and self-possession most effective in dealing with inner (endogenic) impulses and outer (exogenic) pressures and demands of the world. On the other hand, irascible, easily disturbed parents, with short tempers and impulsive and unreasonable reactions, implant similar predispositions in children by example, imitation, and identification. A girl of ten, given to very violent temper outbursts, when confronted with her unreasonable behavior once said to the writer: "You think I have a temper! You think I have a temper! You should see my mother. She breaks the furniture in the house." This incident well demonstrates the sources of self-control and self-discipline.

In child psychotherapy the ego is always involved. We have already taken cognizance of the fact that at the termination of the Oedipal conflict the sexual libido subsides; it becomes more or less latent and is transformed from sexual to nonsexual libido. The reality principle, as opposed to the pleasure drives that reigned supreme in earlier years, begins to emerge and dominates the child's life to a larger extent than it did in the past.

This is what happens in orderly and wholesome development. When there are interferences with this development, the ego will be weak; that is, it will be unable to deal adequately with the pressures of inner impulses and the inpingement of actuality.

Libido organization has a direct relation to ego function. The impairment or inadequacy of one is reflected in the other, and improvement in either inevitably affects the other. The ego is called upon to hold the psychological frontiers intact, but a weak ego cannot hold libidinal strivings and infantile cravings sufficiently in check. Patients who require psychotherapy usually have such ego development. In some, this is frankly reflected in their lives and behavior; others evolve defensive façades that make them appear strong and able to manage their psychic forces. Actually, these are frequently overconditioned reaction formations, defensive pseudo strength, as it were.

The ego is the only one of the psychologic triumverate requiring nurture and special care. The id is nature's endowment, with which each organism comes into life. The superego is to a large extent unconsciously established, first by frustration, fear, and obedience and later by internalization of the parents' and society's rules, laws, mores, and regulations. The ego is the only one of the three that has to be consciously and systematically built.

Although the basic sources of the ego are biologically determined, its educative or developmental processes are inhibition, repression, discipline, identification, and internalization. They are strenuously resisted by the child. Part of the strife so common among parents and children is in this very area, namely, the former's insistence on limiting and circumscribing the id impulses in which the *parent acts as the child's ego* (as well as superego). We have seen that the manner in which the parent and the educator apply these restraints determines whether the child will reject or internalize them. When the latter occurs, discipline is transformed into self-discipline, and direct authority changes to ideal-formation, aims which are common to all good education.

The ego is weakened by (*a*) impaired libido development, (*b*) frustration or blocking of autonomous drives, (*c*) identification with and imitation of faulty models, such as weak and inadequate parents, (*d*) neurotic conflicts and feelings of guilt and fear, (*e*) ambivalence, and (*f*) organic and constitutional deficiencies.

We have already mentioned the relation of ego and libido and how the improvement in one corrects the other. It is equally clear, especially from our discussion on pp. 18 and 19 and pp. 45 to 53, how submission and dependency impair or prevent ego development. If the child is to internalize strong regulative and executive functions, he must be given adequate opportunity to do so through trial and error, experimentation, and reality testing. He must be exposed to situations graded in difficulty and intensity (graded reality) commensurate with his evolving powers, for the ego, like any other function of living matter, is strengthened through use and weakened by disuse.

Another source of ego deficiency is imitating or identifying with inadequate models. The presence in the family of weak or overassertive, domineering, fear-inspiring, or otherwise inadequate parents damages the progressive development of the child's ego toward effective adaptive functions. The ego can also be damaged by identification with persons of importance or popularity in the larger community and by its prevailing ideals and values.

The presence of a neurosis is a constant strain on the ego reserves, since a symptom is the result of and a compromise solution for the struggle between the id and the superego with which the ego is not strong enough to deal. In this tenuous solution the ego is continually called upon to maintain the psyche's equilibrium, which constitutes a strong strain upon it.[9] Another strain upon the ego is inadequately repressed feelings of guilt and fear, thoughts and phantasies—most of them in the unconscious, some in the preconscious and conscious—which must be repressed or controlled. The psychic energies invested in this and other conflicts may strain the ego strength to the danger point. "Nervous breakdowns" and in extreme cases psychotic regressions result. Ambivalence is another source of burden upon the ego energies, for to resolve the pull of the opposing forces in ambivalent feelings leading toward action or decisions absorbs a great deal of ego energy.

More persons than are ordinarily suspected suffer from psychologic debilities and emotional instability because of constitutional and organic defects. Endocrine deficiencies, various types

[9] See equilibrium-under-tension, p. 68.

of organic inferiority, mental deficiency, imbalance of the autonomic nervous system and other types of neurological disturbances of a constitutional origin prevent or delimit adequate ego integration. What seems on the surface a malformation or malfunction of a psychological origin is often actually traceable to organic sources. While in such cases psychotherapy may have only very limited value, it is of utmost importance that the presence of the physical factors be ascertained before treatment is undertaken. It is in this area that therapists may make serious errors. The therapist should be aware of the presence of physical defects so as to determine the course and depth of treatment and to set limits to therapeutic expectations and results. In some cases psychotherapy may definitely be counterindicated.

We have so far discussed the various conditions that interfere with the wholesome growth and functions of the ego as a result of overburdening and dissipating its energies. This is a serious problem. The quantum of psychic energy is more or less constant for any given person, and the greater the demand on it for special intrapsychic difficulties, the less is available for the normal activities required in ordinary living and for personality expansion and growth. Character restriction and constriction is frequently an outcome of the dearth in ego reserves. This quantitative view of ego functioning is understandably open to question. A qualitative approach to the psyche is more acceptable and more commonly employed. But the observable benefits from resolved conflicts and improved attitudes leave little doubt as to the quantitative nature of psychic energy. The general improvement brought about by psychotherapy in control, greater endurance, more energetic behavior, increased interests in job and friends, and general expansion and growth of the personality, all point to the quantitative nature of human energy, which also affects the various types of libido cathexis.

This relation can be expressed in a mathematical formula,

$$EE = RE + IE + GE + OE$$

where *EE* represents total ego energy, *RE* represents that part of the ego consumed in holding impulses in repression, *IE*, the quantum of ego energy required for integrating the psychic forces, *GE*, energy consumed for growth and personality expansion, and *OE* represents the quantum of ego required to deal with outer pressures and demands. If we accept the fact that the maximum of *EE* is specific for any given person, we must conclude that the more is drained off in the direction of any one of the components, the less is available for the others.

A person whose ego is unable to deal with the pressures of his own psyche and the realities of the outside world usually evolves defenses against this failure which become an integral part of his personality. When pressures grow too difficult, self-esteem is threatened, guilt activated, or fear induced, the ego aims to prevent anxiety either by dealing with the stimuli or, when this is too difficult, by avoiding the issues and thus warding off anxiety and pain. The various avoidance mechanisms are referred to as ego defenses. Anna Freud lists these defenses as denial, repression, reaction formation, escape into phantasy, projection, and introjection.[10] Ambivalence, I believe, should be added to this list.

Denial of reality is a very common technique employed at different times by almost everyone. When demands or facts become unpleasant, threatening, or painful, the easiest and most common subterfuge is to deny their importance and even their existence. This mechanism is particularly favored and readily employed by children, since their reality sense is at best not completely formed and denial is not too difficult. Adults frequently misinterpret this as "lying." One, but by no means all, of the several uses of phantasy and fiction is precisely this, namely, escape from reality. Although reality denial and phantasy differ in structure, their functions in this restricted sense are similar. Both serve as ego defenses and means of escape, and both have the same aim, to prevent anxiety. In one, no substitute for reality is offered, while in phantasy, a substitute is employed. The content of phantasy may be entirely unrelated to the actuality de-

10 Anna Freud, "Indications for Child Analysis," in the *Psychoanalytic Study of the Child,* New York, International Universities Press, 1945, I, 145.

nied, or actuality may be so distorted that the ego can accept it.[11]

Repression of particularly painful episodes or occurrences in the life of the child serves the same ends. When they threaten to set up in the ego feelings of shame or anxiety, one of the easy means for preventing them is to eject them from consciousness or awareness and relegate them to the unconscious. This mechanism, however, is employed by children less frequently than by adults. The child's natural impulsiveness and activity drives do not favor repression as a mechanism of defense. One would expect repression of infantile experiences to occur later in life when the superego formation is completed. However, since latency is the period of repression, we must assume that repressive forces operate at this stage in some areas. It is also understandable that particularly painful experiences, especially in relation to parents and siblings, would be dislodged from consciousness and forgotten. The faculty for forgetting (absolescence) is one of the major devices in nature for preventing pain and for more efficient living.

Projection is the most common of all ego defenses and is the last to be given up by the patient. Blaming others is a very simple and easy way to escape the threat from the outside world (punishment) and the impingement of the superego upon the ego. By making others seem responsible for one's lacks, omissions, and transgressions the ego is freed from self-blame and feelings of inadequacy. In addition to warding off anxiety, it also serves to prevent punishment. Projection also serves as a preventive of rejection, reproof, and punishment as well as a form of hostile aggression. We may assume that, unlike the other ego defenses, projection is induced and exists in a more intensive form among children who have punitive parents.[12]

The term introjection as used in this connection denotes the defense against feelings of inadequacy by means of which the ego appropriates from others the means of dealing with a prob-

[11] *Escape into reality* is one of the ego defenses employed as well, but seldom by children, and since it has little bearing on our presentation here, we omit it.

[12] S. R. Slavson, "The Treatment of Aggression through Group Therapy," *American Journal of Orthopsychiatry*, July, 1943; "Deflective Aggression."

lem that seems to it proper and adequate. Children, as well as adults, really believe that information or power they have so borrowed from others is actually theirs, acquired through their own efforts. This raises the patient's self-esteem and builds a more acceptable self-image.

Reaction-formations are frequently present in neurotic children who, being afraid of manifesting their impulses, evolve adaptive patterns of the opposite genre. Thus, excessive submission, ingratiation, and seeming generosity may serve to cover strong hostile and aggressive feelings. This pattern is frequently found in children's attitudes toward their mothers and their siblings. Protectiveness of and concern over a sibling are usually disguises of hostile feelings toward him.

Ambivalence results from a number of psychologic dynamics, but at this juncture our interest in it is as an ego defense. When the ego is too weak to deal with a situation or problems, yet not weak enough to succumb to it entirely or to give it up, indecision is the result. The ego's integrative function fails at this point and avoids making a decision.

Pathological inhibition of certain acts or expression in specific directions represents the ego's defense against committing acts unacceptable to the superego. Inhibition *per se* represents ego development and personality integration when it leads to efficient and effective inner and interpersonal adjustment. Inhibiting mechanisms are not only acceptable but also essential in a wholesome and integral personality, especially when they are employed in a manner suitable to the requirements of the situation. Inhibition requires the attention of the psychotherapist, however, when it is (*a*) localized, that is confined to a specific stimulus or inner impulse; (*b*) when it is bizarre and exaggerated; (*c*) when it has a compulsive quality, that is, it is no longer within the control or the discretion of the individual.

What has been said about ego defenses in the preceding pages applies more to adult psychoneurotics than to children. The ego defenses of the child are much less rigid, much simpler, and less varied. The child's superego, still being weak and unformed, renders defenses against the id less urgent and less intense. The conscious and unconscious are fused in the child.[13] This phenomenon is made possible by the weakness of the repression and censorship of the superego. The content of the unconscious is quantitatively less and qualitatively less rigid in the child; and repression is, therefore, less necessary. The problem of ego defenses in child psychotherapy, therefore, is not as keen as it is in the treatment of older persons.

Like the rest of him, the child's ego is still growing and developing. The defenses are sloughed off as an indirect result of a strengthened ego, and there is seldom any need for direct dealing with them. Just as a strengthened ego deals better with id and libido pressures, it is also more effective in dealing with its own defenses, for it no longer needs their protection. Psychotherapists are frequently puzzled that their child patients improve despite their verbal "unproductivity." Even though some children reveal little of their libidinal preoccupation and their deeper feelings and conflicts, they make good progress under treatment. There is no reason to be puzzled about it if we recognize and accept the fact of the predominance of ego development during latency.[14]

THE PROBLEM OF THE ID AND ITS CONTROL

At this juncture the id urges that are of prime importance in all types of child psychotherapy will be considered. The child is motivated by pleasure drives. He has to give these up for a more realistic pattern of life that involves self-denial and self-discipline which he does unwillingly. He carries on an unremitting struggle for the hegemony of his narcissism against the adults who seek to bring him into line with the demands of socially-determined so-called reality. In this struggle the child first uses direct opposition, such as stubbornness, disobedience, and reactive behavior of various types. As the struggle sharpens, which always occurs when parents are uninformed concerning the laws of child development, are overstrict or overbearing, the child develops various means to gratify id urges and prevent sub-

[13] See pp. 143 *et seq.*

[14] There are, however, children with deep neuroses whose treatment must be focused on the libido.

mitting to their demands. He develops especially strong tenacity to infantile patterns of behavior and reactions, pseudo-stupidity, pseudo-deafness, speech peculiarities, and symptoms. These are pathologic reactions to the effort on the part of adults to dam up the child's id energies.

Often physical illnesses are employed by the child as means of retaliation against, or punishment of parents and others for deprivations suffered. By causing inconvenience, worry, or anguish the child gets even, as it were, for the unhappiness caused him. Misbehavior and pathological symptoms also serve to gain attention and satisfy one's wishes. They are also used as weapons of control and of power, as well as means for exploiting adults. In more pathological reactions to frustrated instinctual drives, other than psychoses, the conflict is converted into physical symptoms, the hostility generated is displaced upon the organism itself or becomes inverted. Masochistic, self-pitying, but withal self-punishing trends appear.

The various means by which the id asserts itself against the restrictions and controls imposed by the superego, other persons, and reality pressures are part and parcel of the instinctual drives. They are forces that work against the inhibitions of the internalized superego discipline from parents and the social mores that seek to control, inhibit, and regulate them. The pathogenic effect of this is twofold. In the first place, it militates against the proper balance between the psychic forces within the personality. As the id continues to predominate, the ego and superego necessarily assume subordinate roles, and imbalance of the total personality results. Secondly, emotional maturation is prevented by the ascendency of the id, and the individual remains the prey of anarchic, unsocial instincts and impulses which lead to rejection, isolation, and social sequestration.

A further disadvantage of prolonged persistence in acting out pleasure urges as described is that they become incorporated into the character of the individual, since character is patterned mostly by repetitive behavior, imposed responses, and necessary adaptations (conditioning). Thus, methods employed to achieve secondary gains by bizarre and deviant means may become part of the personality structure itself. Before this occurs—and here is another advantage in child psychotherapy as compared to adult psychotherapy—the child can be induced to give up behavioral deviations for the therapist if the transference is positive. If the total life setting of the child favors this change, progress is even more assured. For this reason it may become necessary to alter the home and school settings as a part of treatment.

Among the most important interferences with the id urges is the libido repression during the Oedipal conflict, and improper dealing with it intensifies personality disturbances and causes a variety of neurotic manifestations.

When successful, psychotherapy not only corrects the ego formation and regulates the superego, but also the function of the id is altered. Instead of being a source of danger and a tyrannical master, it becomes tractable as it comes under the control of the reality principle. The ego can now repress and control the impulsions of the id with some success, but the id itself becomes less demanding. This balanced condition results from the correction of the libido distribution as well as the strengthening of the ego. In addition, psychotherapy guides the patient toward acceptable sublimations within the therapeutic setting and the outside world, which also serve to convert instinctual urges. This subject will be more fully discussed elsewhere in this volume.

WITHDRAWAL AS AN ADAPTIVE PATTERN

Though at times avoidance and flight are resorted to by all living organisms, normal functioning and survival are served by assertiveness. Both patterns are normal unless their intensity and persistence interfere with or diminish the effectiveness and efficiency of the individual. When an individual is so aggressive as to cause others to shun or to attack him, or when he is unable easily to make contacts with people, some disturbance or pathology requiring corrective measures are present.

Withdrawal, which is largely a result of inadequate security in the child (though interference with growth needs also plays an important part), may take many forms in addition to inactivity and nonparticipation. It reveals itself in mutism, stuttering, compliance, docility, submissiveness, ingratiation, indecisiveness, lethargy, apathy, taciturnity, intellectuality, and many other forms of direct or covert isolation. Inhibition of the spontaneous energies accompanying organic and psychologic maturational processes inevitably arrest the outward flow of energies (libido). When a child is violently repressed or rejected he may become either aggressive or excessively withdrawn. The first reaction is a rebellion against adults and a form of counter-aggression; the second is submission due to fear, though it, too, can be a form of aggression, as in passive resistance. The choice is made on the basis of constitutional predispositions, age, and the influence of parents and other persons involved, such as siblings, grandparents, or other relatives.

Even when there is no direct restraint and punishment, inhibition of the child's spontaneity is the inevitable and automatic result from association with unhappy, limited, restricted, or hostile parents or nurses. When the spontaneous emergence of activity is consistently checked by adults, the child begins to withhold it in order to prevent disapproval. Such physical inhibitions are accompanied by emotional constriction and diminution in intellectual and social growth. When the outer pressures are less intense, the resulting personality may not be inhibited, but instead *restricted,* that is, the individual functions acceptably, but his field of operation is more limited than it might have been if he had been given freedom of action.[15] *Constriction* results when the impulse for expression and activity has been deeply frustrated. Frequently there is present in such withdrawn individuals a conflict between impulse and fear of expressing it, which gives rise to an inner conflict resembling a neurosis. Such persons usually have overwhelming feelings of inadequacy and inferiority.

Another cause of withdrawal is failure in sibling rivalry. Many

[15] Over-protected and infantilized children and those with excessively strong loyalties to people, family, and other institutions are also restricted in their development.

inhibited and restricted children come from families in which sibling rivalries and antagonisms are unusually intense,[16] and the less successful of the siblings in the struggle ceases to make an effort. Having consistently failed either in outdoing or becoming equal to the more successful rival, a child may become resigned to failure. In so doing he also gives up other assertive efforts, and indecisiveness (ambivalence) becomes the rule of his life, enterprise grows repugnant, fear of all competition predominant, and the child evades situations in which effort or aggressiveness are required. The child sees himself as unable to succeed and supports his conviction by failure. He becomes a school failure, has few or no friends, is lackadaisical, slow, and dawdling. The secondary gains in attracting attention to himself through such means have value as well. This is one way in which he can outdo the preferred and more successful sibling. This type of behavior falls in the category of passive resistance, which is common among children.

In addition to the emotional debility, there is present also the element of repressed hostility toward parents and siblings. In some instances this inability to exert effort is accompanied by violent hostility; in others it is disguised by exaggerated affection, submission to and even protection of the more successful rival. Frequently there are present death wishes against parents and siblings, as well as fear of being killed by them.

Any physical, psychological, or social stigma may cause a child to withdraw because of feeling different and, therefore, also inadequate. The stigma may be real or imaginary, physical or cultural. It may be commonly observed that tall persons are usually shy and diffident because of the feeling that they differ from other persons in childhood and especially in adolescence. Their height seemed to constitute a threat to their physically smaller peers. The quiet, benign, and nonaggressive manner serves to diminish the chasm between themselves and others. Children with a physical deformity that sets them apart from their peers tend to isolate themselves. Obviously they cannot feel as free and spontaneous in their games and social gatherings. Fear

[16] See p. 90 *et seq.* and ch. xi.

of rejection and discrimination makes them cautious in their personal relations.

We have already noted that similar effects are caused by cultural differences. Members of minority groups—racial, ethnical, and religious—are led to feel themselves different from their fellows, consequently they feel inadequate and inferior. This results in defensive withdrawal, since being different means being weak, hence subject to discrimination and attack. The adaptation to this cultural complex is usually, though not always, partial withdrawal and isolation.

There is, however, a vast difference between individual and cultural stigmata. In the one, the individual stands alone; in the other, he is one of a large number of persons in similar circumstances. This similarity or homogeneity tends to cut across whatever other differences may exist and bring them together in a *microculture* of their own which gives each support and security.[17] When the number in the minority group is large enough, especially when they live in the same locality, each can adapt himself adequately. Not only do they feel comfortable in their microculture, but also more confident with members of other groups as a result. Numbers yield strength and security. This is intuitively recognized by all persons who have any kind of stigmata, individual or cultural. Members of minority groups usually live in the same neighborhoods and band together in associations. Persons with physical defects also form groups. The associations for the blind, deaf, and crippled attest to this. These and numerous similar organizations operate on international as well as national scales.

Adjustment to stigmata, however, does not always take the form of withdrawal. In many instances it is made on the basis of "reaction formation." The individual counteracts his basic feelings of inadequacy and fear by self-assertiveness, aggression, boisterousness, hyperactivity, acquisitiveness. This holds true particularly for individuals who have had to fight for status or be left by the wayside. Among those who nearly always have to fight

[17] See S. R. Slavson, *Character Education in a Democracy*, New York, International Universities Press, 1939, pp. 37 *et seq.*, and ch. xii.

for status are short persons, and just as the tall tend to be demure and withdrawn, the short are assertive and outgoing. This may be wholly a psychological adaptation to organ inferiority (Adler) or because of inherent vaso-motor constitutions for in considering adaptive patterns, constitutional factor must always be included. Reactions to cultural stigmata may induce in members of minority groups characteristics similar to those described for individual differences. They, too, had to struggle aggressively for status and survival.

In all the above situations we are dealing with defective *self-image,* which is corrected by association with others in a similar quandary. In addition to biologic survival and social security such associations supply, the self-image of the individual is corrected by *universalization,* or as someone aptly described it, "me-too-ism." In his efforts to help children with personal or social stigmata, the therapist deals with their self-image, for it is the feeling of self-regard that suffers most in this situation. In the adult, of course, this is manifested in feelings of sexual inadequacy and the fear of impotence.

Withdrawal may also emanate from deeply rooted feelings of guilt and the fear of being unmasked. In order not to be revealed, individuals may keep to themselves. Guilt may arise from hostile feelings and even homicidal drives toward members of the family, from incestuous cravings, masturbation, or other forbidden acts and thoughts, attitudes or impulses. To relax the bars may "let the cat out of the bag," as it were, and to prevent any untoward act or utterance that may do so, one avoids communication or contact with people altogether or limits it. The guilt-laden person is afraid of being punished for harboring destructive thoughts or indulging in forbidden activities either by an outside source or by his own superego. Unless basic difficulties surrounding such a withdrawal are overcome, it persists into adulthood and becomes the permanent organization of the personality or the basic character structure.

Narcissism as a source of withdrawal is a more or less common occurrence. Where inadequate and unsatisfactory relationships in the home exist, transition from the child's ego-libido to object-libido is arrested. He does not acquire the normal needs to associate with people and draws upon himself for the satisfactions that are ordinarily derived from friendships and association. Inadequate identification with adults in the family may cause the child to grow incapable of object relationships. This is not necessarily a neurosis, but rather a defective character formation that can be overcome, especially by the young child, through friendly, nonthreatening relations with individuals and groups.

Young children can gain much from well-planned group relations. The emotional activation in groups is considerably more effective and more rapid than in a relationship with an adult. Blockings are removed more rapidly because identification is facilitated in a group of children of the same age, and the child is more easily enticed into relationships.

A person who feels that environmental pressures are too great a threat and perceives himself too weak to cope with them may adopt an attitude of impenetrability and aloofness that often baffles the ordinary observer. Such individuals seem little or not at all affected by what goes on around them. They appear emotionally frigid and speak little or not at all. Such persons are sometimes described as "living corpses," but the description of "catatonic defense" is, perhaps, more suitable.

Such defense may be a general adaptation or may appear in specific situations only. One may function in an acceptable manner in some situations, but may become extremely withdrawn in others which represent a particularly strong threat or arouse anxiety or distress. Under these conditions one may withdraw physically. The impelling desire to avoid being hurt or to express resentment and hostility may also lead to a catatonic defense. This condition is sometimes found among children who fear what they may do or what may be done to them. In therapy groups they concentrate on their work with tools and materials and do not look up even when the other members of the group are extremely hilarious and playful. They spend hours, frequently over a period of many weeks and even months, in such a state of withdrawal, but in time they take cognizance of their surroundings by first looking toward the cause of the disturbance within the group and later smiling in amusement. This is followed by furtive and subsequently bolder participation. Provided no intense psychoneurotic fears are present, the unrestrained activity of other children seems to give such patients the courage to break through the overpowering fear of being hurt or destroyed, and soon take part in various activities.

Withdrawal is frequently used by children as a weapon against adults. When the child perceives that withholding annoys the adult toward whom he is antagonistic, he employs withdrawal as spite and as a secondary gain. In some instances he may develop mutism or stuttering. In less extreme cases the child does not carry out routines, does badly in school, dawdles, is late, and acts in a generally irresponsible manner. The greater the adult display of concern or worry, the more pressure is exerted upon him, the more lackadaisical he becomes.

Occasionally this pattern is adopted by a child who is emotionally so involved with one of the parents that he withdraws libido from the other to spite him. Another motive for spiteful withdrawal occurs when a child is forced against his will to take charge of younger siblings. This imposition may engender in the child a dislike of all children. A boy of ten once vividly described his feelings of fear as he sat alone at home watching over his sleeping younger brothers and sisters while his parents were occupied with their own interests away from home. This boy had been extremely withdrawn at home and at school; he had no friends and was not able to play any of the children's games or participate in their interests. Through activity group therapy he was able to overcome his basic dislike for children and acquire facilities for working and playing with them. With the help of his parents, this boy made a satisfactory social recovery.

In extreme cases of withdrawal there may be present an intense drive to return to the ease of the intra-uterine state, where no effort or adjustment need be made. Catatonia is such a state of being, and to a lesser degree, schizoid states. Withdrawal may be a result of neurosis. The blocking of energy is often accompanied by deep neurotic fears of being attacked or destroyed, of achievement, and of the responsibility that it entails. Achievement and aggression may symbolize incestuous coitus, and to prevent anxiety the individual withdraws from activity.

THE PROBLEM OF AGGRESSION

Elsewhere I have defined aggression as "directed activity, having definite purpose, direction, and object." [18] In view of the fact that all life is sustained by aggressive acts, both in the animate and the inanimate world, the use of the term in connection with psychotherapy must be restricted. In abnormal or pathological aggression the factor of hostility is present in a purely unconscious form, but its presence is recognized by the fact that the aggressor aims to provoke, injure, or destroy the object or recepient. It seems to me that there is an error involved when we say that frustration leads to aggression. Frustration *may* lead to aggression, but more often frustration begets hostility. The fact remains, however, that within limits and in so far as it serves the ends of survival and creative effort, aggression is a normal form of behavior. Only when it is excessive, uncontrolled, hostile, or destructive does it come within the purview of the therapist.

A second point to clear up is the difference between aggression and hostility, which will be only briefly mentioned here. Strictly speaking, there is no such entity as aggression. There are aggressive acts, and it is through such acts that aggression is revealed. Hostility, on the other hand, is an "emotional state," which may or may not manifest itself in overt behavior. It is rather a motivation and an emotional quality that accompanies behavior. It may, however, remain unexpressed, as in passive resistance, withdrawal, excessive passivity, noncooperation. In the neurotic it is often manifested as symptoms.

Thirdly, in judging aggressiveness in patients it is necessary to evaluate behavior in terms of the specific culture in which the individual has his roots and by which his character has been shaped. What may be considered excessive aggressiveness in a person in one cultural group may be quite acceptable in another milieu. Table manners unacceptable in one group or neighbor-

[18] S. R. Slavson, "The Treatment of Aggression through Group Therapy," *American Journal of Orthopsychiatry*, Vol. XIII, No. 3, July, 1943. See also pp. 26–29 in this volume.

hood are quite acceptable and normal in another. The manners of children who come to us for treatment, their food anxieties, and similar behavior patterns may shock us, but if considered in relation to their background they may be wholly acceptable. This principle must also be applied to their attitudes and behavior toward each other and toward adults. The patients' directness, indiscretion, "disrespect," and boisterousness may not be at all a problem when viewed in terms of the total cultural environment and early background. All their associates, including parents, behaved in a similar way. They have been "brought up" to such behavior. In fact, were these youngsters different, they would not be acceptable to their neighborhood peers. They would be stigmatized as weak and sissy, become scapegoats, and generally be socially maladjusted in their surroundings. Thus, the needs of survival in certain sections of society require a degree of aggressiveness which may be considered undesirable elsewhere.

To adequately describe a child's outward behavior it is necessary to differentiate between hostile aggression and playfulness, boisterousness, hilarity, provocativeness, assertiveness, outgoingness, and normal aggressiveness.

Agression may emanate from prolonged infancy. As may be expected, a child who has been overprotected and pampered tends to continue his infantile patterns in other relations as well. He is over-playful, provocative, annoying; he seeks attention, cajoles, wheedles, and is demanding. Because both adults and children find this behavior annoying, he is rejected and harassed and becomes socially maladjusted. The social maladjustment of such children is intense, for they soon become targets of counter-aggression from other children or become scapegoats and rejected. Even in the home, where the problem originated, because of the parents' unwise and unrealistic treatment of the child, he causes annoyance and is subjected to abuse and punishment after a certain age. The basic difficulty with such children is that their egos are weak and unable to deal with the earliest types of pleasure drives and demands. They have not established appropriate ego strengths and ego boundaries.

Aggression may also originate within the psyche when the hostility becomes associated with the parental image, which, as we have seen, is charged with hostility.[19] It has also an intrapsychic origin when, as in the case of patients with serious pathology, there occurs disintegration in the ego organization through regression or deterioration.

Aggressive acts may aim at attention getting when the child feels a need for reassurance. Psychodynamically, this is equated with love. When the need for love, affection, and emotional comfort are not met and the child is not satisfied in this area, he seeks any available persons as possible sources of love. It is not unusual to find that run-away children have a vague or unconscious hope of meeting someone on their travels who will give them the love they crave. Receiving attention, then, is equivalent to receiving love, and a child will use any means that will assure him such attention.

Children who have been made to feel weak and inadequate may adopt a pattern of recessiveness or withdrawal, or may fortify themselves against such feelings. Self-maximation, boastfulness, and phantastic self-aggrandizement may appear on the surface as pseudologia phantastica. Actually, they are only compensatory thoughts, wishes, and a desire to impress others. Such children annoy their peers, as well as adults, by their repeated interferences with group activities; they engender feelings of inferiority in their playmates, and consequently are attacked and rejected.

The organically or psychogenically hyperkinetic child is particularly difficult to assimilate in school and play groups, and he finds himself ostracized by his parents, his teachers, and other adults. Hyperkinesis is caused by organic deficiency, particularly glandular or neurologic imbalance, neurotic tension, or repressed energy drives resulting from early frustrations. When constitutional factors are discernible, medical treatment is indicated. When psychogenic factors predominate, appropriate educational and psychotherapeutic measures must be taken.

The reaction to frustration may have the appearance of neurotic behavior, but actually it results from suppressed drives for normal, wholesome activity. We have found, for example, that

[19] Page 24.

talented "problem" children became normalized when they were given an opportunity to work in fields that fitted their special abilities. Because they found fulfillment through creative effort and gained social recognition and status through achievement, they grew poised and happy. They no longer needed to express their cravings by means of substitutive and divertive aggression. For such children suitable activity is *libido-binding.*

Physically over-restrained children and young people often act as though they are neurotic or emotionally disturbed, but when freed of the repressions they behave more normally. The neuro-muscular craving for function and activity must be satisfied, thereby establishing equilibrium essential to poise and social adjustment. Canalization of energy is important for humans, and group activities may be valuable in this respect. They supply opportunities for free, unimpeded expression, help the child discover latent abilities, and direct him toward constructive occupations and interests.

Regulating and sublimating "aggression" of this type should really be the concern of education in the home and in the school. One gains the impression that homes and schools rather activate hostile aggression by rigidity, discipline, frustrations, and suppression of normal activity drives. With young children the substitution of intellectual learning for muscular and aesthetic experience is undoubtedly a major cause for the persistence of this type of aggression. Anxiety about success and failure in school further contributes to an emotional tension relieved by hyperactivity. Frustration of essential motor activity, however, begins long before school age. For their own comfort and as a protection for the furniture parents and nurses inhibit the activities of even very young children. Congestion in the home and the street, the absence of play space, and unsympathetic supervision are among the many elements that serve to inhibit the young child. These result in cumulative tensions, relieved through hyperactivity.

Concomitant emotional tensions and feeling tones are built up in the growing child through prohibitions and limitations that are opposed to his natural development of powers and activity needs. They also constitute rejection. When the adult applies restrictions and metes out punishments that seem reasonable enough to him, the child perceives them as hostile acts. In psychotherapy we must deal with these attitudes.

Children with intense neuroses are unable to enter into a relation with other children, cannot share the therapist, and are frightened by the manifestation of aggression and hostility on the part of the other members in a group. In fact, many of them cannot bear the compresence of others. They can face life only in isolation or under conditions which they themselves determine. Some are unable to accept love and kindness and are frightened by attention and praise.

Although most infantile children have an intense fear of growing up, we have observed a number who, though having this fear, have phantasies and exaggerated strivings to be grown up. This usually stems from faulty identifications with parents of the same sex. A boy whose father is weak, absent from the home, or intensely rejects his wife may phantasy himself the protector of his mother and assume (or act as though he assumes) responsibility for her. The normal striving to be worthy of his mother is intensified and accelerated in these cases. Such attitudes are especially strong when the mother is seductive or dependent and exploits the child for her emotional needs or as a weapon against the father. In many instances the boy is sexually overstimulated and is disoriented in this area as well.

This form of aggression in some children is both interesting and difficult to treat. It is interesting because these children behave like adults. The disharmony lies in the fact that the child is socially maladjusted because he cannot function on the level of children of his own age. It also expresses itself in his relations to other members of the family, especially his father, schoolmates, and playmates. Aggression is directed toward other children in a form that would generally meet with the approval of society. The child dominates others, but along lines of maturity, responsibility, and economy. He insists on good behavior and self-control by the others. Such children are inhibitors, miniature "witchhunters," tyrants, and serve as the "group's superego."

The tyrannical and self-righteous attitudes toward groupmates is supplemented by a subtle and indirect aggression against adults as father substitutes. A major need in the treatment of such a child is to redirect identifications from adults to his peers. This is accomplished in most instances by careful and well-planned group association. Boys and girls who manifestly strive to be prematurely grown up are detrimental to those whom they dominate and frustrate, while they are themselves unable to submit to group authority. Group association should be planned so that it will be possible for them to make friends with at least one child through whom they can make their way into the group. In this we apply the principle of the *supportive ego.*[20]

When early identifications are not in accord with the requirements of "normal" development in our particular culture, or when either one of the parents, especially the mother, is overdominant, boys may develop a character aptly described as an effeminate (castrated) character. Boys who have no brothers, but many sisters may develop such a character. When the total atmosphere is feminine, the boy must fit himself into it. Some become submissive and compliant, lacking initiative and assertiveness, but considerable hostility may underlie this façade. Others become actively aggressive and markedly arrogant and provacative. They may be hostile and even cruel to weaker children. This is considered a character disorder which can be corrected if treatment begins early in life and it is made possible for the child to be exposed to a living situation, such as therapy groups provide, through which he can take on masculine characteristics.

Deflective aggression is found in a great many children and adults, as well as among groups and even nations. When a child is afraid of possible attack, he may use the strategy of redirecting the attack by involving, with himself as instigator, the potential aggressor against himself in an attack on another child. The two then combine to torment their victim. Thus, the child fearing attack saves himself from this peril by redirecting it upon another.

[20] S. R. Slavson, *An Introduction to Group Therapy*, New York, International Universities Press, 1943, p. 153.

III

The Pathogenesis in Interpersonal Relations

TRUE EQUILIBRIUM AND EQUILIBRIUM-UNDER-TENSION

BOTH INTRA- AND EXTRA-PERSONAL EQUILIBRIUM are essential to wholesome growth and development. Tension in whatever sphere disturbs the natural trend toward balance and integration. It draws and ties down energies excessively at the point of stress at the expense of other facets of the personality. Disequilibrium tends to set up activity whose aim is to establish equilibrium of forces. All active phenomena in nature occur because of covert or overt disequilibrium, and the trend toward establishing balance or equilibrium sets up action. Earthquakes and tornadoes are, perhaps, the best example of this manifestation in inanimate nature, but this trend is as universal in organic and psychological life. The trend toward equilibrium is constantly present in man's psyche, even though equilibrium can be maintained only briefly. In fact one of the indications of mental health is the capacity of the human organism as a whole to re-establish equilibrium after periodic disturbances. Persons suffering from autonomic imbalance of the sympathetic nervous system, for example, are left exhausted and debilitated for long periods of time after any disturbance. Psychic disequilibrium is found in all types of neuroses and psychoses. This is most apparent in the manic-depressive states.

In the ordinary course of life equilibrium may be established through a perfect balancing of the forces. This is seldom fully achieved or maintained for any length of time. Most frequently *equilibrium-under-tension* is the prevalent state of psycho-organic life in man.

When equilibrium is disturbed by some outside force, related inner forces reaccommodate themselves in a manner that produces a result which is mathematically equal to zero. As soon as a load is applied to a bridge, for example, the various latent forces change and reaccommodate themselves to again produce a resultant of zero, for if this were not possible, the bridge would collapse. The rearrangement of forces to establish equilibrium in a bridge is particularly striking when the load is moving, as in the case of a railroad bridge. A similar phenomenon, or equilibrium-under-tension, exists in the surface tension of liquids and in animals when the contraction of the muscles balances the forces disturbed by a broken bone. Other common phenomena illustrative of equilibrium-under-tension, so frequently found in nature, are earth formations and water held behind a dam.

Man's organic and psychic equilibrium follows in every respect the same laws of equilibrium that operate in inanimate nature. His inner equilibrium depends upon the balance between psychic forces (id, ego, and superego) themselves and their balance with outer pressures and demands. The most important condition for a child's psychic balance is equilibrium in the family constellation, and its absence is frequently the chief concern of the psychotherapist and other workers in the fields of child guidance and family services.

Equilibrium in the family requires that each member of it has a specific role which he discharges adequately and that the result is emotional harmony rather than the discord of contending interests and drives. In this chapter we aim to outline briefly the place and functions of the persons making up a family group and to describe how their failure to discharge them causes problems in children.

Without underestimating the significance of the sexual nature of the many tensions and maladjustments in children and the importance of the Oedipal conflict, to which we shall give due consideration presently, other factors in the formation of personality and its disturbances must receive our attention as well. Chief among them are the earliest interpersonal relations in the family. These relations may be classified for the purpose of exposition as those arising from (1) the intrapsychic problems of mothers; (2) the intrapsychic problems of fathers; (3) relations with others in the home; and (4) extra-familial experiences. However, it must be recognized that in life there is no sharp demarcation between them and that they form one unitary whole that affects the child's development.

INTRAPSYCHIC PROBLEMS OF MOTHERS

The chief, and often the sole, source of difficulties in the child is the mother who for constitutional or psychological reasons is unable to function adequately as a mother and a wife. Among such women are (*a*) those who have not reconciled themselves to the feminine role, are possessed of intense penis envy, have masculine drives or are basically, if not actively, homosexual; (*b*) those whose Oedipal involvements have not been adequately resolved so that unconsciously they expect gratifications from husband and children of an Oedipal nature; (*c*) infantile, self-indulgent, narcissistic mothers who are unable to give of themselves and instead make unreasonable demands for gratification upon their offspring, such as in oral character organization; (*d*) those whose ego boundaries have not been sufficiently established and who consider children an extension of themselves, sometimes of a phallic nature. This may result from serious pathology and have a psychotic element, but many ordinary women overwhelm their children with dictatorial and authoritarian controls and demands, reflecting their basic rejection of the child which in some cases stems from retaliation against their husbands or from resentment against castration feelings that childbirth reactivates; (*e*) those who have homicidal drives toward their children, self-destructive impulses, and frequently well-defined suicidal tendencies; (*f*) those with weak, ambivalent, and vascillating characters, and (*g*) those who have affect hunger and are over-dependent.

(*a*) To the mothers, who because of basic and deeply unconscious drives reject feminity and the female role begetting children only serves to confirm their state and causes them as a result to function inadequately. Childbirth represents to them castration that further brings home their fancied lack, or childbirth may represent a loss of penis. Rejection of the child follows, which can take the form of neglect, cruelty, rigid discipline, frustration, and restriction. Some mothers in this category may treat their children in a manner characteristic of a reaction-formation. They are overindulgent, overprotective, and pampering. Actually this exaggerated concern only masks destructive and punitive impulses that do not escape the child's notice. Sometimes overindulgence hides homicidal drives. Mothers in this category are frequently in rivalry with their sons (for the possession of a penis). When their sons attend a therapy group, for example, they ask to be assigned to one also. They come to the son's or daughter's group sessions, even though they know that this attendance is forbidden.

The children of such mothers, especially the boys, suffer from the remnants of intense Oedipal conflicts and may feel strongly castrated, with concomitant hostile, aggressive, and self-maximating behavior and possible delinquency. In some cases the mother's desire to possess the son's penis is overtly expressed and even acted out, as when mothers bathe their grown sons or threaten to cut off their penises. When this is the case, the son becomes overanxious. This anxiety may be acted out, or it may result in a "character neurosis," with marked behavior disorders. Girls, on the other hand, unconsciously identify with the mothers' masculine drives, develop homosexual phantasies, but feel emotionally deprived and lonely. In most such instances the fathers are unable to function adequately as models for identification or to assume the paternal role in the primary triangle (father-mother-child relation).[1] Husbands of such women are usually weak, submissive, ineffectual, and dominated by their wives. They are unable to provide for their children's needs for normal psychosexual development because of their wives' all-pervasive domination, and assertiveness.

(*b*) Mothers who remain attached to their own fathers and are subject to guilt-determined submissiveness to their mothers are retarded in their psychosexual development, which in turn is reflected in the treatment of their children. Such libido fixation

[1] Pp. 86–87.

prevents deriving adequate satisfaction from a relation with a husband or children. Instead, they seek from their husbands and even their offspring the love and protection usually accorded by a parent. The emotional burden of this is too much for the children to bear, for the mother's demands are usually extreme, and her expectations of service and protection are beyond the children's capacity to supply. The children feel deprived and at the same time guilty. As a result they become self-deprecatory. The superego development in such instances is accelerated, and it becomes strict and exacting, with resulting guilt and anxiety. Many of these children develop neurotic traits.[2]

The fathers in such families are also ungratified by their relation with their wives and, too, may seek satisfaction through the children, adding to the pathogenic forces operating in the family group. This is especially the case where there is a daughter present to whom the father turns, thereby arresting her psychosexual development. The father may ignore the family altogther or become irascible, quarrelsome, and withdrawn.

(*c*) An infantile, narcissistic mother deprives her children of security, though such deprivations are usually extended to include the child's growth needs as well. The child, especially during infancy, needs care and tender treatment that only love can provide, and obviously the narcissistic mother cannot supply them. In extreme and prolonged instances of deprivation and neglect the anxiety induced in the child from the earliest periods of his life may under various circumstances result in an "impulse neurosis" or a "neurotic character." If the threat to his growth and security caused by the mother's actions and attitudes occurs later in life and is not too intense or persistent, the child's personality disturbance may be clinically diagnosed as "primary behavior disorder."

(*d*) The helpless, dependent children that require treatment as a result of domineering and overbearing mothers constitute a special problem to the psychotherapist. Here we deal with the disorder of character as a whole, not with a specific function, as

[2] Neurotic traits are in important respects different from neurotic symptoms. For this and other clinical categories see ch. v.

in neuroses or in reactive behavior. In the cases under consideration here the total adaptive mechanisms are involved, that is, the child had accommodated himself to a specific environment through which his infantile dependence had been extended and emphasized, his autonomy trends discouraged, his self-esteem and self-regard undermined, and his feelings of helplessness and weakness confirmed. When the total organization is thus involved, we can assume that we are dealing with a character disorder, a character malformation, character distortion, or character deviation.[3]

The overemphasis on and overextension of the dependent trends by harsh treatment, domination, and frustration of spontaneous motility, self-expression, and self-assertion, and the constant need to submit and to comply affect the total personality, not just part of it. Kardiner has well characterized the effect upon character of dealing with dependency. He states that rejection or counteraction of dependency produces an aggressive, stubborn, determined character; the acceptance of it determines a compliant, submissive, and vascilating character, while the evolutionary sloughing off of dependence begets the realistic, discretional, and suitably adaptive character.[4] The domineering mother, who is unable to accept the boundaries of her own ego and the autonomy and maturity of her child, produces one who is weak in character, shuns responsibility, fears assertiveness, and is afraid of success. His adaptive mechanisms are submission, compliance, and ingratiation.

The chief problem here is, of course, a weak ego, but the greater the deprivation, the greater the dependence upon the mother, the more likely is the child to give up the id drives and in extreme cases also the pleasure (libido) drives. The superego, on the other hand, becomes rigid and reflects the parental superego. As adults these children do not live a life of their own. They

3 This category must be differentiated from character neurosis or neurotic character. I am suggesting the various synonyms in view of the variety of meanings in which practitioners employ the term "character disorder." Whatever term is accepted does not matter, provided the meaning is clear.

4 A. A. Kardiner, *The Individual and His Society*, New York, Columbia University Press, 1939.

are almost like shadows of their parents, and many of them do not marry while the latter are alive. Not only are they dependent and weak but they also feel intensely guilty and are therefore unable to cut the silver cord, lest they offend their parents.

A more seriously debilitating effect occurs when a mother, and less frequently a father, is not manifestly circumscribing the child's life and growth by domination, but employs a subtle and disguised method of control. These mothers, too, view their children as extensions of themselves, without independent egos, but indulge them, thus inducing feelings of obligation toward themselves. The child forever remains afraid and too guilty to separate himself. This is a parasitic relation in which the mother is the emotional parasite who feeds upon the child's guilt feelings. In addition to a weak character, there is present in this situation a strong neurotic factor which complicates the therapeutic task, for to gain from psychotherapy the patient must have enough ego strength to make an effort to change.

In all cases of character malformation in prepubertal children group psychotherapy is indicated and essential. Obviously, verbal catharsis and even the acquisition of insight, if that were possible, would not change the *basic structure* of character. Experience with persons and situations shapes character and can be changed by another set of corrective experiences with peers and a permissive and ego-supportive adult. Even when there is a neurotic constellation present in young children, treatment must first be directed toward altering the character and strengthening the ego, which can be achieved through specially conducted groups. Sometimes a *neurotic residue* remains that may require individual psychotherapy. In most children in early latency, even the neurotic elements disappear as the ego is strengthened.[5]

In the treatment of character disorders the paramount fact must be kept in mind that here we are not dealing with a part of the personality, but with its whole structure, which includes the ego. It is inconceivable that the ego could contemplate itself. Insight therapy utilizes one part of the personality in the recon-

[5] See pp. 162–63.

struction and change of another. Experience, on the other hand, forces new adaptations, hence a change of character. It is this fact that led me to recommend institutional treatment in a conditioned environment for psychopathic children and adolescents,[6] since psychopathy is a character disorder.

(*e*) The pathology of mothers having a well-defined self-destructive drive is extremely complex. In such cases there are many pathogenic possibilities. Depending upon congenital, organic, and modifying factors in the family constellation, the children may develop behavior disorders, mixed psychoneuroses, schizophrenia-like reactions, or a combination of them. The inherent rejection of the children by such mothers and their cruelty create reactions that may take many forms, including "borderline" psychoses.

(*f*) Inconsistency in the treatment of a child fosters intense anxiety and a weak ego organization. A child can build up adaptive patterns to or defenses against whatever treatment he receives, even when it is bad, if it is consistent. When a child is treated cruelly, he reinforces himself against cruelty. He either becomes callous, insensitive, aggressive, or may evolve a variety of avoidance techniques which lead finally to a well-entrenched life pattern. This pattern may or may not be socially constructive, but it does establish some equilibrium between the outer stimuli and the inner responses.

Such equilibrium and methods for dealing with outer pressures and injuries to the security and growth of the child cannot be established when the treatment he receives is inconsistent. Consistency itself is a source of security, for one is not taken unaware and is not required to adjust to unexpected pressures. It is better for the child to know that he will be dealt with harshly than to be constantly on tenterhooks as to the kind of treatment he may receive. Both situations create anxiety, but of the two, the latter is the more serious. Parents who oscillate between love and hate, protection and rejection, pampering and sternness lay the foundations for anxiety states in the growing child, who

[6] S. R. Slavson, *The Practice of Group Therapy*, New York, International Universities Press, 1947, ch. v.

may later in life develop what is sometimes referred to as "anxiety character."

(*g*) Some mothers are dependent upon their children and place them *in loco parentis.* They assign to them positions of responsibility that require them to carry emotional and administrative loads beyond their capacities and willingness. The roles here are reversed, so that the child finds himself acting in a parental role to his mother.[7] This strain of functioning in an overly mature manner and performing too-difficult tasks generates considerable anxiety and damages the self-image. Anxiety is produced by the need to undertake activities for which the child does not possess the physical or the psychological powers, while the self-image is damaged because he sees himself in the role of an adult. The probable result of such a situation is a "character neurosis."

INTRAPSYCHIC PROBLEMS OF FATHERS

Because many of the problems emanating from paternal inadequacy have been discussed directly or by implication in preceding pages, only several of them will be specifically pointed out here. These are (*a*) effects of a weak personality in the father; (*b*) pathogenic possibilities in the Oedipal conflict; (*c*) the father's role in superego formation; (*d*) the father's role in ego development; and (*e*) some effects of a broken home.

(*a*) The basic need of the child is for a strong father. It is from the father that the boy draws much of his strength and fashions his personality for the role to which he is assigned by nature and society. The craving for a strong father also stems from security needs, for it is he who provides the livelihood (survival) and exerts final authority in the family (superego). Love, the mother supplies, but the needs for material survival and control are supplied by the father. When the father is weak, the son, seeking to substitute himself in the parental role, debases, provokes, and sometimes even physically attacks him. Upon analysis of such cases we find that the attacks and the provocations represent an effort on the son's part to activate the father to be strong

[7] See Anaclitic Relation, p. 105.

and controlling. In the absence of these characteristics, the son's insecurity and anxiety increase.

When the father is too weak or is otherwise psychologically unprepared or physically unable to assume his responsibilities and duties in the family circle, disequilibrium occurs. The pathogenic effects are further magnified by his reactions to his own inadequacies. He either succumbs to his weakness and enters into a dependent, parasitic, or anaclitic relation [8] with his wife or his children, or he reacts to his weakness by irascibility and reactive overdomination. Because of his weakness he may grow suspicious of his wife and accuse her, even in the presence of the children, of unfounded infidelity. Temper tantrums and beating the children, and sometimes even their mother, is not uncommon. In his helpless rage he terrorizes the family, but actually always feels weak and uncomfortable. Such men are emotionally isolated from the family group, which only serves further to activate their aggressions.

In either case—whether the father is frankly timid or overreacts—the stabilizing force in the family is lacking. The family is at loose ends, but the mother serves as the center of cohesion. Under these circumstances she is inevitably overwhelmed by the many responsibilities and the heavy emotional burden she is called upon to bear. Since the family does not have the father's steadying control, there is an undercurrent of unrest, insecurity, and anxiety. The children are called upon to assert their independence too early in life, which adds further to their fear and insecurity. They are also devoid of an adequate identification model, which weakens their ego organization.

The father's unreadiness to function may stem from a weak, dependent character—a result of his own childhood experiences—physical defects and illness, strongly unresolved Oedipal involvement with either of his parents, feelings of guilt toward them in relation to sex. It is clear that the treatment of children from such families would have only limited effect unless some guidance or therapy is offered to the fathers as well. Their own attitudes and functions have to be improved so that a more

[8] Pages 101–9.

favorable climate for the growth of the children can be established.

Failure to discharge the paternal obligations so necessary for the wholesome care of children is partly due to the conditions of modern life, but it is a serious problem, especially in ethnic or cultural groups, in which violence and neglect reach almost alarming dimensions. In some of these groups the incidence of acute alcoholism and "problem drinking" is very great indeed. Of special concern are the resultant material and emotional deprivations in the children, the inconsistent treatment they receive, the fear aroused in them by the drunken parent's violence, and the interference with normal resolution of the Oedipal conflict.

In other ethnic and racial groups dissolute fathers (and frequently also mothers) are the sources of various personality problems and social maladjustment in their children. They do not supply the secure relations that yield strong character organization. The weak family ties and irregular sexual practices complicate the network of emotional relations. Here, too, the Oedipal ties are greatly confused, and consequently there is confusion in sexual- and self-identifications. The ego ideals are faulty, and identification models, essential to wholesome development, are inadequate or even lacking.

There are also ethnic or nationality groups in which the prevailing pattern is the husband's subservience to the wife. In extreme cases, especially in families with problem children, the husband is in an anaclitic relation [9] to his wife. Under these circumstances the normal male and female characteristics are in contrast to actuality. In these groups the children perceive their mothers as phallic women, with dragon-like, destructive impulses and are actually afraid of them. On the other hand, men are seen as weak and impotent, and thus assume an erroneous place in the psychic economy of the children.

(*b*) The father's usual role in the Oedipal conflict is to accept and deal adequately with his son's hostility and the daughter's overattachment to him. But the father also functions as his son's

[9] See p. 104.

protection against the latter's sexual drives toward the mother. He is a deterrent to those impulses, which without such blocking may create great anxiety in the boy. Because of the son's still undeveloped ego, he needs the support of his father in this intense struggle, which must end in his suppression of incestuous urges. When the father fails him in this respect, either because of absence or of weakness, he lays his unprotected son open to intense conflict. For as the mother's accessibility is increased, the boy is prey to temptation. The child is reassured if the father is a strong, masculine person and at the same time accepts and is interested in him, for in addition to the help the boy receives in the Oedipal struggle, he also has an adequate model of masculine identification in the person of his father.

If the father is overbearing and cruel the boy, in his fear of him, submits, seeks to ingratiate himself, and attaches his libido to the father, which begets an emasculated and effeminate character who may also present psychoneurotic symptoms. This occurs also when the mother is rigid and harsh, for then the boy turns to the father for his primary gratifications, and an "inverted Oedipal" is the outcome, with homosexuality as a possible result. In the case of a girl, this situation begets a confused sexual identification.

On the other hand, when the father is weak, submissive, and inadequate as a male, by identification the son may pattern himself after the father, or he may grow overaggressive and provocative toward his parent and toward other adults as substitutes for him. Aggression here serves to activate strength in others, although he himself lacks it, so that he may receive guidance, control, and support for his own weak ego. A case in point is that of Morris.

At the age of ten Morris was completely disobedient, constantly sought attention, resisted going to bed and to school. He cursed and shouted at his mother and his father and occasionally even beat them. He was careless about his appearance, rarely washed himself unless forced by his mother, nor did he comb his hair. His refusal to bathe himself frequently led his mother to bathe him, but at other times he would not permit her to enter the bathroom when he was in it. He had been enuretic until the age of eight. Morris habitually refused food, and when his mother forced him to eat, he would chew his food and then expectorate it at her instead of swallowing it. When frustrated, he would lie on the floor pretending that he was dead, but once during such an episode, when a neighbor called with her child, he immediately got up and began to play with him as though nothing had happened. He rarely cried, and according to his mother he was never afraid except when threatened with having to be sent to a military school, where he thought they "broke the arms off the disobedient boys."

His mother described how once when Morris attacked her he pulled a handful of hair from her head, leaving a large bald spot, and how he punched her and her husband in the abdomen when frustrated. Once when the family and a number of relatives were seated at a holiday dinner Morris shook the dust mop over the table, spreading dust on the food. Morris had a sister nineteen years old, whom he annoyed by insisting that she do his homework. He crawled into the bathroom through a window when either his mother or his sister were taking baths.

In company with other boys, Morris set fire to trash in vacant lots, which seemed to be a source of danger to neighbors, but he ignored their complaints. He also played dice with boys on the street. He got along well at school, was friendly with teachers and children, was bright and successful in academic studies, and accepted school routine and discipline. Children liked him, partly because of his generosity, and he had many friends whom he brought home with him. Morris was described as having natural mechanical ability and being able to fix anything, including plumbing and furniture. He was always at pains to impress people with his maturity and assumed the manners and mien of an adult.

Morris was described as having always been an active child, but both father and mother dated the beginning of much of his aggressive behavior and physical attacks on them from the age of four, when he was struck by an auto and his shoulder was lacerated, requiring several stiches.

The mother was domineering, restrictive, and overprotective. The father stated that she would not allow the boy's friends to enter the living room. He himself was a weak, submissive man, who cried when describing Morris's treatment of him. He appeared helpless and hopeless in the situation and desperately appealed for help.

The *nuclear problem* here is the incestuous drive toward the mother, stemming from a weak father and a desire for a strong father figure. Morris's striking the mother may be seen as sexual attacks upon her, which is confirmed by his crawling into the bathroom when she bathed. His attacks upon his father are efforts to activate the latter to be strong and protect him against his incestuous wishes toward his mother. This is confirmed by his acceptance of authority at school. At present the father is in a sibling relation to Morris.

The first sexual object of a girl is her father, whom she wishes to have for herself. This is frequently expressed openly, when she suggests that her father marry her or when she promises to marry him when she grows up. This direct expression of her wishes is permissible before the superego has been fully established, but has to be repressed during the Oedipal conflict and later transferred to another man. The mechanism of this process has been frequently and adequately described in the literature and does not require elaboration here.

When the father is either too seductive or unduly restrictive and rejecting of the little girl's wishes for him, disturbances in her psychic organization result. This is especially true when his relation with his wife is unsatisfactory and he unconsciously turns to his daughter for affect gratification. When the Oedipal stage is reached under these conditions, the barriers that should normally be established between the father and the daughter are insufficient, which engenders anxiety in the girl so that she withdraws from him (and later from all men), or she may follow her instinctive drives and become unduly attached to him. Under these circumstances the mother, who should serve as a buffer between her daughter and her husband, does not function in that role, which renders the father too accessible.

An additional factor is that the daughter's natural resentment of the mother is intensified and her rivalry increased. The girl grows disobedient and provocative, negates her mother's authority, and rejects her affection. This antagonism may become crystallized into permanent hostility, which in many instances colors the entire personality of the growing girl and fashions her character. We have found that many of these girls are narcissistic, sexually provocative, coquettish, overly conscious of their appearance and dress, spending much time before mirrors dressing and making up. This is a result of earlier rivalry with their mothers, when they endeavored to overshadow and outdo them in attractiveness and desirability to the father. During therapeutic interviews some actually verbalize their conviction that they could have made better wives to their fathers than did their mothers. It is my belief that coquettishness in women has its roots in the Oedipal conflict, the girl having sought to displace her mother.

When the father is too severe, restrictive, or rejecting, the daughter may turn against him and become overattached to the mother, resulting in an inverted Oedipal relation and possible homosexual identification.

(*c*) It is commonly accepted that the superego stems from the father. This topic has received extensive treatment in the literature of psychoanalytic psychology, and a very brief statement will suffice at this point. The father, representing authority in the family as it is constituted today, exerts restraints to the vagaries of the anarchic impulses emanating from the id. At first these restraints are applied directly by the parent. After a period of such restraint, concepts of right and wrong, good and bad, and a general system of values are internalized and become the individual's superego. Conscience is only the conscious part of the superego. In this process values and censors are detached from the father and become an integral part of the individual's functioning by introjection. It also becomes part of his selective and judicious system.

At the same time that the superego is built through the restraining and standard-setting influences of the father as a person and as a symbol, the hostilities projected upon the father image, which we have already discussed,[10] are intensified, because restraints involve the denial of instinct gratifications. While the child accepts the father's standards, at the same time he resents the fact that he has to deny himself the pleasures he craves. Thus, the father's (as well as the mother's) strictness produces an overdemanding, sometimes referred to as a tyrannical, superego that later in life rejects even permissible pleasures. When the prohibitive forces of the superego are out of proportion to the requirements of a situation, a constricted personality results.[11] At the same time, the conflict between the id and the superego remains unresolved, and neurotic reactions or symptoms ensue.

When, on the other hand, the father is weak or indifferent, the discriminatory functions and the value-system are inadequate or unsuitable. This brings the individual into conflict with his society. In extreme cases psychopathic personalities result from the absence of internalized superego prohibitions under such circumstances.

It was usually assumed that the introjection or internalization of the paternal authority is the forerunner and major source of the superego. Because of the nature of our culture, the constitution of family life, and the function of the father in it, this is still largely the case. However, later investigation showed that the superego can be derived from either of the parents. Within the limitations of biology, the more assertive or effective of the two parents can be the determining factor. Thus, an assertive or controlling mother may be predominant in the structuring of the nature and intensity of superego restraints and prohibitions. As a matter of fact, a girl's superego formation of necessity is

10 See p. 24. 11 See p. 56.

patterned more upon the mother than upon the father, even though both play a part; likewise, in the superego formation of the boy the father plays the major role.

(*d*) As already described, the most serious damage that either the overdomineering or the weak parent, especially the father, may cause in the development of the child's personality is a weak ego. It has been already pointed out that while it is commonly accepted that the superego is a result of paternal influences, the ego as well is a result of the example set by the father (as well as by the mother) and the identifications the child establishes with him. A father with a weak ego will produce children with similar characteristics.[12]

(*e*) In our culture the mother remains with the children in broken homes, and the absence of the father creates special problems. The father's abandonment of the family means to the child that the former does not love him, and because of his own Oedipal wishes to eliminate the father, he frequently blames himself for the father's leaving home and sees himself as the cause of the family's disintegration. The child's wish to have his mother to himself now becomes a reality, which cannot but arouse intense feelings of guilt and anxiety. While he blames himself for what has transpired, at the same time he develops intense antagonism toward his father, whom he sees as the cause of his suffering and unhappiness.

Some of our young patients actually expressed their belief that their fathers left them by choice or because of their own desire that the parent be removed from the family circle. These confusions and guilt reactions are more intense in case the father dies. The child actually accuses the dead father of wanting to leave the family. In other instances, the child sees himself as the cause of the father's demise.

In addition to producing self-blame, the father's absence also engenders in the child the feeling that he is different from others and therefore inadequate. This feeling is often the most destructive consequence of a broken home. It gives rise to defenses that affect character development, with various results—usually

[12] For a fuller discussion of the role of parents in ego formation see p. 18.

oversensitiveness to criticism, feelings of weakness, inadequacy in life situations, and general social maladjustment.

The many pathogenic effects of a broken home have been implied in preceding pages. Depending upon the age of the child when the family rift occurs, the Oedipal conflict may remain incomplete, resulting in confused identifications, intense guilt feelings, and defective libido development. To a boy, the absence of the father, who would normally provide external restraints to his libidinal drive toward the mother, is especially inimical, for it gives rise to psychoneurotic manifestations. When the boy attempts to replace his father and take on the latter's responsibilities, his orderly psychosexual and social development are seriously hampered. The boy's self-image and self-organization become distorted. He grows up without participating adequately in the culture of his peers and the orderly evolution of interests, recreational activities, and occupations. On the other hand, he may feel intensely deprived, due to his father's absence, and invest the mother with phantasies that place her in the role of both father and mother. Under these circumstances his image of the role of a woman is distorted, a distortion that may create considerable difficulty in his later adjustment to women. The girl, on the other hand, invests her libido in the mother, which ordinarily should be attached to a person of the opposite sex, and that results in abnormal psycho-sexual development and general maladjustment.

The young child whose father is absent from the family circle completes that circle by creating one in phantasy. This process is induced largely by the fact that other children have fathers, and in order to be like them, he supplies this lack in imagination. Such phantasies are very important to the child and, like all phantasies, supply the elements that are either actually lacking or are too difficult to accept or manage.

The unequilibrated family can be greatly benefited by a substitute parent in the person of a grandfather, an uncle, or even a brother who is much older than the child himself. The emotional needs and the development of the self-image and identification models can be supplied by such father surrogates.

If these persons are constructive in their attitudes, the growing child can gain much from this relationship.

INTERPERSONAL RELATIONS IN THE FAMILY AS A GROUP

The relations between parents and children are not bilateral,[13] and the interpersonal dynamics in the family group are far from being simple. Family relationships are always multilateral,[14] which is sometimes referred to as the primary triangle—father, mother, and child, each forming an apex. Actually, the emotional network is much more complex. Relations would be triangular if each related to the others exclusively as individuals, but in the family, as in all groups, each relates also *to the relation* between and among the others. Thus, the child relates to his mother and to his father as individuals, but he also enters into and affects the relationship of his two parents. Similarly, the father has a relation with his wife and his child as individuals, but he affects and must consider the relation of the two and his place in that emotional constellation. This applies to the mother as well. In the same way, each sibling has to deal with the relations of his parents and their relation with every other sibling and the relation of the siblings to one another, and his relations to the parents as individuals and as a couple.

This vastly complicates the network of emotions and their ebb and flow in a family group. Every effort to analyze or describe them in general terms or to derive general principles from them is doomed to failure because of this complexity. An effort is made to represent this complex network in a group in Fig. 1.

However, despite their complexity, some understanding of the nature and dynamics of family interactions in childhood pathogenesis is indispensable for the psychotherapist and the educator. But because of this complexity an effort will be made here to describe some of the most common of these relations separately, and it is hoped that the reader will constantly keep in mind the fact that they always coexist, for one interpersonal difficulty or conflict sets off a long chain of others.

[13] Page 215. [14] *Ibid.*

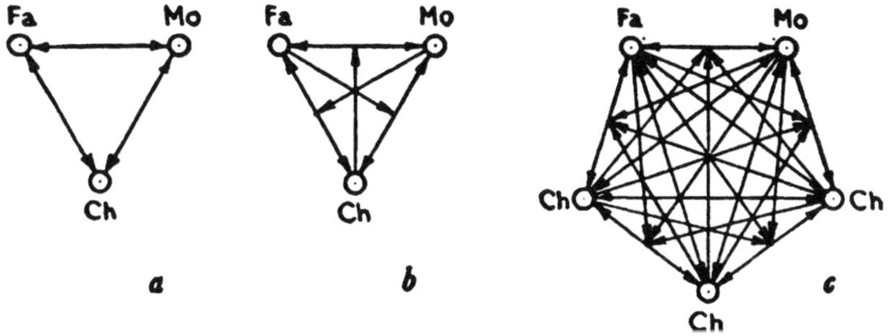

FIGURE 1. A GRAPHIC REPRESENTATION OF EMOTIONAL INTERRELATIONSHIPS IN A FAMILY GROUP

a) The conventional representation of the primary family triangle showing the relationships of the father, mother, and child as individuals.
b) The more involved relationship in a family where the mother, father and child who, in addition to relationships with one another as individuals, also *affect the relatonship* of the other two in the family group.
c) The relationships among two parents and three children where each member of the family is in relation with each of the other four and also affects the relationships of the others in pairs. In order to prevent the figure from becoming more complex, no effort has been made to represent how each may affect other combinations of relationships in the same family, that is, where three or four members may represent an emotional subgroup.

In a well-ordered family, as in all efficiently functioning groups, the status, role, and function of each member are well-defined, and the relationships are stable and lasting. Much pathology results in families in which the mother is dominant and the father plays a recessive role. The security of the child is greatly undermined when the mother, upon whom he depends for love, is stern and punishing. While "only he who loves may chastize," the young child cannot fear and at the same time seek the love and protection of one and the same person without serious confusion. The superego formation and the inhibitive functions of the ego should come largely from the father. When he prohibits and punishes, the security of the child is not threatened as much as when the mother does so, for he is not as intensely involved with his father as he is with his mother in basic dependencies that mean life or death to him. This is only one of the many definite roles that parents have. Another, of course, is that the role of each of the parents in the Oedipal conflict must not be reversed. Still another is that unless each parent lives out his specific role, identifications are distorted and sublimations and ego strength are poor.

Some of the pathogenic conditions in family relations are: (*a*) sexual incompatibility, (*b*) hostility between parents, (*c*) rivalry between parents, (*d*) parental phalanx, (*e*) sibling rivalry, and (*f*) difficulty with relatives.

(*a*) Sexual incompatibility is at the root of much marital discord. Since sex is one of the three major survival mechanisms and therefore charged with intense feeling interference with its full satisfaction generates resentment and hostility toward the marriage partner and guilt because of a feeling of sexual inadequacy. The first is caused by the frustration of pleasure drives and its resulting physical effects. The second, from concomitant feelings in each participant of his own weakness and impotence. We cannot enter here into a discussion of the involved theories of frigidity, impotence, and sexual incompatibility among men and women. We are rather concerned with the effects of these upon the emotional development of their children, for the hostility each of the marriage partners feel for one another can be displaced on a child or, quite to the contrary, a parent may become overattached to a child and seek from it substitute gratifications. As we have already seen, this complicates the Oedipal period.

(*b*) Hostility between the parents for whatever reason—and there are many reasons—sets up intense anxiety in the child, to which we have already referred, causing him to be generally unhappy, depressed, and hopeless in his outlook upon life. In order to assure his own security and status, the child allies himself with one of the parents, which lays the foundation for a general dislike and distrust of all persons of the other's sex. As a result, the child's social and psychosexual development is impaired. He is antagonistic toward teachers, fails in social relations, and withdraws to varying degrees from social contacts. If the rejected parent is of the same sex as the child, healthy identifications are prevented and sublimations for libido urges are not established. Since he strongly rejects the parent, he also builds up defenses against developing the parent's character and traits. Often this leads to confusion in the child's sexual identifications. If the rejected parent is of the opposite sex, the libidinal investment becomes intense in the parent of the same sex, and the Oedipal conflict remains unresolved, with various negative traits as an outcome.

Not infrequently a child whose parents are antagonistic toward one another is ambivalent, and this ambivalence colors his relations with others as well. He grows up to be incapable of strong or genuine feelings and attachments. He may become lonely or grow overly independent and indifferent. This *emotional frigidity* militates against satisfying relationships and the inner gratifications that result from them. To the therapist they present a serious problem in the transference relation.

When a child becomes the emotional battleground of both parents, who vie for his affection, he may form even more destructive character traits. In addition to a prevalent emotional ambivalence, he may develop emotional dishonesty by playing one parent against the other to his advantage. The character of such a child will always be devoid of integrity. This is one of the sources for either psychopathic character or psychopathic-like reactions.

(*c*) When there is rivalry between the parents, some of the reactions listed in the preceding section also appear. In rivalry between parents, however, the sexual element is present in a more intensive form. In such instances the partners may or may not be sexually compatible, but they compete with one another with regard to status and power within the family and outside. Usually this rivalry is the outcome of the masculine drives of the mother, her envy of men, or her need to humiliate them. The roles of the parents in the family are ill-defined, and the child is confused as to his identifications. The Oedipal conflict is also confused, a confusion that is reflected in the child's attitudes toward himself. The self-image is defective, and the libido organization does not follow a direct and orderly development.

When there is rivalry for power and status between parents, their roles are either permanently reversed, or they alternate as one is victorious over the other, with consequent disturbance in the libido organization and the ego development of their offspring.

(*d*) Sometimes parents are so close to one another that the children seem to be intruders. Instead of being the focus of the parents' love, they interfere with the very close relation that exists between the husband and his wife. In such instances, though they are comparatively few, the parents complement one another emotionally, but more often sexually. Their very close tie stems predominantly from the latter area. They are perpetual honeymooners, whose adolescent zest and romanticism do not decrease with the years. This does not mean that the children are treated badly. They are, however, at loose ends, devoid of emotional anchorage, lack a feeling of being wanted, though they may not be overtly rejected. As a result, their affect organization is disturbed.

(*e*) Sibling rivalry as a concept and a dynamic in interpersonal relations and its effect upon personality development is commonly recognized. Sibling rivalry is inevitable, but requires special attention when it is apparently too intense or does not abate with the years. It is understandable that a child should resent a new arrival to whom the mother necessarily devotes her attention. This resentment and the consequent hostility are part of usual human experience. They do little damage to personality as long as the child has the parents' support. When, however, he is neglected in favor of the newly born, much harm may be done. The child sees his sibling as the cause of his own loss and understandably reacts unfavorably to it.

The failure or success in this rivalry becomes one of the major factors in the life of an individual. To a considerable extent it determines the pattern of his personality. Whether an individual becomes competitive or not, just or unjust, petty or tolerant is at least partially determined by the course of this rivalry. Success in competing with siblings gives the child considerable satisfaction and a degree of security, but when they are attained at a great cost, especially when indirection is employed, the child may develop into a selfish, manipulative person, egoistic, assertive, driving, ambitious, and unjust.

Failure, on the other hand, is associated wtih inadequacy and an attitude of hopelessness. Some children become listless and indifferent and give up all ambition and the desire to succeed. Because of their intense hostility, some develop feelings of guilt toward their more successful siblings, and all advantages and achievements in the future reactivate the anxiety associated with the earlier sibling rivalry. The less successful may also become driving and overambitious as a compensation for the earlier failure, but this pattern is seldom found in children; it usually appears later in life.

When intense rivalry occurs between siblings of different sexes, another dynamic appears. The sibling develops the wish to be like the one preferred by the parents or the one most successful in the struggle. This causes him to adopt mannerisms and characteristics of the opposite sex, frequently accompanied by unconscious wishes to be sexually different. Unwholesome identifications are also involved here, frequently with disturbances in psychosexual development and character malformations.

The following case illustrates this point.

Brenda, eight years old, was expelled from school because of "terrific temper tantrums, bizarre and unmanageable behavior, and low school grades, despite her superior intelligence." She wrote invertedly and imagined there were ghosts in the drain pipes. Brenda's mother noticed that she grimaced and laughed in her sleep. Brenda herself felt that she was ugly, though actually "attractive, pretty, and neat," and she expressed openly her desire to be a boy. She complained: "I want to be a boy, but my mother won't let me." She was aggressive, tomboyish, and giggled at anything relating to the bathroom or boy-girl differences and said she didn't know "what girls have," since she "never looked to see." She was interested in mystery stories, animals, and cowboys and went to the movies carrying her own toy gun. During one exciting action on the screen, she whipped out her gun and yelled: "This is a stick-up!" In play at home she pictured herself as a murderess.

Brenda had one brother, four years younger than herself. Her parents felt that she first became a problem at the age of three, after the death of a stillborn brother, to which she reacted by withdrawal, negativism, and temper tantrums. She expressed extreme envy of the younger brother, who was the preferred child, but told her parents that she loved him. To strangers she admitted that she would like to kill him. Brenda slept in the parental bedrom until she was five. The girl suffered extreme trauma, beginning at the age of four and one-half, when electrocauterization of rectal warts was performed daily for two weeks and then at less frequent intervals over a period of several years. She suffered great pain. Brenda's best friend was a boy cousin, age nine, but she also played with girls.

Parents have both been rigid and depriving in their attempt to curb Brenda's aggressions. Her mother had strong masculine drives and forbade Brenda to act like a boy as a reaction to her own wishes in this area. Her father used to be closer to Brenda, but now openly rejected her ostensibly because of her difficult behavior.

The *nuclear problem*[15] of this girl is penis envy, and the *peripheral problems*[16]—confusion in the area of sex; phantasies of castration by the mother, and possibly also of phallic women and girls; hostility toward adults as substitutes for parents; sibling rivalry; desire to be a boy; confused self-image. The clinical diagnosis is character disorder.

Treatment plan. Play therapy by a woman psychotherapist is recommended, to clear up the phantasies that her mother killed her little brother and castrated her, and rectification of the confusions as to the structure of boys and girls. She should be helped to accept, through the transference relation, her femininity. Considerable work will be required with both parents, especially with her mother, who may gain more from a therapy group because of her own masculine drives, which would be difficult to work out in individual psychotherapy other than psychoanalysis.

Rivalry between siblings is intensified when parents are rejecting and unkind. The child's hostility toward the parental

[15] See p. 230. [16] See p. 236.

image is displaced upon the contending sibling. When parents and children are friendly and security and love needs are met in the family group, the children do not have to struggle for affection and status. They are then likely to accept one another. However, in families in which the relation between parents and their relations with the children are not satisfying, siblings cannot accept or tolerate one another. They displace their hostility onto each other.

Here, also, the very opposite may occur. In families in which all children are more or less equally rejected, and in broken families, the siblings may be drawn together in a symbiotic relation [17] for mutual support. They band together against the rejecting parent and present a phalanx of hostility toward him and at the same time draw upon one another for the love which has been denied them. This mutual dependence and in a real sense mutual parasitism is valuable for supplying the security needs, but is likely to be detrimental to the development of the children when it is carried over into adolescence and beyond, because of their limited capacity for object relations.

(*f*) The presence of relatives, especially grandparents, complicates the child's environment considerably. The identifications are nearly always confused in these cases. Grandfathers, particularly, assume importance in some modern homes because of the father's absence during the day, while grandmothers are prone to interfere in the rearing of infants and children. The child becomes the object of conflicting opinions between the mother and the grandparents, resulting in his exaggerated awareness of himself and his importance. The outcome is increased self-awareness, demandingness, and acting out. The reactions are similar to cases of divided loyalty, when parents vie with one another for the affection of the child.

More often, however, a strong antagonism and hostility arises against the grandmother or grandfather because they interfere with the child's direct relation with his own mother. Such feelings may also be generated against aunts and uncles who intervene in the child's relation with his parents. By and large, rela-

[17] See p. 104.

tives in such a setting are subjected to hostile feelings similar to those in sibling rivalry. When there is more than one child present, the children may unite and form a phalanx against the intrusive relatives. On the other hand, when parents are rejecting and unkind, children may turn to their kin and receive some security, substitute love, and support otherwise denied them. In such instances the relatives are of positive value in the child's development, since they furnish the necessary primary relations.

The following case illustrates a large number of principles we have discussed in preceding pages—the effects of the character of each of the parents, their relation to each other, the interference of relatives, physical congestion, school influences, and social dislocation.

Martin, an only child of seven, was brought for treatment by his mother because he clung to her excessively, sought continuous reassurance that she loved him, and was unable to play by himself. He needed the constant companionship of either children or adults. He was described as being exceedingly aggressive at home, but withdrawn when he first went to kindergarten and poorly adjusted at school. Unless urged, he did not participate in play or work with children in the classroom and had pretended to be physically ill in order to avoid going to summer day-camp. The mother said the school difficulty dated from the time a teacher in nursery school had taped his mouth closed because he talked too much. He read well, but wrote with difficulty. His mother reported that even when he was a small child it had been difficult for him to use crayons. Martin had no confidence in himself and declared that he could not do much. He dawdled a great deal and interfered with his mother when she talked to people, tugging at her skirts and speaking so loudly that he drowned her voice when she conversed, particularly on the street.

He had difficulty in dressing himself, which made him late to school, and he refused to wear his ski pants in the winter because he found it difficult to put them on by himself. He felt different in this respect from other children in school, because they dressed themselves. His mother described Martin as having been from early infancy, a nagging, whining child. He never could tolerate her giving attention to anyone else and demanded that the father, when he was at home, should focus attention on him, too.

Martin was described as being very aggressive, demanding, and domineering with the children who occasionally came to his house, and unless they obeyed him, he would become very hostile toward them. As already stated, he hardly ever played by himself either within or outside the home, demanding that either his mother or his father play with him. On the street, if he played at all with children, it was always with someone younger than himself. Martin had only one friend, a little girl who was very submissive to him and did whatever he told her to do.

The mother described Martin as an extremely orderly person, a pattern which she imposed on him. The mother frequently beat the child. When Martin was about six years of age, he had manifested some fear, and his mother dated it as beginning when a television set had been acquired in the home. Martin had nightmares that he was chased by buffalos. He had grown afraid of the dark and could sleep only when there was light in the room. When questioned by the mother about his fears, he said that he thought there were witches in his bed. He was extremely afraid of a dog which he had to pass on his way to school and for a long time insisted that his mother accompany him through that block. Martin was also afraid of the water and would not go into the swimming pool at camp.

His mother was a small, very thin woman with attractive features; she appeared exceedingly tense, but self-controlled. In the interviews, she at first spoke with a quiver in her voice, which disappeared when she became more relaxed. She was the middle child of three living children, one of the sisters having died of meningitis when Martin's mother was fourteen years old. She described herself as being an "introvert," unable to do anything on her own with ease, and having an all-pervasive feeling that everyone was better and more capable than she was. She was extremely "fussy" about cleaning, extremely orderly, and had trained Martin to be orderly as well, which she herself recognized as being "terrible. It is as though something is driving me. I just can't sit still." She was constantly in motion, and she felt that she was under great strain.

Martin was born two years after her marriage, when she was twenty-four years old and her husband was thirty-one. After the child was born, she followed her husband into several army camps. The three had lived in one room. When the child was about one year old, the father was sent overseas, and she returned to live with her in-laws, where she had had a very difficult and unhappy time. She was particularly unhappy when she lived with them during pregnancy. The relatives seemed to have taken over entirely the control of and the responsibility for the child, giving her very little status and making her tense and unhappy about it. However, she had felt too timid to rebel against them, so she put up with the situation until the father returned; the child was then three.

The mother described herself as being disappointed in marriage because the father was an indifferent, lackadaisacal person, having no interest in the boy; she had to ask him to play with the child. The father was attached to his own mother, who banked his money until he was twenty-nine years old and managed most of his affairs. She felt as though she were the man of the house and that her husband was a little boy. He accepted from her his weekly allowance and lived as though he were not married and had no family responsibilities.

Martin had throughout made a special effort to keep the parents apart. He was quite satisfied when she played with him alone, but when the father came in, he became aggressive and hostile toward her. Similarly, on week ends Martin was continually nagging his father to play with him, and when they did play together, Martin would violently chase his mother away should she enter the room. She felt that Martin was antagonistic toward her and did not like her. Although the anamnesis does not contain this information, one may suspect from the symptomatology that the boy had slept in the same room with his parents after the father's return and had overheard them at night.

The *nuclear problem* arose because the father had left the child abruptly when he was one year old, after having lived in close physical proximity in one room. The father's later indifference and the mother's compulsively strict control had evoked in the boy an image of a destructive, hostile world which he had to attack as a defense against being attacked. Acting out is another means of assuring himself of receiving his mother's and his father's attention (love), which he feels he would not receive otherwise. The Oedipal conflict is pronounced here, as was demonstrated by his efforts to keep his parents apart and his desire to have either his father or his mother entirely to himself, but the fact that he can be equally satisfied by either one would indicate considerable confusion in this area. His Oedipal jealousy extends even to other persons, for he interferes with the mother's conversations, pulls at her skirts, and tries to prevent her from giving attention to anyone else. This behavior also has many characteristics of pre-Oedipal behavior disorder. There are undoubtedly strong castration fears present, attested by his nightmares of being chased by a Buffalo (the father), and the threatening figure of the mother is represented by his fear that there were witches in his bed. His need to have a light at night stems also from his castration fears.

Among the *peripheral problems* are behavior disorder, maladjustment at school, fear of dogs and the dark, social maladjustment with children, inferiority feelings, and an unfavorable self-image. *The clinical diagnosis* is anxiety hysteria; possibly mixed psychoneurosis.

Treatment plan. Despite the comparative severity of the symptomatology, which in an older person would ordinarily require intensive psychoanalysis, Martin's age points to the need for concentrating treatment on both parents. The mother's neurotic castration drives and her compulsive patterns as well as her unfavorable self-image and feelings of inadequacy, must be corrected before either her husband or her son can function satisfactorily. The father must be helped to become more independent, to sever his relation with his own mother, and to accept his family responsibilities more maturely. Also, he needs guidance as to carrying out his paternal role by taking his son with him for walks, rides, and boating, and playing with him boys' games, as well as taking him to see others play. Martin may be profitably assigned to an activity-interview therapy group,[18] where he can act out freely without fear of punishment or criticism, but his acts would be interpreted by the other children and by the therapist. The child's social growth had been greatly retarded because, as the mother herself stated, he had always been with her and had had little opportunity to play with other children. The group would provide this opportunity for personal and social growth, and at the same time it would encourage him to detach himself from the parents through his relations with the therapist and the children in the group. The neurotic symptoms would be sloughed off as the child's total emotional climate is changed and his ego strengthened. We have had numerous cases in which such changes in the life of young children have overcome neurotic reactions and symptoms. In the absence of group treatment possibilities, individual play therapy may be substituted.

EXTRAFAMILIAL RELATIONS

The common belief that all psychoplastic influences and relations arise from the home only must be modified to include other areas in the child's biosphere. Elsewhere we have discussed the negative effects of the school and the consequent weakening of the ego and spontaneity. But even before and especially during school age (latency) homonymous (Angyal) or allotropic (Meyer) needs of the child assert themselves. Normally the object libido (Freud) drives urge the child on to seek associations beyond and outside the family group. These associations become increasingly important in meeting the social needs, in establishing identifications, and in building ego ideals. The culture to which a child is exposed is a determining factor in the quality and integration of his personality.

Many of the inhibitive functions of the ego are acquired

[18] See p. 295.

through association with friends and playmates and the susceptibility to id drives is regulated by the group of which one is a part. The need to belong with others, be part of and accepted by a group, is a primary need (social hunger). To be accepted by one's peers is impelling, and much character patholgy is generated by lack of success in this direction. In order to be accepted and acquire group status the child takes on and imitates prevalent modes of behavior, attitudes, and values so that he will not stand apart as different or unique from the others in his particular peer culture. Among them may be many that are considered clinically undesirable and socially unapproved. The child, however, does not as yet have critical faculties or a frame of reference beyond his immediate desires. Even his ego and superego, acquired in the home, are modifiable by these group demands and the climate of his environment. Because of these observations, I have suggested the term *group superego* as differentiated from parental superego.[19] Our observations of groups of children also convince us that the ego defenses are either modified or cast off through adaptive processes in groups. The self-image, as well, is affected or altered by the peer culture and one's status in it.

Despite multifarious individual differences, the culture in which individuals live determines the common elements of the basic character structure. The person conditioned in a culture that emphasizes competition, self-aggrandizement, and personal power differs from the person in a culture in which mutual help, modesty, and creativity are the aims and values. The character of a culture is essentially determined by the ways in which guilt, hostility, and anxiety are generated and dealt with by individuals and groups. It has been demonstrated that while the psychoneuroses are intrapsychic phenomena, their genesis is culturally determined. The regulation of instinct gratifications in a given society and the guilt generated are at the root of the neuroses. The cultural climate impinges upon the child via the family. Competitive values, drives to success, sexual frustrations, and social

[19] S. R. Slavson, *Introduction to Group Therapy*, New York, International Universities Press, 1943, p. 232.

and personal ideals and criteria indigenous to a culture permeate the home and the interpersonal relations in it through the attitudes and feelings of parents, siblings, and relatives and the climate of the home and the community. If popularity and status are the cherished values, the drive for status will affect also the interpersonal relationships in the family group and other microcultural groups: school classes, street gangs, athletic clubs, and other organized and free group activities.

Anxieties and fears that have economic roots do not leave family relationships untouched. Overburdened mothers living in congested conditions are prone to be less patient with a child's normal demands. They are less able to meet the needs of children and thus unintentionally beget in their offspring feelings of rejection and of being unwanted. Fathers whose incomes are small and tenuous and whose jobs are insecure are not likely to be placid and calm with their wives and children. Such factors have a direct influence upon the self-regard of the child and his feelings of security and therefore his growth.

The self-organization and the ego of the individual are also conditioned by the prevalent ideologies. If the ideology is one of mutual help and social responsibility, the individual, from the earliest stages of awareness, adopts these traits as a pattern of life and a quality of feeling. This occurs as a result of identifications and ego ideals, as well as because of a social hunger that impels him to be like others around him and be accepted by them. The balance between inner and outer values, a basic condition for mental health, is established only in a cultural climate that gives each its appropriate place.

A materialistic culture in which achievement and external values predominate over the inner and moral values fosters a character that contrasts in every respect with the ideal of the monastic, medieval society, in which emphasis was upon the subjective. In that society the tendency would be toward a hysterical personality structure, while in a materialistic culture compulsive traits are favored, as expressed in the excessive urge to work and to achieve. Thus, we can see that the effect of the social climate does not end with the family. The total cultural setting shares in the formation or malformation of personality and character.

Despite these modifying influences, and their importance should not be underestimated, the basic adjustment and pattern of reaction to groups is determined by the patterning of the emotional life of the child in the home and the manner in which his security and growth needs are met in it. Whether the child will be aggressive or submissive, courageous or fearful, rigid or adaptable, impulsive or controlled, constructive or destructive is determined by the manner in which primary needs are met and by the quality of intra-familial relations. In fact, whether a child will be able to participate in his peer culture and to have friends and playmates is conditioned by them.

TYPES OF RELATIONSHIP

I have described the various types of adaptation that may arise from early relations, and the following is taken largely from that report.[20] Some of the types are generally known; others are less well defined; while a few I had to formulate so as to throw more light on interpersonal relations in their specific and wider manifestations.

The types of relationship are domination-submission, parasitic, symbiotic, anaclitic, supportive, and equipodal.[21]

Domination-submission. The domination-submisson relationship is a common phenomenon and is considered by some sociologists a basic interindividual dynamic. When one submits to, is acquiescent with, or seeks control from another person who wields power over him, we have the simple type of domination-submission relationship. In evaluating this type of relationship as a pattern of adaptation we are interested not only in the overt acts but also in the unconscious disposition to submit or to domi-

[20] S. R. Slavson, "Types of Relationships and Their Applications to Psychotherapy," *American Journal of Orthopsychiatry*, Vol. XV, No. 2, April, 1945.

[21] See also unilateral, bilateral, and multilateral relations, pp. 214–15, and transference and substitution, pp. 168 *et seq.*

nate, which may or may not be acted out. In some instances, when conditions do not favor acting out, the dispositions are repressed, sublimated, or diverted.[22]

The psychotherapist deals with the individual's need to dominate in contrast to the equally psychogenic disposition to submit. When the child's drive for play, exploration, and experimentation, for example, are too violently frustrated and his growing autonomy is strongly counteracted, he may make adaptations of a submissive nature. On the other hand, when a child is helped to satisfy his native curiosity and activity drives, but his strivings for self-determination are overgratified, he is likely to develop mechanisms of domination. Thus, education, as broadly conceived, determines the nature of reaction and the behavior pattern of submission and domination.

However, the psychopathologist is not concerned with the domination-submission trends in individuals if their adjustment to family, vocational, and social life do not present particularly difficult problems. He is rather concerned with individuals whose domination drives proceed from serious emotional dislocations that undermine his mental health or injure or destroy the group. Even when such domination and aggression are withheld, they still constitute a problem both to the individual and to society. Domination and aggressive drives held in check may find egress through devious channels or through neurotic symptomatology. Whether the domination trend is converted into symptoms or is acted out, it is directed against the persons with whom the patient is most intimate, such as wife, husband, parents, children, or coworkers. Similarly, the submission trend in an individual may create many malformations in social adaptation and emotional imbalance within the individual.

Parasitic. In biology the true parasite is completely dependent upon the host for his very existence. He has no means of sustenance, and in some instances he has no mechanism for digesting food. He absorbs from the host food already digested and trans-

[22] This may be a culture-pattern in which the domination of men over women is the socially approved plan, or where women dominate over men as in other cultures. In some cultures economic status gives one prestige and power to dominate over others who are in less advantageous circumstances.

formed into living matter. The emotional parasitic relationship is the highest degree of dependence, and because of it such relationships among people are referred to as emotional parasitism. Physical and emotional parasitism in man have their origin in intra-uterine life of the foetus and in his helplessness during infancy. There is, therefore, a natural trend toward parasitism in man which is fostered in some families and cultures and discouraged in others.[23]

In the treatment of children with problems we frequently find boys and girls of nine or ten who are still being spoon-fed; they are attended to in the toilet and are not allowed to play with children. This dependence is nurtured by mothers whose emotional needs are such that acting as host to their children is necessary to their own self-fulfillment.

Parasitic relationships are frequently found also among children when a weak child attaches himself to a stronger one for help in activities and for social protection. The source of this parasitism is coddling, overprotection, domination by parents and others responsible for the development of the child. When education does not favor autonomy drives and fails to mobilize and strengthen native power through free and directed activity, achievement, and success, parasitism (and other forms of dependence) are likely to appear. However, by far the greatest source of emotional parasitism is the content of the parent-child relation. A parent who is deprived emotionally, sexually, and socially may fixate the child upon himself and make him dependent. In such cases the parent becomes the host, and the child is the parasite. The mother's or father's needs, on the other hand, may be such that he or she becomes emotionally, if not physically, dependent upon the child. In such instances there is a compelling need to give love as a compensation for one's own past deprivations, which makes the parent dependent upon the object of his love, the child. Here we have a situation in which the child,

[23] In oriental countries girls are trained from early childhood to have little status of their own. At first they depend on the family circle. Later they join the harem of the husband. This is an extreme form of deindividualization within the limits of normality. Even in our culture, parasitic relations are fostered by parents.

through no fault of his own, is placed in the position of host by the parent, who is the emotional parasite.

The degree to which psychotherapy can be effective depends upon a number of factors; (1) the intensity of the parasitic tie; (2) resistance of the parents to the child's maturation; (3) constitutional capacity of the child for growth; (4) the age at which treatment begins.

In the therapy of such children particularly, groups are very profitable. If the environment and the activities do not place too many demands or present too-difficult problems, the child is able gradually to perceive of himself as an autonomous entity and to function independently. If the parents are helped at the same time to give up their need for the child, his libidinal and other personality distortions are greatly lessened. Through example, the other children in the therapy group give the parasitic child courage to try his strength against his environment and overcome some of his fears and feelings of impotence. The group therapist, as well, plays an important role in this development. At first he permits himself to be used by the child as a host, but gradually he removes himself and helps the child to function alone. In the treatment of adults, it would seem that only a thoroughgoing psychoanalysis can be effective in such cases. A transference relation and a living out of traumatic situations that psychoanalysis supplies help one mature emotionally and throw off dependence upon a host.

Symbiotic. In biology symbiosis designates the mutual dependence of two or more organisms upon each other for subsistence and survival. What is commonly described as interdependence in modern society is a form of social and economic symbiosis. The nature of the symbiotic relations, as contrasted to parasitism, is that they are limited, all individuals involved remaining autonomous. A person depends upon members of his family and friends, and they in turn depend upon him for economic security and for emotional reasons. At the same time they have personal and independent lives as well.

A symbiotic relationship in which the need of two persons for one another is uncontrollable and the fear of losing each other is great enough to create distress, fear, and panic is fundamentally neurotic. Suicide pacts are probably the result of such mutual needs. Emotional symbiosis is present in homosexual relations, and often long-lived marriages produce symbiosis, when frequently one mate survives only a short time after the death of the other.

Emotional symbiosis can best be described as a form of mutual parasitism. It is a relation in which each of the persons involved serves simultaneously as a host and as a parasite. Emotional and social symbiosis is the foundation of social living. Symbiosis is present in group integration. It becomes pathological when the participants lose their own identity, become too dependent upon one another emotionally, economically, socially, or in all three areas.

Whether individual or group treatment is employed, both persons involved in such a relationship need therapy. A mother in a parasitic or symbiotic relation with her offspring is an essential element in the treatment of her child. In some less involved cases it is helpful to give her a vital and abiding interest away from her family and her home. Group treatment for such mothers should be effective, particularly if the treatment is aimed to extend out into the community and to provide her with social interests that will minimize her need for the child and make her emotionally more independent. Not only would the mother herself gain greatly from such groups, but the child would be freed to develop his own autonomy and to strengthen his ego. However, where the involvement of the patients is intense and is charged with unconscious libidinal tensions, psychotherapy is necessary for either the child or the mother or both.

Anaclitic. An anaclitic relationship has been described by Freud as one in which one person puts forward another to handle for him the actualities of life or to protect him against them. When a person is excessively afraid to meet new situations and the pressures of external circumstances, he may seek the help of another to intercede for him and to deal with these problems.[24] We often see persons who function adequately within a limited area; for example, they thrive in their professions as long as their clientele continues to come voluntarily, but fail when forced to take steps toward promoting their interests actively, since this arouses basic fears and insecurities that were dormant when circumstances favored them.

The overprotected child or one who has been or is an invalid would tend to develop an anaclitic form of dependence, if not a parasitic one. A child who has been limited and whose functions have been circumscribed may remain in anaclitic relationships to adults. When the personality is not seriously injured, when infantilism has not been unduly prolonged and libidinal distortions are not too intense, anaclitic relationships may be counteracted by extending the reality sphere of individuals and by exposing them to situations of graded complexity and difficulty. When the patient is helped to break through his basic fears and feelings of inadequacy by repeated successes, he no longer feels the need for a protective person. This can be accomplished through the maturing process which is stimulated by individual psychotherapy and in the case of young children by group therapy, where reality is extended from the group into the larger community.

Supportive. In an anaclitic dependence one withdraws and puts forward someone else to deal with situations. In a supportive relation the individual deals with it himself, using others to support him in the process. To survive as a group member, he needs

[24] Until comparatively recently, women were in an anaclitic relationship to men. It was the man who consulted government officials when a litigation was involved; he also went out and battled the world for a living. This has been greatly changed, and the anaclitic relation between men and women has also changed, certainly in a large portion of our population. Women no longer look to a man to deal with the world for them; they do it themselves quite adequately. Sometimes cultural pressures reverse roles, as during the period in Eastern Europe, when due to the absence of profitable occupations prohibited to them by law, Jewish men were driven into the synagogue and the houses of learning. It devolved upon women to earn the family livelihood, deal with, bribe, and cajole officials so as to make the conduct of business possible. In this case it was the men who stood in an anaclitic relation to women. They were almost completely protected by and dependent upon the women for meeting the reality situations of the world. The remnants of this relation are evident in Jewish families today.

the strength that comes from having a friend to protect and help him.[25]

Children themselves establish such relationships with others, usually with those who have similar traits. Aggressives will become attached to other aggressive children, and a withdrawn child becomes friendly with another withdrawn child. We have, however, observed instances in which opposites become attached to each other. An aggressive child chooses a more controlled individual to support him. This may have some connection with the ego-ideal situation, in which the aggressive child feels guilty about his aggressiveness and fundamentally wishes to be different. Therefore, he attaches himself to a more "normal" person in order to live out his ego ideal and for identification. It may also be due to the fact that where aggressiveness is a cloak for basic fears and timidity the child is afraid of aggression in other people and seeks the friendship of one stronger than himself.

Supportive relationships are usually temporary. When the child becomes more secure and more mature, his need for support diminishes or disappears. He detaches himself, moves out into the larger group, and makes contacts with children who earlier seemed to him threatening. Thus, a child who chooses a withdrawn person for his early support, may work out a friendship with a more aggressive child, whom he previously feared. This development is undoubtedly an indication of improvement in the client's personality structure. It involves a perception of inner strength, a growing maturity, a sloughing off of fears, diminishing anxieties, and greater independence. In most cases the child progresses to a state in which he need not attach himself to anyone, but is able freely to interact with all members in a group. Thus, he increases his personal mobility as well as the mobility and flexibility of the group itself.

Supportive relations are somewhat similar to the parasitic and the symbiotic. However, parasitic and symbiotic relations are permanent and charged with greater emotional drives and libido

[25] In activity therapy groups, children find such support in fellow-members or bring friends who are not members of the group, which we encourage. Many children would not come at all without such security. I suggested the term *supportive ego*, to designate such persons.

content than is a supportive relation. As already noted, supportive relations are temporary and transitional. The love-starved child, the child with a weak ego, or one who is constitutionally inferior, handicapped, or stigmatized needs support from the therapist. Big Brothers and Big Sisters are helpful in such situations. In some cases caseworkers and psychiatrists find it necessary to act as supports in individual treatment to the crumbling and weak egos of their patients. To a limited extent, ego therapy, counseling, and guidance rest upon a supportive relationship with the therapist.

Equipodal. In all types of relationship discussed above there are elements of dependence. Even the dominant person in the domination-submission complex is dependent upon the person or persons whom he dominates, for the need to dominate is a symptom of an inner neurotic need. In ideal relationships, persons are on an equal footing or have what is commonly described as a "give and take" relation. Submission and domination roles are adopted at various times by all the individuals involved. There is no drive on the part of one to subjugate or to exploit the others. Such an ideal situation is probably not very often found in life, but it is conceivable, that a person who had lived under favorable conditions in childhood or had been thoroughly psychoanalyzed would be capable of such a relationship. Even if few can attain this ideal, education and therapy must set it as their aim to help people establish the capacity for such relations, which we designate as *equipodal.*[26]

We have discussed relations as they arise spontaneously and are established automatically by people who live in proximity with one another. Some of them are by their nature the concern of the therapist, because they are fundamentally pathological. Others become so because of their intensity and their undersirable effects upon personality.

It is the aim of psychotherapy to help the individual mature emotionally and to eliminate drives to domination or submis-

[26] See also unilateral, bilateral, and multilateral relations, pp. 214–15.

sion, parasitism, symbiotic dependence, fears that produce anaclitic relations, and the need for support and overstrong transferences. We set out to produce changes within the personality that prevent easy interpersonal adaptations and render it incapable of desirable relationships with people.

IV

Clinical Approaches to Child Psychotherapy

THE CONDITIONS DESCRIBED in the preceding chapters can be reduced to clinical categories which are in a sense short cuts for the purpose of communication. It must be kept in mind, however, that the classifications to be outlined in this chapter give only general indications as to the nature of problems and the line of treatment indicated. The psychotherapist cannot rely solely upon these categories, however. In order to plan appropriate treatment and administer it effectively, he must understand the dynamics that operate in the patient's psyche and arrive at a thorough knowledge of the developmental background that led to his condition. This is discussed more fully in Chapter VIII.

PRIMARY BEHAVIOR DISORDERS

It is clear from preceding discussions that when a child is subjected to negative attitudes, harsh treatment, and overt rejection by parents or their surrogates he reacts to it by infantile patterns of demanding, unreasonableness, narcissism, self-centeredness, rebellion, and diffuse aggression. In other words, the child's response to emotional deprivation and threat to his security and growth needs is one of reactive behavior.

Such behavior has a number of aims. One is counteraggression —the child reacts in kind to the adults' treatment of him; another is revenge and retaliation for the pain suffered at their hands; still another is the desire for infantile control over the environment, the retention of omnipotence and power. Attention-getting, a term that needs to be understood somewhat better, may be another objective of reactive behavior. Attention is equated with love, another irrational survival of earlier stages of development.

Reactive behavior is also referred to as "primary behavior disorder." The term "primary" is employed to indicate that the deviant behavior is not a result of or secondary to constitutional or psychological defects or illness, but is a direct outcome of experience. One must note that behavior disorders usually accompany psychoneuroses, psychoses, organic deterioration, and other personality disturbances. Difficult behavior is clinically primary when it is a reaction to the treatment the child receives at the hands of adults. It is important to keep in mind the specific clinical meaning of the term.

Primary behavior disorders are classified as (1) habit disorders and (2) conduct disorders and may or may not be accompanied by "neurotic traits." In habit disorders remnants of early childhood behavior persist, such as thumb-sucking, crying, temper tantrums, language peculiarities, bed-wetting, and masturbation, though the last two can also be neurotic symptoms. The conduct disorders manifest themselves in behavioral patterns, such as school failures, disobedience, destructiveness, hyperactivity, dawdling, and disorderliness.

Disorders of habit and of conduct are continuations of behavior characteristics of the pre-Oedipal stage of childhood and are directed against the parents and their representatives—other adults, the school, and society. A primary or reactive pattern may be spontaneously modified during the Oedipal conflict, or it may originate during that period. When the latter is the case, the behavior disorder is described as of the Oedipal type. Oedipal type primary behavior disorders differ from the pre-Oedipal type in that they are related to the parents as a couple, rather than to either or both parents as individuals.[1]

School problems reflect the child's resentment toward parents; he uses the school situation as a means of punishing them. A girl may become "boy crazy," flirtatious, and even delinquent because she is jealous of the mother, desires to punish the father,

[1] Some psychiatrists attribute "character disorders" to the reactions at this period.

or tries to alienate the father from the mother. Delinquent acts, if not of neurotic, psychopathic, or psychotic origin, may be part of the Oedipal type primary behavior disorder syndrome. Maladjustment in the home, with concurrent good adjustment in school and other outside relations, is another indication of an Oedipal type primary behavior disorder.

A child with a primary behavior disorder shows little anxiety. Although he has been treated badly, he has been protected and was secure at least in his infancy. His parents' negative treatment developed as he grew older, autonomous, and self-assertive. In most cases his history reveals that repressive measures started at this stage. The mother met the infant's need tolerably well, but was unable to deal with his growing independence.[2] Primary behavior disorders usually originate because nurture is displaced by discipline too early.[3] By and large they result from frustration of growth needs, self-assertion, and autonomy, while character disorders are mostly generated because security (survival) is threatened, and neurotic reactions are caused by severe anxiety aroused at an early age.

Anxiety-producing experiences in early childhood add to the behavior difficulties either character deviations or *neurotic traits*, and because behavior deviations usually accompany childhood psychoneuroses, character disorders, and other disturbed states, considerable clinical experience is necessary (in addition to native perceptiveness) to recognize the true "primary behavior disorder." One can arrive at a correct diagnosis only by studying the full history of the case.

The pre-Oedipal behavior disorders manifest themselves at about two or three years of age and are specific. They are directed against a parent or his substitute. It must be kept in mind, however, that similar manifestations observed at an age earlier than two years may indicate some organic deficiency or constitutional psychopathology or psychopathy. Among the important factors to be considered for arriving at a reliable diagnosis are the re-

[2] When rejection, control, and punishment begin in infancy, various types of character disorders result, to be discussed later in this chapter.

[3] Pages 6–8.

ality and intensity of the external stimuli and deprivations. For this a thoroughgoing study of the family constellation is required. Frequently adequate information can be obtained only when the mother is under treatment, as well as the child; often the father also has to be interviewed. When it is found that deprivations and anxiety-evoking conditions have actually existed and there is a realistic basis for the difficulties, we should assume that we are dealing with a basically healthy but disturbed personality. Projective and other clinical tests are advisable before a decision as to diagnosis and treatment can safely be made.

Constitutional factors and the general predisposition determine to a large extent the type and intensity of reactions to external strains. In different children the same conditions and experiences produce intrapsychic difficulties of different intensities as well as of different clinical entities. We have already indicated that when organic and constitutional resources are strong enough to bear up under the strain the child will not become as disturbed as he would were he not so favorably endowed. Primary organic and constitutional dispositions also determine the success of therapy and set its limits.

The treatment of primary behavior disorders depends upon the nature and etiology of the disorder. In its pathogenic center are the defective relations with the mother and other important persons, which leave the child with undeveloped capacities for object relations and inadequate superego development.

The first step in therapy, therefore, is to help him to relate to an adult, to other children, or to both. Following the basic principle of all psychotherapy, namely, that needs of the patient must be met, the young patient is permitted initially to act out his pre-Oedipal and narcissistic indulgences. At this point the emphasis is not on limiting his behavior or on reeducating him, but rather upon establishing satisfactory relations. Only a positive relation will be his motive for giving up regressive, infantile behavior. This he will do for two reasons: (1) because his need for love is met, which serves to increase his security as well as raise his self-esteem; (2) because he now has a constructive model for identification, which corrects his superego formation and the structure of his ego. He internalizes the therapist's values and attitudes, as earlier he should have internalized those of his parents. Whether in individual or group treatment, the therapist assumes the role of the pre-Oedipal parent, and as such he permits all types of self-indulgence, imposing a minimum restraint and control, so that the child may generate his own inner controls (ego) through identification and a positive transference relationship.

After a period of treatment the young patients invariably give up their annoying behavior. When this occurs, the psychotherapist begins slowly to limit aggression. While he continues to be tolerant and accepting and still participates in the child's phantasy and play, the therapist now does so on a more mature level. In individual treatment the psychotherapist conveys to the child that he expects him to behave more maturely and either ignores some of his unreasonable behavior or points out its ineffectiveness and "silliness." Because the child now has a positive relation (transference) with the psychotherapist, he wishes to please him and avoids unapproved acts.

Thus motivated, he gradually brings his impulses under control. At definite points interpretation of the child's motives and the meaning of his behavior is in order. The psychotherapist may indicate that some acts are vestiges of infancy and that his resentments stem from his feeling deprived of adequate attention. The psychotherapist also encourages the child to verbalize his feelings and to talk about his behavior. Even a young child of five or six can be led to understand the reason for his acts. He can be helped to recognize that his enuresis, for example, is a means of retaliating for the lack of attention or because of sibling rivalry. When he is led to see the meaning of his acts and accept it, his ego is strengthened and he can give up his negative behavior for more realistic and more effective aim gratification. In this he is supported by the psychotherapist. The child must be treated with understanding and sympathy as a growing, maturing personality.

In group psychotherapy the controlling and inhibiting role

described is exerted by the other children and the "primary group code" that gradually emerges.[4]

We have seen that when certain relations toward parents exist, the primary behavior disorder may be complicated by the Oedipal conflict. When this occurs the primary behavior disorder is described as one of the Oedipal type and is colored by the sexual impulses the child feels toward the parent of the opposite sex and the fear of the parent of the same sex; but instead of developing intrapsychic conflicts and symptoms, the conflict is acted out. The child provokes, teases, embraces, and kisses the parent of the opposite sex, acts in a seductive manner, and insists on close physical contacts. In some cases of intensive disorder the child may even attack the parents physically, as well as verbally.

The Oedipal type of primary behavior disorder is somewhat similar to the neurotic character. In both, the patient does not internalize the conflict, but acts it out; it is not an isolated symptom as in a psychoneurosis. Because some degree of anxiety is present in the Oedipal type primary behavior disorder, treatment is facilitated. In the Oedipal type of behavior disorder, also, free acting out is part of the treatment process and the transference relation is the major fulcrum in the therapy. Because the psychotherapist is permissive and accepts the child's deviant behavior, he helps him transfer the libido cathexis from the parent to the therapist.[5] Furthermore, it has been demonstrated that in children sexual libido can be canalized into nonsexual expression and that the latter inhibits the former. The ease with which the child transforms sexual into nonsexual libido is one of the reasons for the ease and effectiveness of child psychotherapy.

During the development of the primary behavior disorder there frequently appear mild fears that, though having a neurotic tinge, are nonetheless devoid of the characteristics of a true neurotic syndrome. They are described as *neurotic traits* and are specific, such as fear of animals and of the dark, sleep-walking,

[4] S. R. Slavson, *An Introduction to Group Therapy*, New York, International Universities Press, 1943, p. 153.

[5] See p. 170.

tics, spasms, and hyperactivity.[6] Although on the surface they may appear to be like psychoneurotic symptoms, they are neither as intense nor as organized. Nor are they the result of the conflict between the id and the superego, as are true symptoms. Rather, they are substitutive responses and are much more accessible to treatment, since they are more superficial; that is, they are not so thoroughly interwoven into the structure of the personality as is a psychoneurosis. The differences between a trait and a symptom can be elicited from the history. The former originates in the relation between the child and one of his parents, while a symptom results from the Oedipal conflict, that is, the child's relation to his parents as a couple and the sexual involvements that arise from it.

THE PSYCHONEUROSES

Psychoneuroses are always the result of the Oedipal conflict. Their core is the child's sexual drives toward the parent of the opposite sex and the fear of punishment by the parent of the same sex. This occurs between the ages of four and seven. When the incestuous drives are not adequately repressed, the conflict between the id and the superego continues, and when the ego is too weak to reconcile this conflict or is unable to repress the libidinal drives, anxiety is generated. On the other hand, when the ego can manage the conflict, psychic harmony or equilibrium is maintained. Under special conditions the id may overwhelm the ego and even invade the precincts of the superego. When this occurs a defensive symptom appears to drain off the libido urges from its original aim. The symptom is, therefore, a compromise solution of the conflict and may manifest itself in various psychosomatic phenomena, such as debility, headaches, gastro-intestinal disturbances, aphasia, amnesia, other organic symptoms, or it may be expressed in fears, phobias, compulsions, obsessions, general anxiety, confusions, and similar psychologic states.

[6] It must be noted that some of these may also form a part of psychoneurotic system, especially of anxiety hysteria. The difference lies in their significance and origin.

Anxiety may be localized or specific; that is, it may be bound to specific acts or situations, as it is in a compulsive and obsessional patient and in anxiety hysteria, or it may be generalized or pervasive, as in the anxiety neuroses. In the latter, anxiety is "free-floating," the individual is constantly anxious, even though there is no external basis for anxiety, and may express this fact in psychosomatic symytoms, hypermotility, hyperactivity, and similar manifestations to drain off the energy generated by the anxiety. The stimulus that sets off anxiety may be from without or entirely subjective, resulting from inner conflicts between the forces of the id and the superego which the ego is unable to resolve.

The nature of the anxiety and its significance to the patient may be obtained from a study of the patient's history (anamnesis), especially the period of onset and the circumstances surrounding it.

Some of the sources of anxiety are:

(*a*) *Interference with survival needs.*—Whenever the basic biological needs for survival, such as hunger, love, or sex, are unsatisfied or interfered with, anxiety sets in. The resulting discomfort and tension in the body and in the psyche sets up action to gratify those needs and to establish equilibrium [7] (homeostasis). As a result, anxiety is diminished.

(*b*) *Interference with security needs.*—When one's need for belonging and protection are not met, fear and anxiety set in. This usually occurs when the parents neglect a child, when he is left alone unprotected, or when he is rejected.

(*c*) *Interference with function or growth.*—Anxiety also results from the frustration of the dynamic drives for activity and growth.[8]

(*d*) *Interference with ego or autonomy drives.*—When the growth of the individual's autonomy and independence are interfered with, anger and rage are aroused, which in turn set up a state of anxiety because of fear of punishment or abandonment by the parents as retaliation.

(*e*) *Guilt sources of anxiety.*—One of the most common sources

[7] See pp. 68 *et seq.*

[8] See p. 21.

of anxiety is the feeling of guilt aroused by disapproval from without and the pressure of the internalized superego.

(*f*) *Interference with constructive self-image.*—The ego ideal being one of the important moral drives in man, each seeks to achieve a sense of worth, to be accepted, and to have status. When these needs are not satisfied, the individual becomes depressed and anxious.

(*g*) *Social roots of anxiety.*—Most of the sources of anxiety so far described have social roots, for in the last analysis they arise from relationships and are determined by the conditions, mores, and values of a given society. In some cultures, for example, stealing would induce anxiety in an individual as well as fear of punishment. In other cultures stealing (particularly at certain periods) is not only permitted but even required. Similarly, what constitutes a moral transgression in one society is considered acceptable in other cultures, or what is virtuous at any given time and under certain circumstances in the same society may be abhorrent at other times.

(*h*) *Inadequacy for dealing with reality.*—When an individual feels inadequate to deal with the demands of outer reality, he reacts with anxiety. This stems from awareness of the lack of strength and of impending failure.

(*i*) *Inadequacy for dealing with inner impulses.*—When the id impinges on the ego, anxiety is felt. The symptom is a reaction (or a defense) to the invasion of the superego by the id when the ego is unable to hold the id in check.

The aim of psychotherapy is either to prevent the onset of anxiety, or to establish the ability to bear up under it when it is aroused, or both. This is achieved by decreasing the superego demands, strengthening the ego so that it can hold the id in abeyance, making the individual less vulnerable to group opinion, correcting the libido economy, and reducing the individual's need of the love and protection of others—that is, rendering him more autonomous. However, it must always be recognized that the capacity to bear anxiety has a strong constitutional basis, since the organism, especially the endocrine and vasomotor systems, are intimately and directly involved in it.

As far as psychogenic anxiety is concerned, correcting the states that make the patient susceptible to it may be accomplished by freeing him of the nuclear conflict through bringing into the open the original traumata, by cathexis displacement, and by insight. Egress for emotional tension may be provided by speech and by motor activity.[9]

The difficulty one encounters in treating psychoneuroses lies in the fact that while the patient suffers and wishes to improve (unlike patients with primary behavior or character disorders), he is really unwilling to change, that is, to give up the symptoms or the behavior that serves his neurotic needs. The symptom becomes integrated within his personality and serves to equilibrate the psyche. The psychoneurotic is always defensive about his symptom, for when it is eliminated, a void is established; he can see nothing to take its place. In psychotherapy a positive transference relation is at first his compensation for the loss of the symptom, until the conflict is eliminated. In early stages of treatment the symptom is no longer the only psychic equilibrator; the support of the therapist serves the same end. Later the dislodging of the cathexis, the acquisition of insight, and successful reality testing eliminate the conflict, strengthen the ego, and aid the integration of the psychic forces of the personality.

The most common psychoneuroses are the anxiety neurosis, compulsive neurosis (in which obsessional features may be present), conversion hysteria, anxiety hysteria, and character neurosis. When a patient suffers from more than one of these simultaneously, he is said to have a "mixed neurosis."

Anxiety neurosis is characterized by an all-pervasive anxiety without any special symptom organization. The patient is in a perpetual state of anxiety in whatever he does in his daily occupations and in all his relationships. A *symptom neurosis* is characterized by a definite symptom, usually accompanied by some somatic condition, such as headaches, gastro-intestinal disturbances, psychogenic debility, palpitations, excessive perspiration, tics, and so forth. The term *anxiety hysteria* describes the (psy-

[9] Further details on the dynamics of psychotherapy are given in chapters v and vi.

choneurotic) phobias in relation to a specific situation, such as being in the dark and meeting animals or strangers. An *obsession* is a recurring thought or idea. Under *compulsive neuroses* are classified those states in which the patient wards off anxiety by some specific act or acts, such as striking one's head against the bed a certain number of times before falling asleep and arranging one's clothes in a specific way. A neurotic constellation that pervades the entire personality, but does not appear as a specific symptom, is designated as a *character neurosis.* By this is meant that *all* the reactions and *all* the behavior are subject to and reflect anxiety and conflict. The patient's total functioning, not only some special area, is affected by it, which is characterized by overexcitability, impatience, ambivalence, projection, and an unrealistic perception of people and situations. It may be assumed that this state originates in infancy or very early childhood, perhaps in the pre-Oedipal period, when the early threats to and the frustration of basic needs for security were prolonged and intense and where the ego development was involved.

The psychoneuroses of prepubertal children and of adults differ in one very important respect, which requires different treatment as well. I consider this difference of great importance and the key to my belief that it is possible to treat preadolescent neurotic children by methods other than Freudian psychoanalysis, which I believe is essential for adults. The fact that the sexual urges the child feels toward his parents *are sexual, but not genital,* is the basis of this difference. Since he is physiologically unready for the sexual act, these urges are confined to the pleasures the child derives from being handled, fondled, and washed (which Freud included under the generic term "sexuality"). However, during puberty and early adolescence the genital cravings that are held more or less in check during latency are reactivated as a result of physical maturity and the rebalancing of endocrine functions. The individual then seeks direct sexual (genital) gratification from the parent.

Before and during the first Oedipal conflict the parent is the sexual *object* of the child's urges; he now becomes the sexual *aim* and the subject of genital gratification through coitus. In puberty and adolescence the youngster has to deal with and hold in repression these more proscribed feelings. If his ego and libido development had been faulty in the past, he is unable to do so and a full-blown (adult) psychoneurosis makes its appearance. Even from this brief statement may be seen the important qualitative difference between childhood (preadolescent) and adolescent neuroses.

We have already pointed out how essential it is for parents to exercise tolerance and gentleness during puberty and early adolescence of their children. The child's rising aggressions at this period are activated partly because the gratification of his instincts are forbidden and partly because the youngster has to defend himself against the forbidden impulses just described. It is our conviction, based on extensive clinical evidence, that the reason neurotic prepubertal children improve when treated by activity group therapy, despite the absence of direct interpretation and insight, is due to this nature of prepubertal neuroses. Strengthening the ego, which predominates during latency, is enough for many children, whereas for older children or adults libidinal cathexis displacement with insight is necessary to affect lasting improvement.

Sometimes a psychoneurotic superstructure may overlay a schizophrenic personality structure. Although schizophrenia, being a psychosis, is not within the scope of the present volume, it must be noted that if an early history of strange and bizarre behavior or appearance persisted over a long period it should be further investigated even though the immediate problem has the characteristics of a psychoneurosis. Particularly in childhood schizophrenia do we find that a psychoneurotic façade often covers a schizophrenic character structure or even an active process; to recognize this before treatment begins is imperative. A thorough anamnesis is necessary, but final diagnosis should not be made without using established projective tests, especially the Rorschach. If the clinical picture and test results disagree, the former should take precedence.

One of the indications which should arouse suspicion of such pathology is the early appearance of the symptoms. The mother usually reports that the infant has been "peculiar," withdrawn, unresponsive and that his development was unusually slow. Extreme dependence and constant need to be near his mother and fear and discomfort when she is absent are common symptoms of latent or active schizophrenia. Other children may have found him "peculiar" or called him "crazy," and the word "strange" appears often in the case history. On the other hand, in psychoneuroses symptoms make their appearance during or soon after the Oedipal conflict and are recognizable and easily described. If "peculiar" traits are recorded before the age of the Oedipal conflict, a thorough medical and psychological study of the child should be made to determine whether an active schizophrenic process is to be dealt with, or a schizophrenic personality structure or some organic deficiency is present.

If pathology beyond psychoneuroses exists, it is important to determine that fact, because treatment suitable for the psychoneuroses is counter-indicated for schizophrenia or organ deficiency. Rather than uncover the unconscious and threaten the ego defenses, which insight psychotherapy does, we should strengthen the schizophrenic's ego. An empathetic relation with and support from the therapist is necessary. The psychotherapist has to ally himself with the schizophrenic's world rather than explore it. If treated for a neurosis, a schizophrenic patient may be seriously damaged and latent trends activated into a real breakdown and psychotic episode.[10]

CHARACTER DISORDERS

Character disorders result from pathogenic conditions and relations to which the child had to adapt himself from his earliest years. The prolonged and continuous responses to outer demands, necessitating specific adaptations, determine the quality of the individual and the pattern of his personality that make

10 In recent years some psychotherapists have put forward the idea that schizophrenics can be treated by the "uncovering method." This position has as yet not been adequately established. At any rate, experiments with this technique have been made on adult schizophrenics. It is doubtful if it can be applied to children.

him specific and unique. This we referred to as "character."[11] The term "anxious character," for example, is used to describe a person whose anxiety states consistently had been aroused during his formative years so that his usual responses are marked by anxiety, lack of control, and instability. Persons are said to have "hostile characters" when their earliest years have been marked by frustrations and intense restraint and their personality is organized toward retaliation, rage, and anger. When these are consistent and prolonged, the responses and approach to people and situations are automatically hostile. These states color all responses, and a hostile character results.

The *neurotic character* is one in which acting out, motility, and distractability are parts of the total personality constellation. The behavior of such children suggests at first glance a behavior disorder, but when one deals with them more intimately, one is impressed with some basic differences in the quality of the force and impulses behind their behavior. In a primary behavior disorder the child can be brought under control for a reasonable period of time without arousing serious intrapsychic disturbance. One also observes a measure of self-control in the child when properly motivated. A child with a neurotic character displays signs of intense disturbance when his hyperactivity is impeded or when he is disciplined. Even when fear makes him quiet for a brief period, the inner pressure revealed is more intense and more serious than mere "restlessness." He is not able to remain quiet despite his best intentions, but is rather propelled into hyperactivity.

Some psychotherapists state that "a behavior disorder may assume the significance of a neurotic symptom." I believe there is a distinct psychodynamic difference between a behavior disorder and what we see in the neurotic character. While in both instances the patient acts out, there is a significant difference between the acting out of the child with a behavior disorder and

[11] See S. R. Slavson, "Activity Group Therapy with Character Deviations in Children," in *The Practice of Group Therapy*, New York, International Universities Press, 1947, ch. iv, especially pp. 72–76, for a more detailed definition of character.

that of the neurotic character. What seems to be the acting out of a primary behavior disorder may be the symptom of a neurotic character if it stems from uncontrollable anxiety rather than from retaliatory impulses toward a parent.

Children with neurotic characters were found to be unsuitable for group psychotherapy and difficult subjects for individual treatment, because a specific area or set of factors is not being dealt with as it is in a psychoneuroses. In the neurotic character the entire personality is involved, including the ego and the superego. This makes it difficult for the patient to view his behavior objectively, even with the help of the therapist. His impulses and the well-disguised and repressed anxieties are part of the cognitive process itself. Such children (and adults) cannot understand why they should not act as they do, for their behavior is an integral part of themselves, and they cannot be made aware that there are better ways of behaving and dealing with reality. The psychoneurotic is dissatisfied with his behavior and his feelings; he is cognizant of their nature. His superego is well developed, and he can establish a transference. In the neurotic character, conflicts have become deeply submerged and are translated into action. Object relations are at best weak, fleeting, and superficial. It is difficult to treat these individuals *in situo*. They require a new type of orientation, as do psychopathic personalities, that is, a controlled or conditioned environment such as an institution provides.[12]

The anamneses of patients with neurotic characters disclose a prolonged period of anxiety-producing stimuli and restrictive treatment at the hands of parents and threats to their security since infancy. Such persons had been deprived and were threatened on all levels of ego and libido development, and the resulting anxiety has become "normal" for them which they drain off in action. This is why they cannot remain inactive even when they wish to do so, for in a state of quietus the anxiety becomes too overwhelming to their ego.

In addition to the general and prolonged exposure to the anxiety-evoking situations and relations described, often specific

[12] See pp. 126–29.

situations of a traumatic nature have occurred. Chief among them are severe oral deprivations, prolonged sexual provocation by a parent, sharing a bedroom with parents, witnessing the primal scene, and similar traumata. Among my child patients there have been a considerable number whose difficulties stemmed chiefly or entirely from the fact that they slept in the parental bedroom, had easy access to the parents' beds or slept with one or both parents. Some children alternated between the father's and mother's beds, watched the parents in bed together, and overheard them at night. The sounds in the dark aroused phantasies of the father attacking or choking the mother. If a child is unfortunate enough to be exposed to the primal scene, a traumatic neurosis may be added to the pervasive or diffuse anxiety.

Insufficiently repressed incestuous impulses may also set up restlessness and hyperactivity that resemble a primary behavior disorder. They may be also symptoms of a neurotic character.[13] Castration anxieties may result under specific circumstances in a character disorder, in addition to neurotic symptoms, when feelings of inadequacy and weakness are present or when an organ inferiority, such as small genitals or undescended testicles, is involved.

It is evident from the preceding that patients with neurotic characters may under specific conditions develop also traumatic neuroses. This rarely happens to children. It is found more often among adults.

The *infantile character* is one in which early dependencies have been encouraged and autonomous growth discouraged—when there has been a dearth of growth-producing experiences and the ego is weak. Habit disorders, including language peculiarities, are often retained. Self-controls are weak, and in primary stages of treatment ego integration and character development have to be stressed. Such children act as though they were emerging from the period of nurture, and at the outset the therapist

13 Perhaps it is this behavior that is meant in the assertion that "a behavior disorder may assume the significance of a neurotic symptom." See p. 123. One suspects that the category of "impulse neurosis" may be analogous to what is described here as "neurotic character."

has to limit or restrict their acting out. Since for such children the building of the ego is the first consideration, outer controls must be consistent. There is little value for the child in continuing to act out infantile self-indulgences in the therapeutic situation, for this would make the child even more maladjusted. The therapist has to assume the role of the child's ego, deny him all secondary gains [14] and advantages until he internalizes the therapist's ego and superego.

In nearly all such cases the mother is in need of psychotherapy. Probing and insight are not important for the child, since we do not deal here with unconscious strivings, but rather with a character structure. The aim is to strengthen and integrate the various dynamic factors that had not functioned adequately and whose growth had therefore been impaired. Experiences in an environment that makes new demands upon the child are essential, and activity group therapy has been found most effective in correcting this type of character disorder.

The *psychopathic personality* is a special form of character disorder in which the superego formation is seriously defective or nonexistent. Indeed, so devoid are such patients of regulative principles that they have been considered "moral imbeciles" and that they suffer from organic deficiencies.

To discuss fully the etiology and dynamics of psychopathy would take us too far afield, and the reader is referred to my own statement on the subject [15] and the works of other writers. One of the complicating elements that enters into any attempt to define psychopathy as a clinical category is the fact of constitutional factors and organic inferiorities as they determine social adjustment.

There are definite characteristics that reveal unmistakably the psychopathic personality. They are manifested in the manner in which the patient deals with interpersonal relations and social situations. The psychopath characteristically rejects the moral demands of everyday life. He is evasive, narcissistic, and possesses

[14] Page 70.

[15] S. R. Slavson, "Contra-indications of Group Therapy for Patients with Psychopathic Personalities," in *The Practice of Group Therapy*, ed. by S. R. Slavson, New York, International Universities Press, 1947, ch. v.

a disarming charm that deceives many people, to their disadvantage. One of the chief characteristics is lack of "moral judgment," involving lawlessness and disregard of social mores, rules, and regulations. Other characteristics are selfishness and inability to form meaningful relations. His relations are perfunctory and superficial and are established for material or other personal advantages. Evasiveness, dishonesty, and indirection are the most common techniques of the psychopath, and his social graces and suaveness are his most effective tools in dealing with people.

Some writers believe that psychopathy is caused by specific constitutional lacks; others hold to the view that while there may be a small number of psychopaths who are organically defective, most patients with psychopathic personalities are products of early relationships which caused them from their earliest years to reject the values and standards of the important adults in their lives. One of the most important studies in this field was made by Phyllis Greenacre on a small number of patients diagnosed as psychopathic. She found that early relationships seem to be the cause for this type of character development and the resulting behavior. One of her striking findings is that the fathers or the grandfathers of these patients had been prominent and respected persons in the community, but were emotionally distant from the patients, and therefore their value as sources of superego development was low. Among these progenitors were persons who had public trusts and were in authority: clergymen, judges, heads of schools, civic leaders, and in humbler walks of life, policemen, detectives, truant officers. The mothers of the patients were overindulgent; they had a narcissistic attachment to the patients, and the psychologic separation of the child and mother had not been effected. Greenacre also indicates that the exhibitionistic components of the child's narcissism had been greatly exaggerated in the families, largely by the mothers.[16]

In view of the psychopath's deeply entrenched narcissistic personality and his inability to establish meaningful relations with

[16] Phyllis Greenacres, "Conscience in the Psychopath," *American Journal of Orthopsychiatry*, Vol. XV, No. 3, July, 1945.

people, he is unable to develop a transference relation with a therapist. Experience in group therapy, already reported, leads to the conclusion that it, too, is not effective. Psychopathic persons utilize the group for their narcissistic needs by monopolizing discussions, attacking the therapist and other members of the group, and by exhibitionistic and histrionic behavior. Children steal, destroy and break tools and other equipment, and deface and damage the walls of the rooms in which sessions are held. I have already suggested that the therapy for patients of this category must be less personal than it is in individual and group therapy. Nonetheless, the treatment must be in a group, since such patients cannot establish direct personal relations with individuals. These conclusions point to institutional treatment. They also indicate the importance of authority in treatment, since the superego formation and affect hunger are weak or unformed. Neither appeal to feelings of guilt nor an offer of love and understanding will evoke response in the psychopath.

Because he is motivated almost entirely by self-protective and survival drives, these must be threatened, for only in this way can the psychopath be made contrite enough to seek the help of other people. However, experience shows that when a psychopath is threatened, he quits any situation that gives him discomfort. In an institution all these conditions may be met. The psychopath can live in an impersonal relation in a group, but the group, the community demands, and staff rules set definite controls and limitations. Transgression of these rules evokes punishment or excommunication, both too painful for the narcissistic character of the psychopath. The inexorable regularity and inevitabilities of such a life impress themselves upon him, and he grows aware of extra-personal laws of social living. He may run away, but the inexorable arm of the law reaches out after him and he is returned to the institution. After a number of trials and escapes and much defiance the inevitable reality of the situation impresses itself upon him, and he slowly begins to conform.

In this struggle the psychopath will seek the support and help of others. This is in itself a therapeutic triumph, for the very act of seeking association and help is a step away from his basic emotional isolation and independence. I have already pointed out that this step is particularly constructive when the patient seeks the help of a staff member who is a skilled psychotherapist.[17] As such, he can utilize the patient's need in establishing a relationship, which, if properly dealt with, helps the formation of the superego and the ego. Of course, it must be recognized that this procedure is valid only with psychogenic psychopathic personalities, not when organic and biological factors militate against ego and superego development.

The treatment plan suggested is based upon my conviction, derived from experience with psychopaths in individual, group, and institutional treatment, that the current belief that psychopaths are devoid of anxiety is not correct. My own view is that the psychogenic psychopath has a great deal of anxiety, which he had repressed so deeply and so early that it remains dormant in ordinary situations. His negative treatment in childhood caused him to reject all values, standards, and mores held important to the antagonistic adults whom he had rejected or who were unattainable to him. However, in the process of this rejection anxieties arose, which he repressed, and continued to repress throughout his life. These repressions are so thorough that to the casual observer no anxiety is apparent; actually, what is needed is a situation sufficiently threatening to bring it to the surface. It is this latent anxiety that we must use in the reintegration of the psychopathic personality. It is my belief that further studies in this area would throw new light on the problem.

Types of character constellation that come to the attention of the psychoclinician are broadly described as *withdrawn* and *aggressive*. These general delineations refer to very complicated and varied sets of psychodynamic constellations that have already been described in Chapter II, where withdrawal and aggression were discussed. At this juncture it is necessary only to recall that the psychotherapist addresses himself to those psychodynamic

[17] S. R. Slavson, "An Elementaristic Approach to the Treatment of Delinquency," *The Nervous Child*, October, 1947; "Milieu and Group Treatment for Delinquents," in Proceedings of the National Conference of Social Work, 1948; and in "Bulwarks against Crime," *Yearbook* of National Probation and Parole Association, N.Y., 1948.

elements in the personality that affect character structure rather than to the behavioral pattern of the patient.

My belief is that character deviations and disorders in children require situational therapy [18] as part of the treatment plan. In most cases of this kind situational therapy alone is sufficient. This conclusion was derived from clinical experience with several thousand prepubertal children and can be defended also on theoretic grounds. Character being the cumulative result of prolonged adaptations to actual situations, that is, experience, changes in it can be achieved through experience of a corrective nature, not through verbalization, explanation, and the very limited degree of insight that children can at best achieve.

[18] S. R. Slavson, *An Introduction to Group Therapy*, p. 16.

PART THREE

Psychotherapy

V

Basic Aims of Psychotherapy

THE SETTING IN PSYCHOTHERAPY

PSYCHOTHERAPY deals primarily with the unrational or conative elements in the psyche, and only secondarily with the rational or the cognitive. It is not so much what is done or said as the conditions under which an act is executed, how a thought is expressed, and what significance and meaning it has to the patient that constitute therapy. In this connection one is reminded of the inscription on a book sent by a patient to Dr. Bernard Glueck, which read: "To the man who taught me to understand a lot of things which I already knew." [1] The recognition of disparity between knowledge and understanding is rare. In psychologic processes and human relations "understanding" refers to unrational empathy and perceptions, not to reasoning or logic. Truth is more often perceived than conceived. The subtlety of the therapeutic relation was fully recognized by the early hypnotists and mesmerists and later by psychonalysts. The latter, particularly, rely on a setting and relationship. The couch, subdued light, room furnishings, and arrangement are designed to help the patient relax, preserve libido economy, and aid regression and catharsis.

The setting of the therapy situation is of moment in other types of therapy besides psychoanalysis, though frequently not enough attention is given to it. Play, occupational, and group therapists are aware of the importance of settings and physical arrangements, but those who use verbal techniques, whether individually or in groups, are likely to disregard it. Experience shows, however, that in psychotherapy the physical setting and the total

[1] Bernard Glueck, "Psychiatry; an Instrument of Personal and Social Rehabilitation," *Current Therapies of Personality Disorders*, New York, Grune and Stratton, 1946, p. 5.

atmosphere are of utmost importance, as are also awareness of aims and objectives.[2]

The attitude of the patients and the significance of the experience depends upon whether therapy is conducted in a hospital ward, an out-patient clinic, a private office, a military setting, or an institution such as a "reform school" or prison. The therapist's orientation is another salient factor, for every form of psychotherapy must be based on definite assumptions with regard to the psychic structure of man, the nature and causes of its malformation, and it must function within a sound framework.

COMMON FACTORS IN VARIOUS THEORIES

Each of the many "schools" of psychotherapy seems to emphasize a special dynamic in pathology and to suggest a system or an approach that its proponents believe to be the only adequate treatment method for personality difficulties. Such affirmations as to the personality and its disturbances and the insistence upon one method of treatment ignores the unquestionable facts that personality distortions have many causes, that they stem from different areas of the psychic structure, that the nuclear problem [3] is not the same in all patients, and that treatment must vary. This is as true of group psychotherapy as it is of individual treatment.

The above does not mean that psychotherapy has no systematic theory or organized techniques or that it is devoid of definite principles by which therapists should be guided. But despite some immutable laws in the psychic development of man, possibilities for malformations are innumerable and treatment must therefore be suited to the specific individual and his difficulties. Even when clinical categories are employed as criteria for formulating treatment plans, it is frequently necessary to modify them to suit specific needs of a given patient. While these statements must necessarily remain theoretical at present, the reader

[2] See S. R. Slavson, *An Introduction to Group Therapy*, New York, International Universities Press, 1943, pp. 50–51, and *Analytic Group Psychotherapy*, New York, Columbia University Press, 1950, pp. 117–121.

[3] See p. 230.

will find them further elaborated elsewhere in this volume in support of this position.

Despite the different assumptions and methods employed in the various "schools" of psychotherapy, favorable results are achieved by them all. The question, therefore, arises whether a method of treatment is good if it is employed by a therapist who has confidence in it, whose temperament is suited to it, and who has the skill to use it. The fact that results are obtained by such apparently different techniques needs to be understood.

There are three possible explanations. One has already been stated above, namely, the suitability of a method to the skill and temperament of the therapist. Secondly, the nature of the problems in different patients cause them to respond to one method better than to another. Thirdly, and even more plausible, there are common and basic elements in all the "schools" of psychotherapy which are overlooked because of preoccupation with differences.[4]

Experience shows that despite theoretical unanimity among practitioners in any field of endeavor, including psychotherapy, each differs somewhat in the application of the theory. A practitioner cannot escape the imperatives of his own personality, and inevitably makes modifications as a result of his attitudes, temperament, and understanding. Thus, there is at present considerable variation in the application of such a well-defined practice as Freudian psychoanalysis, even though there is full theoretic consonance.

The fact that treatment has to be suited to the needs of the patient is a sound principle to which all responsible and enlightened persons adhere. Because of the contentiousness of the followers of the various "schools" and the resultant latent and overt antagonisms among them, no effort has been made to evaluate on a research basis the types of temperamental dispositions and personality difficulties for which each particular treatment method would be best suited. A study of successes and failures should readily reveal a definite relationship in this area. Is it

[4] I have discussed these points in *Analytic Group Psychotherapy*, pp. 13–14.

possible that success and failure in psychotherapy depend, in some cases at least, upon the accidental and fortuitous suitability of the type of therapy given a patient? If it does, would it not be more effectual to ascertain criteria of suitability and apply them planfully?

We have found, for example, that in group psychotherapy, at least, five distinct types of technique were necessary to meet the needs of different patients.[5] The indiscriminate use of group therapy by some practitioners has created considerable confusion and has retarded its development. While there are underlying principles in group psychotherapy, experience shows that for each patient a certain type of group yields most effective and quickest results and that for many patients group treatment definitely is unsuitable, while others can be treated only by this method. In the treatment of children, for example, not only is the type of problem an important consideration, but age and sex as well are determining fatcors.[6] Similarly, the techniques of group treatment employed for adult psychoneurotic patients had to be modified to meet the needs of psychotics.

The therapist has to have a thorough understanding of psychodynamics as well as psychopathology upon which he can base his therapeutic activity. He functions in accordance with his understanding of the psychologic content involved and consciously, as well as unconsciously, employs basic assumptions as his frame of reference. One who does not accept the Oedipal conflict as a universal and major source of personality difficulties, for example, would not encourage exploration in that area, nor would he help his patients to gain insight or relief from their inner conflicts about their parents. One who rejects the theories of instinct, libido, infantile sexuality, and primary aggression, must have an understanding of psychologic problems quite dif-

[5] S. R. Slavson, *An Introduction to Group Therapy*, ch. iv; "Current Practices in Group Therapy," *Mental Hygiene*, Vol. XXVIII, No. 3, July, 1944; *Analytic Group Psychotherapy*, chs. viii–xiii, xv; also ch. x in this volume.

[6] *Idem, The Group in Guidance, Handbook in Child Guidance*, New York, Child Development Publications, 1947, pp. 402–12; "Differential Methods of Group Therapy in Relation to Age Levels," *Nervous Child*, Vol. IV, No. 3, April, 1945; "Differential Dynamics in Activity and Interview Group Therapy," *American Journal of Orthopsychiatry*, Vol. XVII, No. 2, April, 1947.

ferent from that of one who is thus oriented. Each would explore a different area of the patient's psyche, and probably they would also have different therapeutic aims.

ANXIETY, GUILT, AND FEAR AS THE SPECIAL CONCERNS OF PSYCHOTHERAPY

Psychotherapy deals largely with persons who have difficulties in interpersonal relations that arise from interferences with orderly growth as outlined in Chapters I and II. It seeks to correct attitudes and feelings by freeing the libido from its anchorage in the self or in special persons, such as parents or siblings (cathexis displacement), by correcting the ego and superego organization, and by improving the self-image.

The most common problems with which the psychotherapist deals are overt and covert anxieties; but in the practice of psychotherapy it is not enough merely to recognize their presence. It is necessary to ascertain their sources in each case. We have seen that anxiety can proceed from conflict, guilt, ambivalence, fear, feelings of inadequacy and other states.[7]

Although anxiety is readily discernible in the psychoneurotic, it is present also in persons having other types of emotional difficulties. It is disguised in some and withheld in others. Even in the primary behavior disorders anxiety is present, though it may be at a minimum or masked. The early rejections and neglect suffered in childhood unavoidably create anxiety. The fact that they have made an adaptation through an anxiety-denying behavioral pattern of aggression does not eliminate that anxiety; it only conceals it. There is anxiety present in other forms of personality disorders as well. I have already stated that in my opinion anxiety is also at the root of the character structure of persons with psychogenic "psychopathic personalities," even though traditionally they are supposed to be devoid of it.[8]

[7] The reader will note that anxiety is employed to describe all states of tension. Fear is the emotion with concomitant organic changes resulting from an outer threat or danger. Anxiety, on the other hand, is employed to designate tensions aroused by an inner threat, e.g., the conflict between a forbidden impulse (id) and the prohibitions of conscience (superego) and the various types of ego defenses.

[8] See pp. 126–29.

One of the main results of anxiety is distortion of reality. In a state of anxiety one cannot but perceive reality in a special way. One sees it either as a threat or as an object of hostility or one is ambivalent about it. The psychotic denies painful reality and substitutes for it hallucinations and delusions, while in persons suffering from the psychoneuroses, where the conflict is between the id and the superego, distortions of reality occur. This is very apparent in projection, a common mechanism of psychoneurotics, where various degrees of reality distortion are present.

Because of the strict superego demands and the ego defenses against allowing repressed feelings and memories to come to the surface, the effect of psychotherapy in its first stages is to increase anxiety. Later, the superego is relaxed as a result of treatment, and the ego is enabled to face and accept one's own impulses and therefore also outer reality.

Although lower animals are able to experience the emotions of fear, love, and rage, they do not feel guilty. The feeling of guilt is a result of internalized mechanisms that operate separately and apart from fear. One feels guilty when no one is near, nor is the feeling conditioned by punishment. When a dog chews on a chair-leg in the absence of his mistress, he does not feel guilty. It is only when she puts in an appearance that he will crawl and whine. This he does because of the association of the act with punishment and his fear of it, not because he feels the internal threat of a superego.

Fear is an important devise of nature to assure survival, for without fear animals would not be aware of danger and would be destroyed. In our culture fear is synonymous with weakness, and it is creditable to deny that one is afraid, though such denial has an adverse effect upon mental health. When in war soldiers are told by their officers not to be ashamed of being afraid, the latter are better able to bear the strain of battle. The shame of being afraid only adds to the strain. It is when fear becomes an indefinite, indefinable, all-pervasive feeling and is experienced even when no specific external threat exists that it becomes pathological. Fear of a recognizable, real danger is normal. In psychotherapy fears are allayed by the sustaining relationship (transference) with the therapist (substitute parent), who is friendly, accepting, and supportive, while insight (and understanding) convince the patient of the unfounded basis for any specific fear. However, the ultimate aim of the treatment is to dissolve the intrapsychic states that cause one to be afraid.

In a sense, the feeling of guilt is a mechanism of self-punishment, as contrasted with punishment by an outside agency. It is true that the origin of conscience is fear, but civilized man internalizes a guilt-evoking principle (superego), which is distinct from fear of external punishment. Some psychoneurotics systematically place themselves in situations and deliberately commit acts that preclude the satisfaction of their basic needs for pleasure; they fail in their undertakings, or provoke rejection and punishment. Actually, they may seek punishment for unconscious or repressed wishes and acts committed in the past or fear the responsibility that maturity and success entail, or feel unworthy.

Hubert, twelve years old, an adopted son and the only child in the family, whose foster father was a prominent professional man in a small town, was referred for psychotherapy because of habitual stealing at home and elsewhere. He had been adopted when a small child. The parents were indulgent, and being financially well off, gave him many educational and social advantages. He came to the attention of a social service agency because he had been systematically stealing for some years from the small department store in the town where the family lived. Because of the father's social position, for a long time no one suspected the boy of stealing. When he was finally discovered, it was found that he usually returned the objects he had purloined a day or two later. Again because of the position of the family in the community, the police were not called in; instead, the parents were apprised of the facts. The latter attempted to deal with Hubert in a kindly manner, but one day, when they were away from home, the boy stole a sum of money and some of the foster mother's valuables, and disappeared. He was later apprehended in another city and returned to his foster family.[9]

A study of the boy's difficulties revealed that his relation with his foster mother was not entirely wholesome. Due to her emotional needs for a child and her sense of guilt because she was unable to have one of her own, she provoked the boy and acted seductively with him. Her overprotection and infantilization were a defense against a deep-rooted hostility toward him, for he personified her failure as a woman. On the other hand, Hubert had developed a strong sexual attachment toward her. His phantasies in relation to his foster mother aroused in him feelings of guilt and jealousy and fear of his step-father. The stealing episodes were aimed to activate punishment, which he felt he deserved. Since he was not caught in the act of stealing, he returned the objects, thereby doubling the chances of being discovered and punished. When he could not accomplish this end, and in a state of intense anxiety, he decided to run away from the relationships that caused him distress. The boy also resented his foster parents, whom he saw as the cause of his separation from his real parents, and running away expressed his unconscious hope that he might find the latter.

In treating psychoneurotics, especially, the aim is to reduce the feelings of guilt and the consequent anxiety. This is achieved largely by draining off the hostile impulses and phantasies that are in conflict with the superego; correcting the sense of right and wrong by transference, identifications, and the permissiveness of the therapist (and fellow-members in group psychotherapy).[10]

There is always an element of education in psychotherapy through which one may reevaluate his development in the light

[9] This case was first reported in the author's "Elementaristic Approach to Understanding and Treatment of Delinquency," *The Nervous Child*, Vol. VI, No. 4, October, 1947.

[10] One of the major values of a group in this connection lies in the fact that feelings of guilt are diluted by the discovery that other persons have the same prohibited impulses and strivings and that one is not unique in these respects. The feeling of being "different" is diminished. This dynamic is known as "universalization."

of evolving emotional maturity, ego strengths, and a new perspective. The infantile nature of fears and their groundlessness in reality become apparent, but a word of warning is necessary in this connection. Education alone is not enough to correct intrapsychic states that produce fear and anxiety. Psychotherapy strengthens the ego so that it can deal with the fears; it reduces the inner conflicts between the id and the superego by redistributing psychic energies (libido), and helping one to see himself in a more sanguine light (self-image). Thus, a number of therapeutic processes occur simultaneously that fortify the individual to deal with himself and with his environment.

AMBIVALENCE, REALITY DISTORTION, AND EGO ORGANIZATION

Ambivalence is a more complicated dynamic than is fear or anxiety. The latter are devices to deal with danger and threats. Ambivalence, on the other hand, is a state of struggle and indecision which causes emotional and physical debility, since so much energy is consumed in the resolution of conflict preliminary to every decision. Psychotherapy seeks to remove this indecision and in its stead develop emotional clarity and certainty. Where there has been fumbling, uncertainty, and oscillation, decisiveness replaces it. When a patient is able to bring forward his repressed, negative, guilt-evoking impulses and phantasies and recognizes and accepts them, conflict is reduced or eliminated. Having established a desirable balance between negative and socially approved drives, he is able to act decisively and unfalteringly. Conflict is reduced through the therapist's understanding and his nonpunitive attitude and the growing emotional balance in the patient. These also reduce guilt feelings and strengthen the ego to deal with conflict. In groups, universalization and identification among the members are of great help in this connection.[11]

Group discussions are especially valuable when projection and rationalization are employed as defenses against guilt. Such defenses readily yield to the friendly interpretation of the mem-

[11] S. R. Slavson, *Analytic Group Psychotherapy*, pp. 93–97.

bers in a group. Projection and rationalization cannot always be dealt with directly by the therapist, since they are important defense mechanisms to which patients cling tenaciously. One must follow the rule that defenses must not be attacked before the patient's ego is ready to deal with the conflict. The therapist must wait until the ego is sufficiently strengthened so that it no longer needs the support of its defenses. As in the case of ambivalence, the disappearance of projection, rationalization, and other ego defenses are by-products of psychotherapy as the patient's psyche becomes integrated.

One of the chief difficulties of emotionally disturbed persons is that they resist the everyday educational and developmental possibilities offered in the course of living and interacting with others. What is commonly understood by education in its broadest sense is negated or rejected by the narcissistic rigidity and defensiveness of such patients, and as a result they remain emotionally retarded and become socially maladjusted. The aim of psychotherapy is to overcome this resistance to the impact of the outside world so that its influences may shape feelings and condition attitudes. In larger terms, the major aim of psychotherapy is to eliminate self-encapsulation by eliminating or reducing self-protective or retaliatory rigidities established in childhood and to weaken the defenses built up as a reaction to earlier stresses and traumata. Only when this is accomplished are the adaptive and affective functions freed for growth. When flexibility gains ascendency over defensive rigidity, object relationships are facilitated. The primary dynamic in achieving this is transference.

It is evident that one cannot accomplish social integration without inner balance. One may develop a variety of disguises and amenities, such as politeness, obedience, ingratiation, submissiveness, cynicism, aggressiveness—all of which militate against emotional independence and individuation [12] so essential for growth and wholesome functioning. Most of these devices mask resistance and hostility, for, as is well known, they are overdetermined reaction-formations to a hostile character organization or defenses against being hurt, feelings of inadequacy and

12 See p. 32.

insecurity, and similar attitudes. Through catharsis, which can occur only in a transference relation, psychotherapy accordingly releases aggressive drives that are controlled or repressed.

We have seen that the ego is called upon to repress hostile impulses, as a result of which a large part of its strength is preempted thus diminishing the quantum of its energies available for social adaptation and personality expansion.[13] Much character constriction is a direct result of limited ego functioning caused by demands upon it to hold inner conflicts in check.

THE NATURE OF CHILDHOOD AND PSYCHOTHERAPY

There is a sharp difference between psychotherapy for adults and psychotherapy for children.

The most outstanding characteristics of a child are his comparatively weak ego organization and his limited ability to deal with inner impulses and external demands. The second difference, which is a direct outgrowth of the first, is the basically narcissistic quality of the child's libido organization, his lack of ego control, hence, impulsiveness, his still narcissistic character, hence, self-indulgence and feelings of omnipotence. The third distinction is the surface nature of his unconscious. One is impressed with the readiness and almost complete unself-consciousness with which young children act out and speak about matters that are embarrassing to an older person. This can be attributed to the incomplete superego development, the lack of repressive forces (ego), and undeveloped sublimation channels. Finally, the child's identifications are in a fluid state.

The child is still in the developmental process, and the struggles between primitive impulses and restraint have not as yet been resolved. He is still working out a pattern for his life, which eventually will lead to some inner balance. Because of this formative state, the child's emotions are labile and his behavior is inconsistent. He is experimenting with himself and with his surroundings and is therefore subject to frequent changes of mood. He is transilient, and his concentration span is short. In some respects this is the result of organic instability due to growth;

[13] See pp. 46–50.

in others, to congenital temperament; in still others, to emotional drives. The child's social awareness is rudimentary; the superego is as yet unformed. His identifications are unstable and ego ideals are easily discarded for others. Friendships are temporary until later, when they become comparatively fixed. Generally, the child is less restricted in his own world than are grown-ups, and the capacity for change and reintegration is much greater.

What is even more important to the psychotherapist, the child is in thrall to his primitive impulses. He is little able to submit to their frustration, and because of his still unregulated drives he is given to rages and fits of anger. He is intensely concerned with freedom of locomotion, action, and expression and with his impelling needs for exploratory acts and play. His phantasy life is rich, and reality and imagination are under certain conditions interchangeable, if not identical. In this state of flux and change the child is impelled by the laws of biologic and organic growth and by his psychic evolvement, as well as by the resentments and hostilities built up in the course of his brief life.

For the child, functioning as he does on primitive levels and with ideational capacities still unformed, physical activity is of fundamental importance. The child still has to discover intellectually the realities around him, and he still has to become acquainted with them. Physical activity, however, is very important to him and has more than educational value. Such activity is also the most significant source of mental health. The human organism is constantly producing measurable electrical energy. In fact, nerve impulses are electrical currents which are propelled by electric potentials generated through the chemical action in the body. This potential energy must in turn be transformed into dynamic (kinetic) function if the body-and-mind equilibrium is to be maintained. Blocking the discharge of energy produces organic and psychologic tensions.

It has been adequately established that discharge through the vasomotor system of the body equilibrates emotions as in athletic activities, in anger and rage, and in other forms of acting out. It has been shown by actual measurements that the blocking of activity of young children in the school room retards their physical growth, especially in the first years of school, and it would not be too difficult to demonstrate that psychological development is also adversely affected by the limitations and frustrations it imposes.

Play therapy has been devised for young children because of the inadequacy of language as a medium of expression. When the child is supplied with appropriate materials, he conveys symbolically his phantasies and preoccupations. Release therapy, introduced by David M. Levy, has demonstrated that young children can overcome certain states of traumatic tension of recent origin by abreacting in a properly equipped environment with appropriate furnishings and materials. Many therapists supply objects such as guns, soldiers, darts, clay, dolls, and water with which young patients can express aggressions and anal and sexual preoccupations.

Activity group therapy has also demonstrated that such materials and occupations and free play in a group setting can serve not only as a means of communication but also as self-regulation and that the effect is fundamental change in personality structure. These improvements have been confirmed by Rorschach tests.

THE IMPORTANCE OF ACTING OUT

The value of encouraging activity, or "acting out," in the treatment of very young children was demonstrated in four selected cases very briefly outlined here.[14]

Susan, the only child of a divorced refugee mother, was brought for treatment at the age of five and one half years. She greatly feared being separated from her mother, had temper tantrums, and vomited. Susan had food fads, dawdled at mealtime, and was extremely sensitive to food odors. She was afraid to go out on the street alone and afraid of Negro men. These

[14] These cases have been reported in the *Journal of Social Casework*, Vol. XXX, No. 4, April, 1949, and I am indebted to its editors for permission to reproduce them. My thanks are also due to Gusta Thaun, Diana Tendler, and Betty Gabriel, all of the staff of the Jewish Board of Guardians, for supplying the material for these case histories.

symptoms first made their appearance when Susan was three. At this time the mother worked as a domestic and lived away from home.

The symptoms were exacerbated when Susan began to attend kindergarten at the age of five. The mother was then periodically employed as a waitress or domestic, living with the family where she was employed. Susan usually lived with her maternal grandmother, a rigid, primitive woman. When treatment began, however, Susan was living with her mother at the latter's place of employment. Both spent week ends with the grandmother. The child's condition was diagnosed as incipient psychoneurosis; that of the mother as mixed psychoneurosis.

From the first, Susan violently acted out aggressive and hostile feelings. With a white face and a menacing look she would grow violent and hurl herself at the therapist, hatred expressed by her eyes and by her clenched teeth. It was not sufficient for her to aim a gun at the therapist; she wanted to catch the therapist's nose in the trigger of the gun, saying that she wanted to see her limbs fall off when the gun was fired. Susan would often become desperate—tear up the desk blotter, spill ink, tear up books and paper, stamp on toys and clay, and make every effort to throw something out of the window. If, by chance, the therapist had to answer a telephone call during the interview, Susan would viciously attack the toy cupboard, hoping to destroy it before the therapist ended her telephone conversation.

Difficulties at home enhanced the ferocity of her behavior with the therapist. In order to prevent injury to herself and the therapist, it became necessary to restrain Susan. This, of course, only heightened her drives to attack the therapist physically, but she refused to leave at the end of each session. She would violently cling to each object in the room, desperately resisting being forced to leave, or else she would lock herself in the room or the hall closet, screaming loudly: "You lousy stinker, you! You're not getting away with this. I'm coming here for a million years. I'm going to make you my mother, or teacher, or something;" or "You make me wrong; everything I do is your fault."

The therapist recognized that to render treatment effective

she would have to (1) be able to keep herself physically separated from the child, (2) avoid the need to restrain her, (3) provide more leeway for her actions, and (4) supply opportunities for certain types of activity which could not be carried on in the therapist's small office. These conditions could be met in the "activity room."

In the larger room, Susan's first response was to become tense and anxious. She excitedly asked many questions, but was delighted with the size of the room, the many facilities, and the variety of toys. In contrast to the constant need to restrain Susan, that so resembled her grandmother's everlasting "don'ts," the therapist could now permit her to handle freely the various tools, toys, and paints and to use and wash the kitchen equipment. She messed around a great deal with paints and splashed water. While at the beginning of the first period in this new room Susan continued to whine "You don't let me," she gradually recognized that this was not the case. Susan was inordinately curious at first and broke cupboard locks in her desperate need to discover the contents. She would insist that things were being concealed from her and that she was being denied access to them. She screamed, "You liar! You thief! You crook!" Susan was given the keys to every closet. At the same time, the objects that she tried to "steal" were clues to the immediate and specific content of her conflict that was emerging at the moment.

The size of the room permitted Susan long periods of rope-jumping. She constantly maneuvered so that she would get into physical contact with the therapist. She attempted to lift the therapist's dress and to caress and touch her. Susan's intentions became quite clear in this setting, since there was no longer any need to attack the therapist under the guise of resisting restraint. The unconscious drives became obvious even to the child. This was interpreted to her and traced back to the origin of her need. In play with the therapist, Susan would yell: "You stinky, smelly, lousy you! I don't have to smell you anyway. I smell my mother, and gee, it stinks."

Susan then told how she and her mother would sit together closely on the toilet while Susan had her bowel movement. Susan constantly questioned her mother about how the excreta smelled. There was excitement about the intensity of the smell and many comments about it. There would be a proud announcement when the movement was starting and much acclaim as to its size. Susan would warn her mother that she was getting feces on herself and on her mother. Susan was also taken into the maternal bed, where each fondled the other's rectum. She cleverly repeated this type of behavior in bed with the maternal grandmother. These facts did not come out when treatment was carried on in the confinement of the small office.

Susan's growing independence and maturity were demonstrated after several sessions, when she told the therapist to go up to the activity room by the regular stairway, while she herself used the dark back staircase, of which she had once been afraid. Later, Susan agreed not to splash paints all over the room. The therapist and Susan agreed that only more controlled activities, such as painting a real picture, sewing, or making cut-out designs, were permissible. Because the relationship was now a positive one and because of proper timing, progressive restraints were acceptable to the child. She did, however, return periodically to some of her earlier uncontrolled behavior.

The change in Susan's demeanor was not immediate. It was a long-drawn-out process of regression and progression. However, because of the advantageous physical setting, the struggle was no longer between the therapist and the child; it was now between the latter's own impulses and her growing ego. After she realized this, Susan once said: "I really don't have to do this like a baby; I could really do this like a big girl and do it nicely." Another time she said: "You know, sometimes grown-ups are right."

It is evident that in this case in order to reveal her problems the child had to have the space, the freedom, the materials and the security in relation to the therapist that made it possible for her to play out and act out her libidinal drives and preoccupations. For this purpose restrictions and physical confinement had to be minimal.

Jerry, age three years and eleven months, at the initiation of treatment, was "wild, destructive, uncontrollable by the mother." He started strangers' parked automobiles, set fires, tried to jump out of windows, and occasionally stayed away from home for hours. When first brought to the clinic for treatment he was discovered driving a horse-drawn milk wagon on a main thoroughfare. Much of this uncontrollable behavior, involving very dangerous activities, had been in evidence since he was two years old.

The child was under observation for a short time at a mental hospital, where it was found that he had a superior intelligence and no organic defects, but that he was reacting to a punitive, hostile environment created by an immature, rejecting mother and an infantile, impulsive father. It was recommended that Jerry be placed in a day nursery and that his mother be treated in a child-guidance clinic. This plan was carried out, but at the end of the year Jerry was dismissed from the nursery, and individual psychotherapy was undertaken for him also.

Jerry reacted with a great deal of hostility and resistance to the therapist. He was very destructive, attempted to set fire to her office, threatened to jump out of the window, made frequent demands, and freely expressed, verbally and physically, aggression that proved to be too violent to control.

The child seemed to suffer from a severe primary behavior disorder, with potentialities for severe psychoneurosis if repressive forces were brought into play too soon. It was essential to provide for him opportunities for discharging primitive impulses and wishes in a free environment. It was suggested that Jerry be allowed to use a larger room where he would be able to act out with less restraint and confinement. Three sessions a week were arranged for him in such a room, specially equipped for release activities.

When told of the new arrangements, Jerry's instant question was, "Can I make fires?" When told that he could, his attitude was one of eager anticipation.

Jerry's behavior during the first two sessions, although hyperactive and exploratory, was not overaggressive. He made fires in a tin can and suggested that he and the therapist eat together beside the fire. After requesting to be "boss," he later magnanimously decided that he and the therapist were "bosses together." However, he accepted without too much complaint her insistence that she was in charge. He explored every nook and cranny of the rather large, bare, and rather unattractive room, and he told the therapist that this was the most beautiful place he had ever seen. He suggested that the therapist go into the junk business with him after he had assembled a pile of old bottles, tools, and cooking utensils that were in the room. With the money they would make they could go into the candy store business and earn enough money to buy and furnish a house, where he could live with the therapist and sleep with her in the same bed.

During the third interview he became more erotically aggressive, demanding that the therapist exhibit herself to him and displayed in his comments much confusion with regard to his own sexuality. These conversations took place during an interview when he made several fires. At the following sessions he showed more marked erotic aggression, piercing a clay female figure through the abdomen with an arrow and then telling the therapist that he would like to do the same to a "real lady," the therapist herself. Immediately Jerry rushed up to her and asked for a kiss. He also asked her to go into the bathroom with him to defecate, but quickly withdrew his request.

During the period when Jerry was treated in this special room, the expression of positive and negative feelings became accentuated, and he more freely acted out his impulses and desires in a setting in which the therapist was able to assume a more permissive role. Jerry seemed better able to conform outside the treatment room, being fairly well behaved en route, but he used much more profane language.

After seven interviews in this large room it was possible to use a small room in the clinic which approximated some of the freedom available in the large room, but where more limitations had to be imposed. This he accepted.

Another favorable development as a result of adequate opportunities for acting out is clearly seen in the cases of John and Ben, two boys, approximately ten years of age. Both were uncommunicative in the interviews, and both had been treated individually for about a year.

John, an only child, was referred for treatment because of moodiness, lack of friends, and complaints of aches and pains for which no physical bases had been found. He had a tendency to identify very strongly with sick people and was sensitive, fearful, and high-strung. He had facial tics and a persistent cough, had always been finicky about food, and accused his mother of wanting to poison him. He daydreamed a great deal, was unable to concentrate in school, and was inordinately afraid of criticism. In individual treatment John remained silent for long periods and would not volunteer any information. He answered only definite questions, but then admitted that he was worried and afraid of being criticized by other children.

Ben was referred to the child guidance clinic for treatment by his teachers because he disrupted school routines by talking loudly out of his turn and wandering about the classrooms. He was insulting to teachers, lied, stole, and had "nervous twitchings" which led the family physician to the diagnosis of chorea. Ben had been an inveterate thumb-sucker since infancy and had the unpleasant habit of dripping saliva on his clothes and nearby furniture and other objects. Ben's father was severely neurotic and had had several "nervous breakdowns." The mother, a domineering, hyperactive woman, was disappointed in her husband, and as a result had turned increasingly to an older son for emotional gratifications. Ben was rejected from birth, since the mother had wished to have a girl-child. She had been separated from her husband since Ben was five years old.

When the boy was placed in a nursing home at that age, he changed from an exhibitionistic, overactive individual into a quiet, subdued, and conforming child who cried a great deal. When he returned home at the age of seven, he was found to be a "very spiteful and tough guy."

Because very little progress was being made in treatment with either John or Ben, it was decided to bring them together in the psychotherapist's interviewing room in the hope that they would activate each other. This they did readily. They utilized the play materials available in common play, spending much time in finishing the construction of a doll house and furnishing it. Though they vied with each other in this work, they frequently planned the furnishings together. This activity was later continued in a different form in a larger room, when two girls were added to the group.

It soon became apparent, however, that the room in which the two boys met was inadequate in both size and arrangement, and the interviews were transferred to the "activity room," where there were a greater variety of toys, wood, clay, paints, an electric stove, and simple kitchen equipment.

At first the boys spent much time in volleying a tennis ball in the room and in running about at random. Some weeks later the two boys, while talking quietly, decided that they would "write a newspaper," which they named "Atomic News." John and Ben were to be the sole contributors to this publication. Later the boys made a toy jeep, and during this activity the definite characteristics of each emerged. John was planful and followed directions supplied with the materials for the jeep, while Ben was distractible and complained that he was tired.

The therapist interpreted this to him by asking him whether he always felt tired when he had a difficult job to do. Although he indignantly denied this, by this interpretation he was activated to a renewed interest in the jeep, and he resumed work on it with John.

During these occupations Ben frequently returned to his thumb-sucking and drooling, at which times the therapist nonchalantly handed him a paper tissue. On one of these occasions he stuck the tissue in his pocket and stopped sucking his thumb. Once John stated that he liked to work on difficult problems, to which the therapist responded that he had already solved several such problems. This pleased John very much, and his growing self-assurance was further intensified. He reacted by saying: "You bet!"

The activities of the group, however, particularly after the girls were added, were not limited to manual work. The children discussed a great many problems, such as their family relations, their hostilities, and their attitudes toward each other. When therapeutically indicated, the therapist interpreted the material. Once they openly discussed stealing, and it was found that all the children had stolen at one time or another. Ben was not the only culprit in this regard. Since that discussion, all the children, including Ben, have given up stealing.

During one such conversation in the group John described some of his compulsive behavior, which, he said, he has now overcome. He said that when he now has an urge to do the same thing repeatedly and to do it in exactly the same way: "I say to myself, 'I don't have to do it this way,' and I don't."

When Ben arranged some pieces of felt gracefully and commented that he had designed a hat such as was worn in 1848, one of the girls said she thought he would be a dress designer. John remarked that his father was a designer of hats and a pattern maker. As a result Ben proceeded to make various types of hats, all of which he tried on, prancing up and down the room.

After approximately six months the two boys and the two girls in the group began to rearrange their doll house. This toy had been taken out of the room, and they decided to bring it in for "spring cleaning." All the children participated in washing the outside and the inside of the house, as well as the furniture. Each chose a room to furnish, and when there were criticisms and differences of opinion, one of the children said: "That is how it usually is. No two minds work the same way."

Once, when all the children were present and it was raining, Ben suggested that they all talk. He said that when he had been ill recently he was very much afraid of the injections he was to receive, but that he had not actually minded them very much. Ben and John compared the lengths of their pencils and pretended that they were hypodermic needles, which clearly revealed the castration phantasies associated with injections. Once, when they were talking about birth and operations, John remarked that he had improved a great deal since he came to the group. "I don't talk so fast except when I am excited. Also my mother says my posture is better and I am neater." By this time he had entirely given up drooling and thumb-sucking. His school marks also had improved.

At another time, when the children were discussing illness, John stated that a few days earlier, when he had not felt very well, his stomach felt "as though it was going up and down on a washboard." Ben replied: "I feel that way once in a while, too." Then Ben went on to tell John that he ought to keep busy so that he would not have time to think about himself.

The improvement in John was particularly noticeable when at home he once accidentally cut his wrist, and a number of stitches were necessitated. He described how panicky his father became and described his father as "very nervous." John said that he was not the least bit excited, and he later commented: "It's so different from what I used to be like. Before I would be afraid that I was going to die or lose all my blood. This time I was not afraid." He also commented about the loss of the facial tic. All the children also became aware of the fact that Ben had given up his thumb-sucking.

At the risk of anticipating a discussion to appear in Chapter VI of this volume, it may be useful to describe briefly the dynamics of these four cases at this juncture, since it will serve two purposes: first, it will convey more clearly the general orientation of this volume; secondly, it will lay the background for Chapters VI–VIII.

Susan's nuclear problem was her abnormal fixation on the anal level and her preoccupation with feces and the products of her own body, especially the odors. Her rectum was erogenetic and has been the source of much pleasure as well as of an intense feeling of guilt. Her mother both pleased and attacked her via her rectum, and Susan had to defend herself against such attacks from other adults. It was one of the reasons, though not the only one, why she attacked the therapist, screaming that she did not have to smell her as she has smelled her mother. Her neurotic sexual conflict in relation to her mother has further complicated her personality, and she developed specific fears and anxieties. One of these that requires special attention is her fear of Negro men. The blackness of the Negro is associated with the mother's black pubic hair, and the male figure represents aggression, which probably in some way is connected with her father or the fact that in her opinion her father may have castrated both her mother and herself.

It is also possible that phantasies that birth occurs via the rectum have become associated in the child's mind with the important role the anus plays in the psychic organization of the mother and of Susan. Therefore she equated herself with feces and developed fear of the toilet, where she might go down the drain as do the excreta. This is suggested in her wish to see the therapist fall apart or disintegrate when she shot at the latter. Such disintegration Susan observed when she watched the feces wash down from the toilet bowl after she had flushed it. Her suspicion that the therapist was concealing things from her, her accusations against the therapist as a thief and a liar, and her desire to investigate all the cupboards were all parts of her wish to understand more about the sexual mystery engendered by the mother's furtive and secret play with her. When Susan said "You make me wrong," she was accusing the therapist of creating difficulties for her as her mother did.

There are sufficient grounds here for the development of a serious behavior disorder. The father left their home when Susan was very young, and the mother both rejected and neglected Susan, partly because of economic necessity and partly owing to her own deep disturbances. However, unless Susan is treated successfully, she will develop a neurotic character. The relationship between Susan and her mother was such that reactive aggression on the part of the child was inevitable, and Susan acted it out against all persons having a maternal role. The child makes this plain when she says: "I'm going to make you my mother, or teacher, or something," but the overwhelming anxiety that the intimacies with her mother produced are being structured into her character.

The chief aim in treating this child was to disanchor the libido from the anus and reallocate it so that the various erogenous zones would assume their appropriate importance in the total libido organization. This was accomplished by removing the secrecy from and therefore her preoccupation with activities in this area by encouraging her to act them out and later to talk about them. Once the libido is detached from any given area in this manner, the self-regulative trends of the organism distribute the thus liberated libido among the various psychic and organic centers, resulting in a more integrated or balanced organism.

As these preoccupations diminish, the anxieties are also reduced and the associated symptoms vanish. As Susan no longer feared an attack from the therapist or her mother, she tested her newly acquired strength by using a dark back stairway to the room and walking alone, unaccompanied by the therapist. Other fears have also disappeared.

In this respect the therapist functioned as a focus of cathexis displacement.[15] Susan has withdrawn from her mother the libido cathexis and attached it to the therapist, who has dealt with it therapeutically, thus weakening her tie with her mother—a desirable and necessary development in this case. The therapist further helped in every way possible to free Susan from the feeling of guilt associated with her behavior by being permissive and accepting her as she was.

Were it not for the fact that Jerry had been under observation in a well-equipped, reputable hospital, one might suspect constitutional psychopathy[16] because of the inordinately early onset of the deviant behavior, which occurred when he was two years old. If we are to eliminate this possibility and the possibility of a psychosis, it must be assumed that Jerry was acting out a very definite and intense Oedipal conflict, in which his father played a major role. The father's weakness and infantile character left the boy without the protection against his sexual impulses toward his mother, who undoubtedly was seductive as well as rejecting. We may also deduce from the case history, especially from the character of the treatment sessions (his asking

[15] See p. 170.

[16] See p. 127.

the therapist to exhibit herself, for example), that he slept in the parental bedroom, frequently in the same bed with his mother. The nuclear problem of this boy is, therefore, a feeling of anxiety stemming from his incestuous urges toward the mother, on the one hand, and fear of these impulses because of the father's inadequate protection against them, on the other.

During the treatment interviews Jerry acted out the strong male figure he wished his father to be. He wanted to be "boss" and then go into business so as to make it possible to act out the male role by going to bed with the therapist as his father does with his mother. Following this his reactions grew more erotically colored, and he made fires, asked the therapist to exhibit herself to him, vicariously had intercourse, and suggested further intimacies.

Obviously, considerable work with the parents would have to be done in this situation. Sleeping arrangments, if that is one of the difficulties, should be changed; the father's role in relation to his wife and son needs to be fundamentally altered; the mother's attitudes toward her own sexuality, her relation with her husband, and the use she makes of her son must be explored and corrected. Jerry himself can be helped by encouraging him to act out and bring to the surface the guilt-producing and fear-evoking impulses and preoccupations. The transfer of his erotic drives from his mother to another woman is of utmost importance and should be employed as a basis for interpreting his unconscious wishes at a level of his development and perceptions.

Although there is little information given on John and Ben, it can be stated with some degree of certainty that John's nuclear problem is castration anxiety, while Ben's is an infantile character. The strong rejection on an oral level evidently accompanied by strong rejection by both his father and his mother caused John to be afraid that he would be poisoned by the latter. This was also the probable cause of his generalized fear of illness and death. Having received no love from his parents, he turned for affection to himself, developing hypochondriacal or conversion symptoms, the nature of which is not clear from the material presented. The facial tics and persistent cough may have deep significance, or may be means for attaining secondary gains. Ben, on the other hand, presents no psychoneurotic problems, with the exception, perhaps, of the unexplained "nervous twitchings," which may be weapons of aggression against the mother, who was annoyed by them. In addition to the character disorder of the boy, there was present also a primary behavior disorder with regard to his habits and conduct.

In John's case we find also a considerably improved self-image following the treatment. He now recognizes that he was weak and that he had made too much of simple situations in the past. He now sees himself strong and powerful, able to withstand and control them. He recognizes that he is now in control of his tendency toward compulsive behavior and that he did not become panicky when injured. John's self-esteem was raised and his ego greatly strengthened. Similarly, Ben's ego gained ascendency as a result of the friendly relations with the therapist and fellow group members and the acceptance he had received from them, as well as the encouragement and praise of his creative activities.

Neither of these boys responded to individual treatment by a woman therapist. Their distrust and dislike of women was too great to make it possible to develop a direct transference. The modification of this transference with the same therapist offered by a group was essential before a positive relationship was possible. Once the resistances and defenses were lessened, both boys allowed themselves to relate to the therapist, to each other, and to the two girls in the group, which in turn aided catharsis and insight. These cases also demonstrate the suitability and even the essentiality of groups for children in latency.

The above cases indicate clearly that for very young children, particularly, the setting is of primary importance in treatment. Because of the nonverbal nature of the children's communication, adequate opportunities for acting out are essential.

THE AIMS AND VALUES OF PSYCHOTHERAPY

Psychotherapy for the very young child serves (1) as a corrective biosphere (environment); (2) to release emotional tension through acting out and verbalization; (3) to supply targets for the discharge of hostility through play materials and through direct aggression against the therapist as a parent substitute; (4) to provide opportunities for a centrifugal attachment to the therapist (object relation); (5) to establish corrective attitudes toward parents; (6) to attain the satisfaction of being accepted by an adult; (7) to supply the support of the therapist; (8) to help overcome fears of being "bad" (punished); (9) to lead to a better inner adjustment through balancing the psychic forces of the id, the ego, and the superego; (10) to eliminate rigidities and ego defenses and therefore to strengthen adaptive powers; (11) to diminish the defensive patterns of projection, displacement, and distortion; (12) to reduce the feelings of guilt and anxiety; (13) to correct the self-image; (14) to lessen narcissistic self-centeredness and self-indulgence; (15) to weaken the barriers to self-expression and communication; (16) to eliminate fear and avoidance patterns; (17) to achieve self-acceptance and therefore more tolerant attitudes toward others.

VI

The Dynamics of Psychotherapy

Psychotherapy consists of four fundamental corrective aims: (1) redistributing the libido; (2) strengthening the ego; (3) correcting the structure of the superego; (4) correcting the self-image.

LIBIDO REDISTRIBUTION

We have seen how attitudes of parents or their surrogates toward the three elemental functions—eating, evacuation, and sex—may either fix a child's libido on an infantile level or aid its progressive development. The patient's intensity and preoccupation with these functions, his concern and anxiety related to them, prevent their being weighted properly as parts of the libido economy of the organism. As a result, the personality is unbalanced. We must note in this connection that it is vastly easier to correct these malformations in children than in adults, because the organization of their libido is still in a fluid and formative stage. This makes easy movement from one area or level to another.

Adults are more innured in their way of life than are children and adolescents; their psychological patterns are more set; they are rigid rather than flexible; their lives are fixed rather than labile; their defenses are mobilized, structured, and entrenched. The result is comparative inflexibility and lessened capacity for change. In the neurotic these characteristics are even more intensified: rigidities are greater, and defenses are less accessible.

In psychotherapy we count on the patient's regression to the stage (or situation) in which his development was arrested or his libido fixed; these are also the points of greatest anxiety. This regression occurs through catharsis and may be made manifest either by language or by action. In the case of children the therapist depends upon activity catharsis [1] even more than on verbal communication, and he must be prepared to understand the latent meaning of behavior, as well as of speech.

A patient allows himself to regress only when he (*a*) trusts the therapist (*b*) feels that he is understood, and (*c*) is assured of not being punished or disapproved.[2] In dislodging libido fixations from any given area the third factor is of most importance. The objectivity with which the therapist deals with the child's actions and thoughts and his willingness to talk about subjects usually prohibited in our culture serve to divest them of their importance and diminish their emotional significance. Because they are no longer so important the libido investment in them is correspondingly decreased. Once the regression occurs and is dealt with by the therapist (parent figure) with equanimity and calm, the excessive libido attachment becomes gradually dissolved. This can be even more facilitated by interpretation, though in young children acting out has the same effect.

Thus, we see oral children whose thumb-sucking, lisping, salivation, voraciousness, and other symptoms of orality diminish or disappear. Children whose anal preoccupations take the form of messing with clay, paints, and water and who act out defecation by dropping pellets from their buttocks discard these and similar activities, thereby reflecting a diminution of the libido attachment to the anal area.[3] Other young patients stop bed wetting, fire setting, masturbation, and erotic play. These and similar results are obtained because the libidinal significance of the symptomatic behavior has been diminished by the therapist's tolerance and understanding, and therefore the orifices lose their exaggerated significance. The child's bestowal of his libidinal wishes upon the therapist also serves to detach them from himself and his cathexized areas.

[1] S. R. Slavson, *An Introduction to Group Therapy*, New York, International Universities Press, 1943, p. 187.

[2] For a more detailed discussion of these processes see "Transference and Substitution," in this chapter.

[3] Harriet Cary Montague reported a case of a seven-year-old boy who actually acted out defecation in a therapy group. See her "A Case of Regression in Activity Group Therapy," *International Journal of Group Psychotherapy*, Vol. I, No. 3, Sept., 1951.

STRENGTHENING THE EGO

From our discussion of the disturbances of the ego and its functions[4] it is clear that in order to correct the child's ego organization it is necessary to (*a*) remove interferences with its growth; (*b*) decrease the load it is called upon to carry; and (*c*) diminish the intensity of the defenses it has built up.

Again we rely upon the fact that the child's psychic functions and powers are in a state of growth and evolution. Unless the distortions are extreme, as in full-blown psychoneuroses, which are rare in children, the removal of impediments releases the endogeneous powers for growth. Since imbalance in the libido also affects ego integration, libido redistribution has a salutary effect upon the ego, which is automatically strengthened, because it no longer has to keep under control id impulses.

Because in the pregenital stage the young child has not fully achieved individuation, he is still tied to and dependent upon his parents, they can easily counterbalance or obliterate any improvement. Extra-familial agents, such as therapists and teachers, can do little against their adverse influence or resistance. The child's ego development must be helped and encouraged by members of the family such as siblings, grandparents, and other relatives who have to be involved in guidance and therapy. In effect, these persons must cease to act as the child's ego, thus preventing his internalization of controls. He must be freed by them to proceed from the points of earlier fixations toward progressive integration. His growth must also be motivated by their praise, appreciation, and respect.

Some psychotherapists believe that libido regression during psychotherapy brings in its wake regression or weakening of the ego. This may be the case with some patients, but we are inclined to consider the process rather a strengthening of the ego, since some of its defenses are let down sufficiently to permit the id impulses to come through and be examined.

The blocking of ego development may be removed also by the substitution of more wholesome identification models, who

[4] See pp. 45–53.

by their behavior demonstrate to the child desirable ways of dealing with reality. Such models help to counteract the effect of weak or overbearing parents, older siblings, relatives, and others. The therapist is of great importance in this connection, for his personality as a therapist and his own ego organization condition the psychotherapy.[5] In meeting the young patient's idealized picture of a parent, the therapist motivates him to give up his traits and his undesirable behavior.

Ego defenses must receive special consideration in psychotherapy, for they are integral parts of the personality structure and are valuable because they serve to ward off and prevent anxiety. A direct attack upon them strikes at the very core of the system of self-protective mechanisms the child has built up, and this is an attack upon his psychological survival. This psychic armament must be respected and preserved until the patient no longer needs these defenses and is ready to give them up. Premature criticism, reproof, and even an objective analysis of them may set up a train of anxiety which only strengthens them. If one finds it necessary to deal with ego defenses in the course of psychotherapy, it must be (*a*) undertaken after a very strong positive transference had been established and (*b*) timed so that the patient is ready to recognize their existence, understand how he had employed them, and be ready to give them up. As we shall see presently, the ego defenses constitute a large part of resistance to treatment, but they cannot be attacked in the therapeutic process.

CORRECTING THE STRUCTURE OF THE SUPEREGO

The formation and function of the superego have received extensive attention in the literature of depth psychology. Briefly, the superego is that segment of the tripartite psychic structure of man which evalutes and decides whether certain drives and wishes may or may not be gratified. It is the superior judge that evaluates desirability and permissibility of urges and acts whose judgment and demands the ego, as the executive, carries out. Be-

[5] See ch. vii, especially pp. 198–208.

fore an act is committed or a pleasurable thought entertained its validity and virtue are passed upon by the superego. The value of this mechanism is obvious, for without it social man is at the mercy of the anarchic and pleasure-motivated id, the hegemony of which would result in a group life and interpersonal relations fraught with untold difficulties or render them altogether impossible. If a certain act may be permitted, the ego aids its consummation; however, when the impulse arising from the id is not acceptable to the superego, the ego inhibits the impulse or prevents the act from being carried out.

This selective evaluation of outer reality and ultimate power over the inner forces are the result of the child's experience with reality in which the parents occupy the predominant role and which reaches its highest peak in the Oedipus complex. The original standards of value, of right and wrong, good and bad, arise from parental prohibitions and their judgments, which are modified and enhanced by experiences with other persons of significance, groups and culture to which I have already referred as "group superego." It is also quite clear that these internalized values are not entirely a result of fear of being punished or abandoned, though it plays an important part. The factor of identification, first with parents and later with others as ego-ideals, plays its role in the final formation of the superego.

From a study of the nature of the superego and of the id it becomes clear that they may be antagonistic to each other. The pleasure and hostile drives of the id are examined, approved, and disapproved by the sober and exacting superego. The id urges and the superego restraints may place the two in antagonistic camps. There is an almost constant struggle between them, with the ego acting as the regulator. Too great pressure from either places the ego in a equivocal and difficult situation. It has to serve two masters, as it were, and establish harmony between them. We have seen how strengthening the ego aids its mediatory functions, but frequently, as in the case of psychoneurotics, demands and restrictions of the superego are as exorbitant as they are lenient in psychopaths and psychotics. These overly strong demands have to be diminished through psychotherapy.

The two major drives in the child with which the psychotherapist has to deal are the hostile aggressive drives against parents and siblings and the incestuous urges that have not been adequately repressed during the Oedipal period and their consequences. These are the most common difficulties for which neurotic children come to us for treatment.

The therapist's major function is to free the submerged aggressive drives that are transformed into neurotic reaction-formations. In the average person repressions and sublimations are adequate to deal with aggressive and destructive impulses, but in the person who comes for psychotherapeutic treatment these repressions have not been successfully accomplished. Before inhibitions and sublimations can be established, a regressive discharge of the primary impulses and urges must occur. It is from this point that the therapist begins his reconstruction or repatterning of the psychologic texture of the personality.

This change can be accomplished only in free and unhampered catharsis, which is possible when the patient feels secure with the therapist. The therapist also supports the patient's ego so as to permit the coming to the surface of impulses, thoughts, and phantasies. Upon further analysis it becomes clear that in the mind of the patient the therapist actually becomes identified with the patient's superego, which was first derived from the parents and serves as part of this intrapsychic dynamic. The therapist is in effect that part of the superego that prohibited expression, but this is now permitted because the therapist does not punish or criticize as the parents did. Thus, the therapist relaxes the internalized (unconscious) superego, which may have been too rigidly formed because of parental control. He also becomes, at some stages in the treatment, as the reprojected superego. The therapist becomes in part responsible for the child's acts. This is sometimes evidenced by the child's requests for advice and permission. In some instances he showers upon the therapist blame, as though the therapist were responsible for the child's acts.[6]

[6] Susan screamed: "You make me wrong; everything I do is your fault!" (see p. 146).

The superego structure may be inadequate and its restrictive functions too lax, permitting socially impermissible acts. This occurs when the moral and ethical values of a family are below those of the larger community, when the parents themselves have unsuitable standards and are therefore unsuitable models for identification and ego ideals. In such instances the id urges take precedence; they set the rules for conduct to an extent that is not acceptable to others in the environment. In primary behavior disorders both the ego and the superego are inadequately formed in relation to the id to establish a workable balance. The transference relation with the therapist in these cases corrects the superego structure of the patient through identification and introjection of the therapists' attitudes and values. Extreme cases of superego deficiency, other than among psychotics, are found in psychopathic personalities, where superego development is at its minimum. A more detailed discussion of the process of the diminishing of superego demands as related to ego organization and the id will be found in other parts of this volume.

CORRECTING THE SELF-IMAGE

We now come to our fourth major psychotherapeutic objective, the improvement of the self-image. The self-image is the perception an individual has of himself in relation to other persons in his environment.[7] In the course of his life everyone builds up specific feelings about himself, his appearance, abilities, strengths and weaknesses, adequacies and inadequacies. He *perceives* himself as good or bad, worthy or unworthy, strong or weak, successful or a failure, desirable or not. The elements that go into this complex are numerous and extremely complicated in their manifestations, as they are also in their genesis and etiology. In the formation of these attitudes toward self, physical and constitutional factors play a part. Height, size, general physique, size of genitals, and general appearance contribute to the emerging critical and evaluative attitudes of the individual. Less evident

[7] Trigand Burrows employed the term "social image" to describe this phenomenon. I suggested the designation "self-image" as more fully representing the feelings involved.

are the internal factors, such as heart and gland action, nervous constitution, native musculature, liver, and other organs that affect and determine organic kinesthesis. A disturbance in the balance of their functions and their structure generate self-awareness and feelings of debility or inadequacy.

The self-image is also conditioned by the way in which the individual has been regarded by others: whether he has been praised or blamed, treated derisively or respectfully, encouraged or discouraged, and how well he fitted into his setting. A short person, for example, feels less weak and less stigmatized if he grows up in a family of persons of similar height and has play-mates no taller than himself than does one who is shorter than is everyone around him. A red-head is less self-conscious when other red-haired persons are within his environment, and one whose metabolism is perfect and whose energy reserves are ample feels stronger than others who are less well endowed in these respects.

The aspects of the self-image with which psychotherapy is most concerned are those that have been derived from persons in the immediate family. The same conditions that contribute to the malformation of the ego operate also in setting the self-image. The weakening and debilitating effects of parental rejection, disapproval, frustration, and physical punishment beget in the child images of himself as unworthy, weak, or bad that persist throughout his life. In most instances such self-derogation is not justified by facts. It is rather a result of personality problems, and in turn is contributary to them.

The Oedipal conflict is an important factor in this regard. Feelings and conviction of weakness emerge if the father is overpowering, thereby impressing the child with his weakness, a feeling that is carried into and fused with the final image of the self. Similarly, in a child to whom love is denied the conviction is engendered that he is unworthy of being loved.

The permissive atmosphere of the therapeutic setting and the accepting, if not approving, attitude of the therapist tend to dissipate some negative feelings and thus correct the self-image. In child psychotherapy there is predominantly an atmosphere of acceptance, though at certain times restrictions have to be applied. The effect of such security, acceptance, and respect upon the young patient is to instill in him a growing conviction that he is loved and therefore worthy of love. It is also necessary to encourage the child in his efforts at reality testing and to insure his success until his skills and his ego are ready to function independently. With each successful step in his endeavors, encouraged by the friendliness and consideration of the therapist, the child's perceptions of himself take a more favorable turn, and a more hopeful and more sanguine outlook emerges.

In addition to these specific favorable conditions in psychotherapy, the self-image is constantly corrected by the removal of impediments to growth, the improvement of identifications, the lessening of anxieties and fears, and the establishment of better working relations among the psychic forces that had been hitherto at loggerheads and in conflict. The resulting integration of the whole personality is reflected in better organic functioning, improved metabolism, and more general inner harmony. To achieve these results, however, the cooperation of members of the family and the school staff are necessary for the same reasons as in ego strengthening.[8]

The therapeutic processes through which the many corrections in personality structure and social adjustment are achieved consist of six dynamic elements: (1) transference and substitution; (2) catharsis; (3) insight; (4) ego strengthening; (5) reality testing, and (6) sublimation.

TRANSFERENCE AND SUBSTITUTION

Transference is the process by which the patient attaches to the therapist feelings he has had toward his parents. The term is employed to indicate that the patient transfers these feelings from parent to therapist, whom he must accept *in loco parentis* and react to him with the numerous associated emotions of hate, love, dependence, hostility, and ambivalence. As we have seen

[8] See also "Developing Self-acceptance," in S. R. Slavson, *An Introduction to Group Therapy*, pp. 197 et. seq.

so clearly expressed by two of the children on whom we reported in Chapter V, the therapist also becomes the sexual object of the patient. Because they were young, these two children expressed their libidinal drives toward the therapists. Such feelings exist in patients of all ages and both sexes, but because of fear, or embarrassment they do not always find such clear expression. The sexual urges the child feels for the therapist are the reactivation of identical urges he had entertained toward his parents, which he now transfers upon the substitute parent, the therapist.

Transference, the cornerstone of all psychologic treatment, is also the basis of group psychotherapy, even though in the latter its manifestations are vastly modified and varied, quantitatively and qualitatively.[9] I have also attempted to show that "the importance of transference has been vaguely recognized even among the ancients and more clearly so in more recent centuries. When Socrates recognized the existence of mental illness separate from physical sickness, he prescribed as its cure 'sweet words.'" [10] Although at first the term "transference" was employed by Freud and his associates to designate the libidinal involvement with the therapist as an extension of the Oedipal conflict, the term was later employed to include other relations in derivative psychotherapies and in everyday relations among people. This wider use of the concept in its various meanings in both quality and intensity led to the recognition that there are different "levels of transference."

It has been found that some patients prefer a therapist with one type of personality and manner, while others respond to other attributes and characteristics. Therapists find it difficult to establish a workable relation with some patients, but receive instantaneous response from others. For successful psychotherapy with children therapists must be gentle, friendly, sympathetic, and responsive. These qualities are prerequisites, because children are essentially dependent and need security and love. Adults are more autonomous and self-reliant, but they, too, need

[9] S. R. Slavson, *Analytic Group Psychotherapy*, New York, Columbia University Press, 1950, pp. 15–36; also "Transference Phenomena in Group Psychotherapy," *Psychoanalytic Review*, Vol. XXXVII, No. 1, January, 1950.

[10] *Analytic Group Psychotherapy*, p. 15.

sympathy and understanding. If a child's initial response to the therapist is friendly a favorable prognosis is justifiable even though there will always arise in the child negative, hostile, and aggresive feelings in the course of treatment. The alternate and frequently simultaneous positive and negative feelings with regard to the person of the therapist give rise to considerable ambivalence and alternation of affect, which in turn result in positive and negative phases in the transference.

The patient strives to be liked and accepted by the parent surrogate, the therapist. He wants to be loved by him, as he wanted to be loved by his parents. The patient perceives what the therapist would like him to be and to do and strives to please him. In fact, this is one of the motivations for improvement. The desire to please the therapist and gain his love may be a subsidiary factor, but must be taken into account in evaluating the dynamics of recovery.

The accepting attitude of the therapist helps the patient to overcome his resistance, which in turn releases repressed feelings, because he is sure of the noncritical and understanding approach of the new parent figure. He feels that the therapist will not scold, punish, or humiliate him because he harbors "bad," immoral, or cruel impulses and intentions. He need not be ashamed and therefore defensive. This narcissistic core that is always encountered in patients is among the most serious impedimenta to successful treatment. The core is built up not only in relation to others but also from the impelling need to maintain one's own ego-ideals and an idealized self-image.

In addition to the direct libidinal drives in the transference relation in psychotherapy, the element of displaced hostility to the parent who blocked the early pleasure drives has to be reckoned with. The negative phase in the transference is largely due to stored up resentment the patient, as a child, feels toward his parents. As the therapist represents a parent, the related emotions are activated and attached to him. The therapist then becomes the person who frustrates the patient's infantile strivings and thus becomes the hated person. This was well illustrated by the young patients described in the preceding chapter. Dealing with these negative feelings when they are manifested against the therapist is the pivot in all psychotherapy.

In addition to other reasons, patients usually resist the development of a positive transference. There are many exceptions to this, as in children with affect hunger, for example. Establishing a transference is an admission of one's emotional inadequacy, which implies dependence. This feeling in many instances the ego is unable to accept. It also connotes a separation from or a rejection of the parent, that arouses feelings of guilt and anxiety. The child feels that in becoming attached to the therapist he is disloyal to his parents, a feeling that is intensified when he is insecure in their love. Still another reason for this resistance is that because of the child's painful experience with loved persons (the parents) in the past, he is afraid of entering into a close relation with another adult. This is well illustrated by the following incident.

A severely psychoneurotic boy of seven under treatment by a woman psychotherapist asked his mother to call her on the telephone and tell her that he no longer needed any treatment. The mother rightly told him that he would have to tell the therapist himself at his next interview. On the way home from that interview, the boy said to his mother: "I like Mrs. Smith, mother. I like her very much. But you know, when you start liking somebody, you get afraid."

The basic feelings the patient entertains toward the therapist are charged with the same sexual urges he has toward his parents, which have been hitherto inadequately repressed. We shall designate this type of transference as *libidinal transference*. This we do as a device for differentiating it from *identification transference*, where the therapist serves as the patient's ideal and identification model.[11] Observation of children under individual treatment confirms this conclusion and is unmistakably apparent in group psychotherapy.

The manifestation of positive and negative phases of transference resembles the alternation of feelings toward parents. To some extent phases reflect (*a*) the child's feelings toward his

[11] See ch. vii.

parents *at the time of the interview,* (*b*) the associated emotions aroused during the interview, (*c*) the threat to ego defenses, and (*d*) the need to discharge tensions. The direct expression of hostility by aggressive acts toward the therapist is essential to successful psychotherapy. The hostile, threatening phantom—the parental image—upon whom the child discharged his aggressions in phantasy is now a real person, against whom they can really be acted out without fear of being punished or abandoned. This discharge of hostility frees him from the burden of suppressing or disguising feelings. It allows him to reconstruct his image of the real parent, who now looms in a more favorable light, thus making available added ego energies.

This occurs, however, only when the therapist deals helpfully with the child's aggressions. In accordance with requirements of the situation, among which are (*a*) the specific central or nuclear problem, (*b*) the state of the transference relation, (*c*) the age of the patient, (*d*) the stage in treatment, and (*e*) the aim of treatment, he may either accept, tolerate, approve, disapprove, use passive or active restraint,[12] interpret, or even apply mild, direct control. The negative phases of the transference are revealed by resistance manifestations such as absence, tardiness, evasiveness, noncommunication, irrelevant talk, carefully prepared communication in advance, various irrelevant play, as well as by direct aggression. However, for successful therapy the child's feelings toward the therapist must be basically positive. Frequently seemingly negative behavior masks positive feelings. It is only upon the background of a positive transference, irrespective of how it reveals itself, that treatment can be built. Positive transference is essential for the free flow of catharsis and resultant regression. The first step in treatment, therefore, is to convince the child of the therapist's good faith, worthiness, honesty, empathy, and understanding. The child has to feel secure that he will not be reproved, disparaged, punished, or betrayed.

We propose the terms *"basic"* and *"transitional"* to describe these types of transference. It is upon the foundation of the basic

12 See p. 221.

positive transference that the structure of psychotherapy can be built, even though we encounter from time to time negative transitional phases. These blockings (resistances), of which transitional negative transference is only one manifestation, are the very essence of psychotherapy. The child must discharge hostilities and manifest aggressions, or he will not improve. Where no hostility is discharged, no therapy takes place.

I have suggested that the transference in children in the pre-Oedipal and Oedipal stages in many respects differs from transference in older persons.[13] Observation of young children throws doubt upon the genuineness of the transference as usually defined. While the adult patient redirects his early childhood feelings onto the therapist, he is at all times fully aware that the latter is not his parent. He may feel toward the psychotherapist as he does or did toward his parents, but he knows that they are entirely different persons. The narcissistic nature of children is such that they do not make this differentiation, and they treat other adults *as though* they were their parents. In treatment they psychologically substitute the stranger for the parent, and when they act out their love and hatred toward the therapist, they do so as though the latter were actually their parent—in phantasy they substitute the therapist for the parent. Since the very young child is still very much a part of the mother and their mutual relation makes one an extension of the other (anaclitic relation), it is impossible for him to detach himself completely from the parent as does an older child or an adult. The nearest he can come to it is to substitute other persons for the parents. This he does also with objects, pets, siblings, nurses, teachers, playmates, as well as with the therapist. I suggested the term "substitution" for this phenomenon rather than "transference." Another reason for the child's inability to develop a true transference, according to other writers, is that he is still in daily and intimate contact with his parents. They are the chief objects of his love and dependence, and therefore he is unable to cast them off.

One of the effects of psychotherapy is the gradual acceptance of the therapist as a real rather than an idealized person. This is

[13] *Analytic Group Psychotherapy*, pp. 29 *et seq.*

essential for all forms of psychotherapy. The growing sense of reality and the strengthening of the ego in the patient should make it possible for him to accept the therapist's personality as real, with the faults and foibles common to all human beings. A child can achieve this objectivity less successfully than can older patients. However, one should aim to help him accomplish it as far as possible. No patient should continue his unrealistic beliefs in the perfection and the saintliness of the therapist, for it prolongs the patient's transference relation and militates against emotional maturity. Dissolution of the transference is essential in psychotherapy, a process that is seldom fully achieved in practice. Every effort should be made, however, to achieve it, for a patient who continues in transference after treatment is unfree to develop, grow, and mature. The phantom of the therapist can be an impediment, as is the phantom of a parent. The pre-Oedipal role of the psychotherapist has to be changed as the patient's personality matures and changes. The therapist-patient relationship is changing and dynamic, and the therapist must emerge as a real rather than an idealized person.

The young patient needs to be helped to understand and when possible to recall that before the traumatic experiences occurred parents and siblings were sources of pleasure and kindliness; they were not cruel or unpleasant at first. This recollection changes the child's perception of his parents and the affect attached to them. This important development is greatly furthered by a more realistic frame of reference in the person of the psychotherapist. As long as the contrast between the person of the therapist and the harsh parents and other important adults predominates in the patient's mind, he is less able to accept the reality of the therapist. But as the chasm between him and the others is narrowed, he can accept it with greater ease and more realistically. The child now sees his parents also in a new light. Just as he viewed the therapist in the light of his parents at the outset of treatment, he now sees that his parents are similar in some essential respects to the therapist. This process I have called *transference in reverse*.[14]

[14] *Analytic Group Psychotherapy*, p. 105.

A more realistic conception of the therapist is equally important in group psychotherapy, where the therapist also changes his role as the children mature emotionally. The following illustrations taken from play-group psychotherapy exemplify the more realistic role the therapist assumes as the young patients become ready for it.

Charles, between five and six years of age, started to pour paint into a pan of water and said: "I am going to squirt it at Fanny [the therapist]." Morris became interested, and Rhoda said: "That's a good idea." The therapist said: "I don't want the paint on me." Charles started throwing things around and hurled some water against the wall. He then took a saw and Morris a hammer, and they said: "We are going to hit you, Fanny." Morris said: "I am hitting you on the ash can [buttocks]." Both attempted to strike the therapist, who said: "Wait a minute, boys," and removed the saw from Charles' hands saying: "Charles, see the saw? There are these edges on it that we have to keep in good order to use it." She then replaced the saw. Charles said: "I am going to find another one." Morris dropped the hammer and said: "We aren't crazy here," and went back to work on his clock. Charles said: "Oh, our paint; where is the paint?" The therapist pointed it out to Charles. Charles took a bottle of red paint and began to pour it into a pan. He said: "I will throw this around." Morris said: "Don't throw it around." Charles said, "I will be careful. I will get it just in the pan." Here the authority exerted by the therapist was taken over by one of the children, who assumed the role of the restraining person.

At another session Charles and John began to set fire to bits of paper on the electric grill, which the therapist considered to be dangerous, though such actions are not prohibited to older children in activity group therapy, where a special setting is provided for fire-making. The therapist, therefore, decided to restrict this activity and told them they could experiment with other objects, but must not set fire to paper. The boys gladly fell in with this idea and tried to set fire to various uninflammable objects, such as crayons, pieces of metal, bits of clay. Although this involved a considerable amount of movement, going back and forth for things to heat, there was less distractibility than in the earlier sessions of this group, indicating increased self-control and purposiveness.

CATHARSIS AND RESISTANCE

The second basic dynamic of psychotherapy is catharsis. By catharsis is meant the patient's discharge of memories and thoughts that oppress or disturb him with their associative feelings, a process that should lead back to the traumatic situations in which his problems originated. Freud and his collaborators found that in the treatment of psychoneurotics symptoms disappear when the patient is helped to regress to earlier stages in development, to recall painful memories, and to relive past traumatic situations. The process by which this regression occurs is catharsis. The traditional aim of catharsis is to overcome repression and dislodge painful memories, thoughts and strivings from the unconscious and bring them to consciousness. Originally the method employed was to set a situation in which the patient would talk freely of all matters that come into his mind, relive the significant points in his experience, respond to them emotionally, and acquire insight into his reactions by discovering their true significance.

The primary means by which this may be accomplished is *free association*. By this is meant that the patient communicates whatever comes into his mind whether or not it has any recognizable relation to the preceding ideas. Breaks in continuity have special significance. They may denote fear or efforts to evade or to resist revealing emotionally charged thoughts and memories. All this constitutes the resistance that one always encounters in psychotherapy. The value of this undirected talk is its power to lead the patient to sources of anxiety and traumatic experiences. In the psychotherapy of adults we rely on verbal communication, but actually there is considerable "acting out" even in psychoanalysis, where the physical situation is controlled by the fact that the patient lies on a couch and the analyst is out of sight. Patients flail their bodies, arms, and legs, tense their extremities, redden or pale, shout at and abuse the analyst, even rise from the couch to walk excitedly about the room.

In the less controlled therapeutic settings (where the patient faces the therapist, for example) catharsis is not so emotionally charged, regression is not as thorough (for lying down is an act of submission and therefore regression). Catharsis, therefore, does not usually extend as far into the past as it does in psychoanalysis and is not as emotionally charged. Children are prone to act out their current stresses and past difficulties. Verbalization usually, but not always, accompanies actions, and both are employed in the cathartic activity.

Catharsis can be (*a*) verbal, (*b*) activity, (*c*) vertical, (*d*) lateral, (*e*) free-associative, (*f*) directed, or (*g*) vicarious, or it can take the form of (*h*) associative thinking.

Verbal catharsis is that form in which the patient communicates to the therapist his thoughts, feelings, preoccupations, and fears in words. It can deal with events which he had experienced and lead back to the earliest traumatic situations. When this happens, we may designate it as *vertical catharsis:* it leads from the present to the past. We employ this connotation to differentiate it from *lateral catharsis,* by which we mean that instead of concentrating on background and developmental material, the patient talks of his contemporaneous problems and preoccupations. In the first instance he draws upon his unconscious and preconscious; in the latter, predominantly upon the conscious. The former relies upon free association, while in lateral catharsis *associative thinking* is employed, that is the content is drawn from immediate and current events and thoughts rather than from the past.

I apply the term *directed catharsis* to that catharsis which is suggested, controlled or guided by the psychotherapist. Examples of this are the situations in which the psychotherapist asks the patient a series of questions, directs him to talk about a special subject or period of his life, or asks him to remember and relate his dreams. *Vicarious catharsis* occurs in group psychotherapy when one patient covertly participates as a spectator, while another patient talks about or acts out problems, situations, and feelings identical with his own. I have used the term *activity catharsis* to differentiate the many patterns of behavior, acts, and conduct of a patient during therapeutic interviews other than speech. It can be observed in its purest form in activity group therapy, but it is also present in play therapy and in other forms of psychotherapy.

In the early stages of therapy associative thinking takes precedence; the patient has to deal first with "top realities" in his life. This is necessary because they constitute the greatest and most pressing concerns of which he is aware; it gives him a chance to become acquainted with the therapist and more comfortable in his relation with him, but it delays revealing more anxiety-charged matters. When he becomes more comfortable in the relationship, that is, when a positive transference is established, the patient brings to interviews material of a more free-association type. Associative thinking may be a form of resistance if continued for too long a period, except in guidance or counseling. Compulsive and hysterical patients usually either omit or condense this preliminary stage and deal with their life histories almost from the outset. Such ready revelations may also represent resistance.

Free-association and associative thinking and vertical and lateral catharses are not mutually exclusive. In sound psychotherapy all forms appear. In free association and vertical catharsis deeper levels in the individual are reached, and the therapist, through interpretation, activates repressed memories. In associative thinking and lateral catharsis, on the other hand, his major function may be to help the patient strengthen his ego and understand his role in the setting of which he forms a part.

The predominant characteristic, but by no means the only one, of vertical catharsis is to purge the unconscious, while that of the lateral catharsis is to ventilate feelings, which serves to reduce tensions, guilts, and fears. Lateral catharsis and associative thinking may improve one's functioning and social adjustment. These, however, must not be mistaken for true psychotherapy; the aim of the latter is to effect more or less permanent change *within* the structure of the personality. In the one, the patient is temporarily relieved; in the other, the nature and relation of the intrapsychic forces are more or less permanently corrected.

Associative thinking is much more effective with children than with adults. The child represses less, and, as we have already shown, the unconscious is near the surface. In his case ventilation of feelings and support from the therapist are important detensors, which set up self-corrective trends.

For precisely the same reasons activity catharsis, that is, revealing and abreacting to intrapsychic problems through behavior in a specially designed setting, is essential in child psychotherapy. Through our work in activity group therapy we were able to establish the value of activity in psychotherapy with children, though it is also implicit in "play therapy." In the past, however, this fact has been obscured by interpreting the behavior rather than relying upon the corrective effect of the activity itself and the setting. This oversight arose because (*a*) the methods of treating children were derived from the treatment of psychoneurotic adults, (*b*) childhood neuroses were erroneously assumed to be the same as those of adults,[15] and (*c*) the automatic growth and self-corrective processes of the child in a favorable environment were not fully appreciated. The study of numerous improvements and recoveries through activity group therapy with prepubertal children has shown that action catharsis and regression in behavior, coupled with support of the ego and substitute gratifications, offer appropriate therapy for the majority of children with personality problems.

Prepubertal children, whether under individual or group treatment, require opportunities for communicating their inner difficulties through play and other types of action. Young children require clay, water, fire, paints, brushes, dolls, mannikins, masks, guns, soldiers, rubber darts, doll houses, and doll's furniture, including beds and toilet fittings. Older children need also

[15] See p. 120.

tools and equipment such as wood, metal, and aeroplane models.

Doll houses with a number of rooms and bedroom and bathroom furnishings are particularly valuable for uncovering unconscious preoccupations. In his play with them the child reconstructs many of his phantasies. He places both parents in bed and the child in another room; or the child and the mother in one bed, with the father in another room. The latter is often left out altogether. Fathers are frequently left outside and barred from entering the house. Dolls representing parents or siblings may be thrown down great heights and presumably killed. The bedroom may be placed on an upper floor, or it may be the first room at the entrance. The bathroom also receives diverse consideration, with the toilet bowl as the center of attention. Play with water, fire, clay, and paints reflects preoccupations with basic organic functions such as urethral, sexual, and anal-sadistic phantasies. Chewing, shouting, and eating assuage oral cravings. All these are *libido evoking* occupations that favor libido redistribution as contrasted with *libido fixating* activities in activity group therapy, such as work in arts and crafts and games like ping-pong, checkers, or cards.

The materials supplied to children should vary in complexity and resistivity to accord with the child's age and development. Very young children should have materials of low resistivity and complexity. They need to be soft and pliable, such as water, paints, clay, and plasticene. Older children can use profitably materials such as wood and metals. Gradation of resistivity has the added value of developing power and improving the self-image in the weak.

Release through play and activity is beneficial for all children and is a requisite in good education. Acting out, however, has therapeutic value when it is related to the child's central or nuclear problem. Although in the course of treatment, especially in its beginning stages, it may be diffuse and unfocused, it must finally take shape and become related to his specific problems. If this does not occur, infantile immature trends are only reinforced through acting out. Climbing, for example, is a healthful occupation for all small boys, but it is of special value when it reflects growing masculine aggression in a castrated boy or is a form of reality testing.

In adults acting out is a form of resistance and a reflection of a weak ego that is unable to inhibit motility and impulses. It is also a regressive pattern by means of which one seeks mastery over a situation. It also serves to drain off emotions. In children, however, acting out is a natural means of communication because of their state of psycho-organic development. Every form of psychotherapy in which play and activity are used is a means of reaching the child's conflicts. It needs, therefore, to be viewed in the same light as verbalization, and its latent meaning understood. It is vastly more difficult to understand behavior than language, but the child psychotherapist must acquire the necessary knowledge, insights, and perception to do so.

The principle of free association operates in play as it does in verbalization. Therapeutic physical activity reflects and is associated with feelings, preoccupations, and unconscious strivings and urges. Therefore the play situation has to be as free-flowing as is conversation in the interview, so that the sequence of feelings may be revealed in a regressive train of events. Studies of children's activity in individual and, especially, group psychotherapy show that there is an unmistakable sequence characteristic of free-association in activity and behavior.

The nature and sequence of a child's actions reflect his problems, his difficulties, and his tensions. The relationship of acts to each other in a free-flowing chain (as in the free association of ideas in a verbal interview) lead to his central or nuclear problem. They illuminate repressed or surface emotions and reveal latent meanings even to a larger extent than does ordinary play.[16] The psychotherapist must recognize and understand them and deal with them therapeutically. He may interpret, explore, probe, or accept them without comment. The therapist's unresponsiveness is also interpretation, for the child perceives the intention and the meaning of such passivity. In activity group therapy,

[16] All play and free activity of children have latent meanings and special psychological significance. In this respect the play and activity in the therapeutic situation is not very different from the ordinary situation at home, playground, and school. They are, however, used differently in treatment.

for example, all the interpretation is passive, for which I have suggested the term *action interpretation*,[17] but its meaning does not escape the young patients.

Free access to a large variety of *libido-activating* and *libido-revealing* materials is required if free-association activity is to be stimulated. It should be emphasized here that the child must have free access to materials or toys. Restraint and limitations on the use of materials and toys block the free flow of the unconscious and free-association activity catharsis. Materials, toys, and tools unsuitable or dangerous for a given child for any reason should be removed before the child enters the room. This is in conformity with the principle of passive restraint, to which reference has already been made.

The therapeutic setting or environment in play or activity psychotherapy is planned and *conditioned* so as to activate catharsis by *visual suggestion*. However, its suggestiveness should not be adapted to a specific aim that may not reflect the child's needs at the moment. Spontaneous preference has to determine choice, for it has to be assumed that the choice reflects psychic needs at a given time. Free-associative play and activity therapy should provide not only free choice but also free use of the equipment.

There arise in the course of treatment emotional constellations that in the therapist's judgment require clearing up before the young patient can proceed. In interview therapy probing and interpretation are employed in such instances. In play therapy a special setting and suitable materials serve the same purpose. If the therapist knows that a child is attempting to work through his fear of animals, for example, and that he has gone far enough in treatment to be able to face this fear and to reveal the traumatic conditions in operation, he may provide a special setting or situation related to that fear. For another example, the therapist sometimes provides bathroom equipment for a child ready to undertake the correction of his anal preoccupations. Such

[17] S. R. Slavson, "Catharsis in Group Psychotherapy," *The Psychoanalytic Review*, Vol. XXXVIII, Jan., 1951.

specific conditioning of the therapeutic environment should be used sparingly, but it is very helpful and effective when employed at the appropriate time.

In child psychotherapy acting out serves also as a preliminary to verbalization; it also helps to diminish anxiety and resistance. Perhaps its greatest value is that when behavior is accepted by the therapist the child is convinced of the latter's affection, essential in establishing a positive transference.

Although the nature of the child's resistances is in some respects different from that of adults (their ego defenses and superego restraints, for example, are not as strong), there is considerable resistance present here as well. Children, too, struggle against revealing themselves. They are afraid of being reproved, humiliated, or punished for their socially disapproved cravings and wishes. Just as during the Oedipal stage he had striven to be worthy of the parent, the child now desires to be well thought of by others, especially the therapist. He does not want to appear "bad" or weak. Perhaps the chief reason for warding off certain types of catharsis is the child's fear that the therapist will disapprove of his interests and preoccupations with sexual ideas. As a defense against these fears, resistance sets in, and frequently it is also the cause of negative transference. Consequently, it is necessary that the therapist, who in addition to being a parent figure, also represents the mores and restraints of society, must help free the child from his fears before he can allow himself to regress.

On the other hand, the behavior of some children seems regressive, but it actually reflects their state of immaturity; for example, children with prolonged infancy, children without siblings, and psychopathic and other narcissistic personalities. Their behavior is a result of an arrest in development rather than a process of regression. This important difference is frequently overlooked. Arrest in development connotes that an individual has never gone beyond a certain level. Regression, on the other hand, occurs when an individual who had reached a level of development returns to an earlier stage under conditions of stress, illness, or anxiety.[18] It is a retreat along a path that the patient has already traveled, as it were. He can regain his former position under psychotherapy and progress again.

In the case of true fixation the path has to be first cut through. In ordinary development this is the task of education, but in specific cases growth is dependent upon special therapeutic help because of the malformation and disinclination to growth that had already been established. Sometimes, when educational influences have been inadequate, the therapist has to assume the role of educator. One of the encouraging characteristics of regression as it occurs in psychotherapy is that the return from the point of fixation to more mature levels under favorable conditions requires less time than did the original journey.

Regression has two categories. One is *regression in therapy,* which is temporary. It occurs in a transference relation, and the patient recovers in a brief time. The other is *pathologic regression,* which manifests itself in psychoses when the individual returns to an earlier stage in libido development and ego organization, where he may remain permanently or for a long period.

The usual forms of resistance are irrelevant or superficial conversation, resisting efforts by the therapist to explore the patient's feelings, engaging the therapist in games, projecting his own feelings and attitudes onto others, blaming other persons, negative transference toward the therapist, abrupt changes in the conversation, tardiness, failure to keep appointments, forms of blocking free association.

Among the more subtle unconscious resistance patterns are repetition and stereotypy—defenses against self-revelation that frequently cause considerable difficulty in treatment. Repetition, of course, may also serve to inform the therapist that the patient has not been understood or helped by the treatment to work through or to solve a given problem. The situation must

[18] The complementary nature of fixation and progression has been pointed out by Freud, namely, that at every stage of progressive development there lurks in the background the earlier fixations to which an individual retreats under stress.

then be clarified. Stereotypy may represent resistance not only to the therapy but also to growing up in general.

INSIGHT

Our third factor in psychotherapy is insight. Insight is a rather ambiguous term that has been incorporated into psychiatric terminology probably because of an inept translation from the German. The difficulty is that it is easily confounded with understanding, whereas it actually means something quite different. Insight is rather an emotional accommodation and flexibility within the patient's psyche that transcends mere recognition or intellectual understanding. Although it stems from the therapist's interpretation (as differentiated from explanation), insight can be attained only after emotional growth and cathexis detachment have been achieved by the patient. For example, one cannot interpret to a patient (*a*) without a positive transference, (*b*) before a point is reached in catharsis where the interpretation becomes *relevant* and therefore *meaningful,* or (*c*) before the patient's *readiness* had been effected by his growth and his emotional freedom.

Interpretation is quite different from explanation. "The latter is an ideational process to establish the relation between cause and effect and give intellectual meaning to a phenomenon. Explanations deal largely with manifest phenomena and involve the emotional factors to a minimum. In psychotherapy, however, the emotional elements are predominant; it concerns itself largely with the latent content of what a patient says rather than with the manifest. It is not enough for a patient to analyze his problems and reactions intellectually. In fact every therapist knows that this is often one of the most tenacious forms of resistance. Patients are prone to use lucid verbalization (rationalization) as a means of warding off therapy. Volubility is used as a defense against the therapist's effort to penetrate the patient's inner world; it may also be employed to ward off anxiety. The therapist's technique in dealing with this will, of course, vary in accordance with the patient's psychodynamics. While he may press a patient who is psychopathic or one with a character disorder, he will deal more cautiously with the anxiety hysteric, for example." [19]

Because interpretation plays so important a part in psychotherapy (though less in child treatment than in work with adults), a brief statement concerning it may not be amiss here. As I have indicated, explanation deals with the rational and ideational aspects of a situation and with its manifest and observable content and meanings; interpretation attempts to bring forth the latent and unconscious implications, meanings, and content of a manifest act or statement. Interpretation, therefore, is one of the therapist's tools in helping the patient to break through his defenses and the façade by means of which he keeps his hostilities and aggressions hidden and to uncover censored and repressed feelings and urges. Interpretation also aims to give thoughts, cravings, and phantasies different and less significant meanings in the light of a newly evolving personality and more mature understanding.

It is important that in giving interpretation the psychotherapist shall take cognizance of the patient's readiness for uncovering its relevance to the immediate content of the catharsis and the levels at which therapy is aimed. A patient who is not ready to face his unconscious will either not understand the "interpretation" or will violently deny it. He will do so because of resistances emanating from ego defenses, the feeling of guilt, the need for secondary gains, or the fear of maturity and its consequent responsibilities.

Relevance, the other requisite, depends upon the psychological context rather than on logical relations. The relation of one emotion to another must first be established, by regression and free association, before the patient can recognize it or accept it. It is essential to follow strictly Freud's admonition that interpretation be given only when the patient is almost ready to see latent meanings himself; only then does it become relevant and significant.

Interpretation must be directed toward the patient's immedi-

[19] *Analytic Group Psychotherapy*, pp. 54–55.

ate revelations, not to some hypothetical or remote aim that the therapist may have in mind. Although the psychotherapist may justifiably feel that the patient should be made aware of some problem at a specific time, the technique of forcing upon the patient an explanation would not be effective unless the latter is concerned with that particular matter at the moment. The therapist has to be poised and ready to introduce the subject when the patient gives him the lead; he may not force it into the therapeutic interview simply because he thinks it is important. Catharsis is the process of gradually uncovering layer after layer of memories, feelings, attitudes, and traumatic experiences until the core, or nucleus, is reached. This process cannot be speeded up without losing the advantages of emotional growth and strengthening of the ego that accrue during a slow and gradual procedure. A technique that renders psychotherapy rationalistic and didactic and allows the therapist's activity to predominate yields a minimum of maturity and insight for the patient. A badly timed direct approach to the nuclear problem may intensify the patient's defenses rather than help him free himself of them.

Interpretation cannot be assimilated by a patient if his ego is not ready to accept it; nor can his defenses be attacked before his ego has been sufficiently strengthened. If the patient is not ready, he may not return for treatment, or his anxieties and resistances may be vastly intensified and the transference relation undermined. It is even more serious to make an error in transference. When the therapist rips open defenses, as it were, and strips the patient emotionally, he appears like a cruel, unfeeling parent who has to be fought or shunned. Properly employed interpretation activates and strengthens transference. The therapist-patient relation is fragile and highly cathexized and can be destroyed by even a slight misjudgment.

During treatment the patient's verbal communications and actions must be viewed as steps in catharsis leading to the uncovering of nuclear problems. Awareness of this by the therapist is essential in utilizing whatever the patient says and does toward the ultimate aim of dissolving his fixations and conflicts. Such awareness also gives the cathartic manifestations meaning that they would otherwise not have.

Despite the fact that the therapist should not anticipate or direct the interviews, he should have in mind a focus and direction for the therapeutic effort, that is, reaching and solving the nuclear problem. Diffuse and uncanalized production by a patient is a sign of resistance, and in helping the patient overcome resistances, the therapist also helps him focus and find his way toward his basic traumata. Questions, statements, and interpretations by the psychotherapist must follow the direction and preoccupations of the patient, except when the latter seeks to avoid self-revelation or when his change of the current of the interview is obviously resistance. In such instances the therapist may interpret these as he does any other form of resistance.

In attempting interpretation the therapist must be certain of all the implications of a given situation. When in doubt, it is best to remain passive and leave it to the patient to follow the trend. The therapist must have clear reasons for whatever he says or does. It is far better to remain silent and inactive than to make a wrong move. The rule we have evolved for group psychotherapy—"do nothing, say nothing; when in doubt, don't"—is applicable also to individual treatment. The last admonition, particularly, holds good.

To be able to meet the many demands on him and to exercise judgment, the therapist needs to listen with *relaxed attention.* This also makes possible "free-floating attention," that is, the readiness to register and perceive the patient's vagaries, variations in content and direction, changes in affect, hesitation, repetitions, and the numerous nuances and subtleties that are characteristic of an interview. To achieve this the therapist must have not only knowledge and insight but also emotional clarity, and he must be free from intrapsychic interferences that may arise from his own emotional problems and preoccupations.

Interpretation may be directed toward a patient's anxiety, transference, or defenses. Each requires different treatment. The capacity to bear up under anxiety varies with each patient, and one should not be expected to exceed his particular limits. This is especially true when interviews occur less frequently than daily and the periods of strain are, therefore, prolonged. The exhausting effect of being in a state of anxiety for long periods between the interviews should be avoided. The therapist may, therefore, deem it advisable to allay anxiety by recognizing it in the patient, making a few general remarks on anxiety, its causes and effects, expressing sympathy, or interpreting it in a way that would reduce it. This is particularly essential in the treatment of children. Because of the low level of their ego development, anxiety is particularly destructive. The general aim should be to have the child leave the interviews with a feeling of gratification. It is permissible, for example, to allow a child to take a toy or a book or some other token of acceptance from the therapist's room at the end of the interview. Encouragement, reassurance and sympathy can be employed to reduce anxiety. It must be noted that these suggestions are at variance with the practice of psychoanalysis and other types of psychotherapy with adults, where anxiety should run its course and be used in the therapeutic grist. This is unsuitable for child psychotherapy.

The interpretation of transference is essential in all sound psychotherapy. This applies to psychoanalysis, as well as to therapies of lesser intensity, and to children, as well as adults. Its importance is made clear by the basic goal of psychotherapy, which is to uncover, to explore, and to eliminate the repressed hostile feelings and libidinal drives toward parents. The exploration and interpretation of transference attitudes toward the therapist serve to clarify the patient's feelings toward his parents. For this reason psychotherapists must utilize every opportunity for transference interpretation when it is relevant and otherwise indicated. However, this may be fraught with danger, and great caution must be exercised, for as already pointed out, an error in the use of transference may abrogate the therapeutic relation. Experience shows that it is almost impossible to overcome or to correct an error in dealing with transference.

Errors in this area are particularly serious in the psychotherapy with children. Children are seldom as keenly aware of problems within themselves as are adults. They do not suffer from them to the same degree, nor are they hampered in their functions as jobholders, parents, and members of the community. Inadequacies are not as blatant and as frustrating to a child. He therefore does not feel that treatment is imperative and is ready to give it up. The therapist has to "seduce" the child, as it were, into treatment, and since transference is the predominant motive, an error in this relationship may well mean the end of treatment.

Interpretation of defenses presents its own peculiar and very serious risks. Any premature threat to defenses creates anxiety and resentment that may well destroy the transference relation. By and large, defenses can be expected to disappear as the intrapsychic and practical needs for them disappear, but under special circumstances it may become advisable to make the patient aware that he is using them in lieu of facing and dealing with reality. To do this, however, one must be certain that (1) the transference is positive and firmly established, (2) that the ego is strong enough to give up its defenses or at least to examine them, and (3) that they are recognized as no longer a function of the personality, but rather vestiges of the past and a continuation of habit patterns.

Sometimes resistance and defenses are confounded or are used interchangeably. This is a grave error. Defenses are the props of the psychic life of the individual; they are the web and woof of human mental life and attack on them affects the entire psychic structure. Defenses are relinquished when buttressing forces are generated through the transference relationship, strengthened ego, and a growing awareness of one's processes and mechanisms. These accrue from emotional freedom, flexibility, and intellectual comprehension, which constitutes insight. Ego defenses can be interpreted in the later stages of the treatment only.

Sometimes probing may become necessary, but it should be used very sparingly. Probing may frighten the child and make him resentful. It should be employed tentatively and experimentally, so that the therapist can abandon it gracefully when the patient displays discomfort, embarrassment, or anger. Probing may become suitable as well as necessary with children. Their defenses are not strong and ordinarily they are not able independently to recall events and to formulate ideas. But the therapist's questions must always be specific rather than general. When fears are discussed, for example, a child should be asked whether he is afraid of a specific object, situation, or animal rather than whether he is afraid in general. A child cannot comprehend such general queries that make it necessary for him to take stock of his fears, usually an impossible accomplishment for him. In addition, his mind is distracted from his specific problem or fear and turned to generalities; this changes the course of catharsis and free association and strengthens his resistances.

The word "why" should be used sparingly. It is difficult for an adult, to say nothing of a child, to understand the basic motivations for an act or a feeling. Questioning by this means carries an accusative connotation, as well as an emphasis upon explanation and intellectualization. Rather, the aim should be to uncover feelings, not merely to stimulate understanding. Asking "why" one does or feels as he does not only embarrasses the patient but also directs therapy into the wrong channels, namely, conceptualization.

One of the situations that lends itself to probing is phantasy. The therapist is in a real and significant sense the bridge between phantasy and reality. The child gives up his phantasy for the more realistic gratifications he receives from treatment. Through this relation and because of his newly acquired ego strengths, the patient can accept reality with greater equanimity so that he does not need to escape into imagination or attenuate it by phantasy. The therapist can speed up this transformation and can further the maturing process by probing and interpretation. Again, as in the case of defenses the procedure has to be carefully planned and sensitively carried out. A direct and violent attack on a child's phantasy might shock and frighten him as would an attack upon his defenses. In fact, phantasy can be considered as a defense against too-difficult reality demands.

Interpretation, explanation, or probing should never become so insistent and persistent as to make the patient feel that he is pressed or pursued. Some psychotherapists erroneously persist in a line of thought or explanation so long that the patient feels either hounded or trapped. When this occurs, patients often escape into irrelevancies or selective silence, or they submit and passively accept the explanation offered. This, of course, is of no value. Even the most experienced psychotherapist cannot be entirely certain when a patient is ready for insight or to accept an idea or explanation. When the therapist finds it necessary to persist in pressing a point, it is a fairly sure sign that the timing is wrong. He would do well to desist and suggest the subject again at a more propitious moment.

Interpretation and insight are of necessity on a much simpler level with young children than with adolescents or adults, but even preschool children acquire insight and display considerable perspicacity in understanding interpretation. It has been observed that a considerable depth of insight arises spontaneously from the child's awareness of inner changes, his improved facilities to deal with impulses and the outer world, and his less rigid, less hostile, and less defensive attitudes.[20]

It may be expected that at best only limited levels of insight are acquired by the child. His immaturity, language, and conceptual limitations necessarily allow only elementary awareness and comprehension. However, limited as they are, they are important in his progressive development and in his emancipation from inner problems. In child psychotherapy we have to rely upon the mechanics of libido redistribution, the buttressing of autonomous growth trends, and ego strengthening, especially the latter, more than on the acquisition of insight.

EGO STRENGTHENING

Ego strengthening has already been discussed at considerable detail on pages 16–20 and 45–53 and do not require additional treatment at this point. The reader is referred to the sections

[20] I have suggested the term *derivative insight* for this phenomenon, which I first observed in activity group psychotherapy. The phrase designates the awareness a child acquires of himself through his automatic growth and inner security. In activity groups in which no interpretation is given, children become aware of the change within themselves and of their former motives and reactions. I believe that derivative insight is present in all types of therapy with adults and with children as a result of the patient's emotional growth as defined here.

where the subject is described; it is mentioned here only for the purpose of completeness.

REALITY TESTING

Reality testing, as differentiated from reality perception, is part and parcel of normal development, as well as of psychotherapy. No person can mature and no patient can improve even under the best psychiatric care without coming into contact with reality and testing himself against it. The patient must match his "conditioned" perceptions with their real nature. Dealing with outer reality—actuality—is an integral part of psychotherapy (as it should also be of education), for in the last analysis it is his attitude toward actuality that is at the center of the patient's problem. He either distorts, attacks, or withdraws from it. Even when sequestration is necessary for a particularly disturbed psychotic or neurotic patient, such a step is considered only temporary and transitional. The patient is transferred as soon as possible, first to a less supervised ward, later to an open ward; he is then placed on a daily or a full parole, and ultimately discharged. This procedure follows the principle of *graded reality* testing as applied to hospital patients. A patient completely isolated from others and for prolonged periods cannot possibly improve even under the constant care of the most expert psychotherapist. Isolation militates in every way against mental recovery, which requires a constantly broadening base. Each person, healthy or sick, draws upon his environment, incorporates it, and makes it part of himself. He is literally nurtured by it, and making it inaccessible is tantamount to making the very source of life unavailable to him.

Recognition of the importance of real situations in psychotherapy does not mean that they have to be included in the therapeutic process itself. Out-patients are constantly exposed to the realities of daily living, against which they test themselves. Their success or failure to cope with it forms a goodly part of the content of the interviews and certainly a major part of the patient's self-awareness. The frustrations he experiences, the deprivations he has to bear, as well as his growing sense of power, are all in the foreground of his thoughts and concerns, both in individual interviews and in group sessions.

As already shown, the ego is strengthened by success in dealing with reality and is weakened by failure. Self-esteem is buttressed and the self-image is altered beneficially by functioning effectively in realistic situations. However, the situations that a patient undertakes to deal with should be commensurate with his powers, which are progressively enhanced by treatment. Of this the patient has to be made aware by the therapist, and failure and success must be viewed in the light of the patient's capacities. The psychoneurotic patient, particularly, tends to demand too much from himself and is too strongly affected by failure.

In child psychotherapy direct experiences in real situations are more important than are ideas. The response he receives from others, the freedom and success of his efforts, are vastly more revealing to the child than are explanations. The therapeutic setting for children must include sufficient challenging reality against which they can test themselves. Psychotherapy with children should be predominantly of an active nature, whether it be in individual or in group treatment.

A group presents an important and inescapable segment of reality, and if the child is able to accept and deal with multiple relations such as a group presents, it should be included in the therapy for prepubertal children. Groups are particularly important to children in latency. At this age the child should have the pressures and complexities of the group graded and controlled so that they may not further traumatize him. The environment needs to be conditioned in accordance with his capacities. In play, activity-interview, and activity-therapy groups [21] the setting is designed on the principle of graded reality, in which each is free to do whatever he desires and in whatever manner he wishes. The child may participate with the others or withdraw from them; he may work, play, or idle. In this permissive and flexible environment he can test himself against other children and the physical and social environment planfully provided for him. Because of the unpredictable and frequently un-

[21] See ch. xi.

controllable reactions in groups, many children are not prepared for such strains and should not be exposed to therapy groups. Despite these reservations, a large number of children in latency can be helped by group therapy if it is properly fitted to their needs.

SUBLIMATION

Sublimation is the psychologic process of redirecting psychic energies and instinct gratifications into channels and forms and toward objects acceptable to the ego, superego, and the social mores. The alternative to sublimation is repression, which blocks the routes of the instinctual forces. In sublimation the psychic forces are not blocked, but are rather recanalized. They move forward in their original direction, but are changed in form, or content, or both, by another set of forces. Thus, a child sublimates anal interest by playing with clay or mixing paints. Aggressive-sadistic drives are sublimated by games; sexual preoccupations by play with fire and scattering sand and salt. Many creative and constructive endeavors and important achievements of individuals are sublimations of primary aggressive and other drives.

Sublimation should be carefully distinguished from displacement. In the former both the form and the object of the impulse are altered. In striking a ball, when the real aim is to strike a sibling, the child's original impulse is redirected to a different aim, namely, ball playing and winning the game (defeating the sibling). In displacement, the child would strike a playmate or a pet instead of his brother. The impulse to hurt someone has not been altered, only the recipient (or the object) of the aggression is different.[22]

In addition to the other values already outlined, active play psychotherapy applies sublimations for the id urges in play and work and is, therefore, of value because it allows energies to

[22] The psychoanalytic interpretation of sublimation is the transformation of sexual into nonsexual aims. While I accept this definition, I have broadened it for our purpose here, because we are dealing largely with children in the latency period; also because we assume the existence of primary aggressive drives which are nonsexual in nature. I consider them part of the biologic struggle for existence.

flow outward and helps the patient to find better ways of achieving his aims and to adopt acceptable patterns of self-expression.

One of the difficulties of the adult neurotic is that not having established adequate sublimations he is constantly in the act of unsuccessful repression that drains his energies. He is unable to canalize energies into acceptable aim fulfillment. The child redirects his energies into sublimatory activities with greater ease. Play and even serious work afford him suitable and acceptable outlets. Most activities appropriate for children are unsuitable for adults; clinics and hospitals and sometimes also private psychiatrists, therefore, use specially planned ancillary forms of activity for them as sublimations, in addition to the regular interviews. Among these are occupational therapy, individual and group recreation, dramatics, plastic and graphic arts, and similar occupations.

A major advantage of group psychotherapy with children is that it affords ready opportunities for sublimation. Children find it easy to sublimate primitive impulses into manual and play activities and in interpersonal relations in a group. Aggressive work with tools and materials, group play, fights, and struggles serve these ends.

In treating children it sometimes becomes necessary deliberately to expose them to activity and interests that help the sublimation process. Though usually sublimations in appropriate activities are selected by them spontaneously, some children require help in joining group games, sports, and intellectual pursuits. Sublimation channels, like all other steps in psychotherapy, should be supplied when the patient is ready to utilize them constructively.

If treatment is successful, all patients—children as well as adults—independently seek out sublimating activities and interests commensurate with their strengthened psychic forces and the reorganization and improved balance of these forces. As the primary drives are decathexized through libido redistribution and a strengthened ego, the urges for direct infantile gratifications are diminished. The individual can accept altered and substitute satisfactions more consistent with his emotional maturity. In this the transference upon the therapist plays an important part, for the example set by him and his role as an object of identification predispose the patient to give up infantile strivings and behavior.

VII

The Psychotherapist in Reality and Phantasy

WE SHALL HAVE AN OPPORTUNITY to discuss at greater length the art and science of psychotherapy.[1] In the present chapter the therapist as a person, his educational qualifications, and his functions will be the center of our attention. It may be helpful to point out that knowledge of the process is not sufficient for the practice of psychotherapy. The psychotherapist's disposition and his natural facility for the art are at least as important. To make this palpable, we shall discuss it under four separate headings: (1) personal qualifications; (2) educational backgrounds; (3) skills and functions; (4) special problems.

PERSONAL QUALIFICATIONS

Success in psychotherapy is achieved as much because of what the psychotherapist is as by what he does. The patient is always alertly aware of the therapist's quality of personality and of his reactions. He registers the therapist's frustrations, embarassments, hesitancies, confusions, disapproval, anger, and the numberless other reactions of one individual in direct relation to another. Much of this is obviated in psychoanalysis with adults because the analyst is out of sight of the patient. In psychotherapy with children such an arrangement is both impossible and unsuitable, if for no other reason than the child's physical activity during interviews. In facing the patient, the therapist reveals himself and his unconscious reactions, which inevitably affect the therapeutic process and relationship.

Some individuals are said to possess a "therapeutic personal-

[1] See ch. viii.

ity." While each one, as a result of his own experience, has a vague notion as to the characteristics of such a personality, it may be helpful to define as nearly as possible what that means. Personality, as a concept, is in itself as complex as it is elusive, and this intangibility is only enhanced by the adjective "therapeutic." However, despite these obvious difficulties an effort should be made to construct a workable definition, even though it may be extended and functional.

For work with children a psychotherapist should not have left his childhood so far behind him that he is unable to empathize with his young patients. Even if he has succeeded in working out his earlier problems through a personal analysis or has had a favorable childhood, he must remain psychologically close to the earlier level in order that he may feel with and understand the struggles of his young patients. A person with too rigid controls, inflexible and devoid of lyrical qualities and some enthusiasm, cannot make any contact with children. Children do not respond to or have confidence in the matter-of-factness, coldness, and detachment that is erroneously attributed to "maturity." The successful child psychotherapist needs to possess warmth, spontaneity, imagination, and some of the "unrational" qualities usually attributed to children themselves, except that he should have integrated these qualities into his total character so as to have them under control. He should have what may be termed *controlled spontaneity*. In a child or an immature adult spontaneity is not under control.

To work with children a therapist should have had a difficult childhood himself and have worked through his problems sufficiently to have gained the knowledge and the wisdom which serve as instruments of his craft. A person who has not suffered cannot have empathy or be able to understand—using the term in its deeper sense—the suffering of others and the results of suffering. The danger here is that if the therapist has not overcome his own fixations and feelings of resentment and hostility he will *identify* with his patients only too well and countertransference will result. He will reinforce undesirable feelings in the child instead of helping him to rid himself of them. Identification with patients vitiates therapy; it is rather empathy that is necessary. One's own difficult childhood aids empathy, but too strong survivals of one's childhood feelings prevents it. It rather encourages identification, which is undesirable.

The above discussion is intended as a background for the suggestion that development varies greatly in individuals. The childish traits retained by many adults often escape detection, for most of us base our evaluations on impressions rather than the examination of subsurface forces. My own experience with several scores of psychotherapists was that the most successful child therapists are those whose basic personalities are fixated to some extent in childhood. Although all of them were manifestly psychologically adult—they seemed to be well-controlled, serious-minded, aim-directed persons, with a good sense of values—actually there was a side to their character that was not in keeping with this picture. They possessed a child-like quality, which in ordinary parlance might be considered immaturity. It is this quality, their closeness to the child's psyche, that activated positive transference in their patients and made it possible for them to "understand" children.

Perhaps an instance from experience may illustrate this point. A young woman of twenty-eight who was acknowledged as an extraordinarily gifted and resourceful teacher of five-year-old children asked to be "advanced" to teach a class of eight-year olds. As consultant to the staff, I advised against it on the ground that the teacher in question was basically not mature enough to deal with children of that age. I pointed out that her superior gifts with children under six proceeded from her own emotional development. Perhaps it should be added in passing that she had undergone a prolonged psychoanalysis. Because of the teacher's insistence, the director of the school did not heed my advice and transferred her to an older group. The teacher broke down in the middle of the school year and was forced to take a leave of absence. She had lost complete control of the older children because she had neither the understanding nor inner resources to deal with them. It is evident to all those who have worked with children in any capacity—in education, recreation, or therapy—

that the quality described is the basis for empathy and the surest means of evoking positive transference from a child. The psychologic chasm, added to the size and the intellectual distance, between adult and child creates a barrier that is difficult to span in any relation, especially in psychotherapy.

To have empathy with others, perceive their feelings, and respond intuitively to the nuances of their mental processes are primary, not acquired, gifts that are enhanced in persons who have coped with their own unconscious. No person can help a patient to come to grips with his unconscious who has not done so himself, for he would otherwise become embarrassed and distressed at the revelations of his patients and therefore be incapable of dealing with them. Since people are so much alike in fundamental cravings and problems, the patient inevitably activates the unconscious of the therapist, who because of his frustrations may develop various countertransferences.[2] By act or by his manner he may discourage the patient from proceeding, his mind will wander as a defense, or he may become manifestly disturbed. Under these circumstances the therapist is incapable of giving the "floating," or free, attention essential for psychotherapy. These and numerous similar responses by the therapist will be perceived by the patient and will block transference, free association, and the other dynamic processes of psychotherapy.

Therefore, it is recommended that psychotherapists have a personal analysis in order that they may better "understand" their patients and be able to deal with the emotions activated in them by the patient's communications. The therapist should be devoid of "blind spots" in his own emotional organization. One therapist, for example, reported that she felt antagonistic toward mothers of children whom she treated. She became aware of siding with the children against their mothers. She also recognized that she was displacing upon them hostility toward her own mother, but was unable to control those deep-rooted feelings.

Another therapist had overemphasized the incompatability of husbands and wives among her patients. More or less normal

[2] See p. 208.

tensions inevitable in all marital relations became exaggerated in her mind, and she could not see any other way out in these situations except dissolution of the marriages. She succeeded in creating considerable discontent in many families and caused a number of family break-ups. Quite evidently this exaggerated overemphasis was a result of her own Oedipal conflict, but in this case the therapist was not aware of it. In another instance a psychotherapist, whom I controlled, suspected homosexual interests on the part of her women patients, often without foundation. Although one can expect a high incidence of homosexuality in women under treatment, this therapist's unconscious preoccupation with homosexuality caused her to project it onto the women she treated.

Some therapists with certain cultural and family backgrounds have a censorious attitude toward children's rough, unmannerly, or uncouth behavior. Despite their efforts to be objective, permissive, and accepting, they actually disapprove of such attitudes, even though they may successfully control overt expression of their feelings. There are also therapists who because of their own identifications and attitudes toward themselves can understand one sex better than the other. Because of his basic hostility to children, as a result of sibling rivalry in his own life, a therapist may react by overpermissiveness and laissez-faire that defeat the ends of treatment. All preferences, antagonisms, and fixations decrease one's usefulness as a therapist, and unawareness of such attitudes may do considerable harm.

We have mentioned in passing the importance of intuition in dealing with people therapeutically. Every psychotherapist knows that patients do not communicate all their feelings or reveal the entire content of their unconscious. Even when resistance is minimal, it is not possible for the patient to know or be aware of everything that his psyche contains. He may recognize those elements in his personality that disturb him or cause interpersonal maladjustments. However, much is structured in the unconscious or preconscious that may be the center of the problem, but has not been brought forth. The therapist needs to be able to perceive these elements and at appropriate times to use them as part of interpretation. This perceptiveness may be characterized as "intuition."

Perceptiveness is a major equipment of the therapist. The actual skills of dealing with problems can be acquired by training, but the use made of these learnings and the aptness of their application will be determined by the responsiveness to the immediate situation at hand and the capacity for empathy with the patient's state at the moment. The therapist has to possess them as a part of his native and acquired professional capital, as it were. Training and education can strengthen them, give them realistic foundations, and help to make it possible to use them appropriately and with skill. But training without native talent is a building without a foundation.

To the students of this volume it is not necessary to contrast extensively sympathy and empathy. The definitions of these two terms are in a sense inherent in their etymology.

Empathy, like feeling with others, is made possible by having suffered and successfully worked through and overcome that suffering. Sympathy is the emotion of an individual who is still preoccupied with his suffering. In one case a person emotionally understands because he has had the same or a similar experience; in the other, a person's own suffering is activated. Suffering, said Schopenhauer, is the crucible in which the human soul is purified; but, it must be added, only when it results in wisdom and detachment. Suffering can also embitter one: one "goes sour," as it were. This is manifested by unhappiness, self-pity, general disturbance, a hostile and unkindly disposition toward people, jealousy, and ill-wishes toward friends, neighbors, and relatives. Some succeed in emerging from suffering with deepened feelings, broader human understanding, increased forebearance—in other words—wisdom. The change is partly conditioned by a stronger ego organization, greater frustration tolerance, a philosophical (objective) outlook, or a combination of these. Experience with depth psychology as a patient has a salutary effect in this respect and is one of the reasons why a personal psychoanalysis is recommended for prospective psychotherapists.

Both sympathy and empathy are necessary in psychotherapy.

Sympathy is appropriate for some types of therapy; empathy for other types. But the therapist has to be capable of both. However, sympathy may have a negative effect upon the therapeutic process. Since it is rooted in identification, it may engender countertransference. Although the therapist has to be an empathetic person, he must guard against identifying with the patient's suffering, which is inherent in sympathy. The absence of detachment in the therapist militates against the process that helps the patient mature and become less dependent. When the therapist becomes himself involved in the patient's emotions, he supports the infantile fixations, instead of helping progressive growth and maturity.

In psychotherapies, other than psychoanalysis, and sometimes in that too, it becomes necessary for the therapist to take cognizance of the patient's feelings and dilemmas. This he has to do in order to support him and make him feel less alone and less helpless, but he must do so without any actual feeling about the patient's predicament. To be a successful therapist one needs to be able to respond to the patients' suffering and confusion without actually assuming them or being infected by them. In order to help, one must have imagination, for without it no one can respond appropriately to a patient's needs.

Detachment in the therapeutic relationship is the basis for the relaxed and "floating" attention [8] that the psychotherapist has to exercise, a detachment not possible when one becomes involved emotionally by sympathy, identification, resentment, or in any other way. Detachment leaves the therapist free to follow the patient's vagaries and to recognize the unifying thread in them that gives them meaning. Detachment results from freeing one's libido from cathexised early fixations and disanchoring (detaching) the emotional investment in traumatic foci.

"Detachment," as we use the term here, does not mean either insensitivity or lack of a desire to help people. On the contrary, without it no therapist can be of any value. He must be a sensitive person, but he should be sensitive to others rather than to himself. In a sense this means empathy. This point is quite im-

[8] See p. 201.

portant, for frequently detachment and empathy are considered mutually exclusive. Rather, they belong together in psychotherapy, and unless the detachment is of a primary nature, which may be a symptom of pathology, they coexist. Detachment is not callousness.

A genuine desire to help people is a prerequisite to being a good psychotherapist; without it one is bound to fail no matter how profound are his theoretic knowledge and educational qualifications. The absence of such a desire, no matter how well guarded or disguised it may be, unfits one for the job of psychotherapist, for without it one cannot exert his best efforts. Also, true inner motives cannot be hidden long from a patient. A word, a gesture, a grimace, or a nuance of facial expression betrays one to his watchful eyes—and the patients' eyes are ever watchful. Because of the patients' intense need for assurance, support, and acceptance, they are very alert to the real feelings of the psychotherapist. Children unfailingly distinguish genuineness from pretense; the true from the feigned. Their intuition and perceptions have not been as damaged as have those of adults.

One of the attributes that militate against the effectiveness of a psychotherapist is narcissistic preoccupation with his own processes. When one is too aware of himself, of his cleverness, insights, and good technique, one loses sight of the patient; there is no longer free-floating attention. It also interferes with the transference relation and with the adjustability and flexibility necessary to meet the changing moods and latent content of the patient's verbal or action catharsis. Nor should the therapist use patients as research subjects. This aim-attachment[4] is a form of countertransference which would interfere with free association and therapeutic catharsis on the part of the patient and free-floating attention by the therapist. This is especially undesirable when dealing with neurotics and others who tend to be particularly suspicious. Combining treatment with research is therefore inadvisable.[5]

[4] See p. 210.

[5] This extreme view may arouse opposition on the grounds that the develop-

Relaxed and free-floating attention require freedom from rigid ego defenses and preoccupations with one's self. When the therapist has painful thoughts and feelings aroused in him by the patient, he must be able to face them without disturbance, for once his attention is detached from the patient, free-floating attention ceases, and he becomes absorbed by his own problems and conflicts.

Another important qualification for a successful psychotherapist is ability to be passive. Even when the therapist is required to participate in the interviews or to assert himself as part of the treatment plan, basically he must be a passive person. This capacity stems to a large extent from temperament, metabolism, and other somatic factors. To a considerable degree, however, such passivity can be achieved through psychotherapy, self-discipline, and the extent and nature of frustration tolerance. The latter must be highly developed in psychotherapists or they will block or interfere with the patient's catharsis. Tenseness in the therapist and his drives for energy discharge in talking or uncontrolled physical movement impede the therapeutic process.

The psychotherapist must be free from belief in the "omnipotence of words." The experienced and sensitive psychotherapist knows that words are effective only in relation to a content and setting. The psychotherapist may not have a rationalistic or intellectualized approach to the patient's problems and to life in general. He may not believe that all that is necessary to obtain a cure is to "explain" a problem, "show" the cause, and induce "understanding." Such oversimplifications of the dynamic process in treatment may actually be the therapist's reactions against his feelings of inadequacy, lack of training, impatience, or inability to remain passive.

Therapies that employ explanations and rationalistic meth-

---

ment of a science and a profession depends upon research. This dichotomy can be resolved by keeping records and notes of the interviews and other pertinent facts, which can be later studied, classified and analyzed. This technique which I have employed for thirty years in a number of fields proved more reliable than setting the stage for research. It more faithfully represents what occurs in an actual situation than an artificial setting that frequently adds to or excludes elements from the natural situation. In the latter case the findings are untrue or at least unreliable when applied to the actual practice.

odologies strengthen defenses against the disturbing intrapsychic conflicts or induce submission to a parental person, the psychotherapist. Symptoms may sometimes be cleared up by these and other superficial methods, but since the basic conflict remains untouched, they either reappear after "treatment" has been terminated, or other symptoms take their places. Therapists, therefore, who prize intellectuality and invest confidence in its efficacy are prone to make many errors and affect no desirable results. Because of this special bias they cannot respond flexibly to the unrational and illogical reactions of their patients.

Despite the subordination of intellect to empathy and of reason to the principle of self-induced insight and understanding by patients, the psychotherapist must be capable of quick and unerring responses. Confidence in the therapist's ability and the transference feelings are strengthened in a patient when the therapist can formulate what the patient is unable to formulate himself[6] and when he conveys by some other means that he understands the patient's problem. We have seen how repetition and stereotypy set in when the patient feels that he is not understood. If continued for too long, this can turn into hostility and negative transference. To be understood is the major need of all patients, and when the therapist is intellectually and, especially, emotionally not equipped for it, therapy bogs down.

Finally, an even temperament and consistency are of utmost importance for the successful psychotherapist. We have seen that inconsistent treatment of a child by its parents is one of the major pathogenic factors in family life. Inconsistency or anything resembling it cannot be countenanced in the therapeutic setting. The security and the growth needs of both the child and the adult patient require an even and placid relationship. The patterning of the relation and the personality of the child in the transference should be supported by the solidity and security of a therapist's predictable and constant manner and mien. Impulsiveness and variability on his part increase anxiety and block

[6] This must be done with great caution. The therapist should not anticipate the patient. He should rather aim at clarifying the confusion in thinking and formulate preconscious insights and understanding that are present at the time.

the patient's growth. This does not mean that the therapist may not change his role, which he must do with the changes in the ego-strength of the patient and the transference relation. But the change itself should be planned and consistent rather than reflect fluctuation in the therapist's emotional state. The therapist's steady, strong, and even demeanor strengthen the child's ego. The child feels protected and, as a result, improves.[7]

Because countertransference so strongly reflects the personality of the therapist, it will be included in the discussion on personal qualifications.

On pages 201–2 we have given some examples of countertransference, that is, feelings induced by patients in psychotherapists, usually the result of identification with the patients. Such feelings in a therapist are a part of countertransference, which, as we have already seen, blocks or vitiates the therapeutic effort and process. In addition to identification, at least three other types of countertransference are discernible—*negative, positive,* and one for which I have suggested the term *aim attachment.*

Therapists are frequently irritated by a child's nagging, provocative, consistently challenging, and repeatedly annoying behavior. Even though the therapist understands the child's mechanisms and aims intellectually, his unconscious registers the child's tacit hostility. His deeply ingrained and largely unconscious precepts of decency and of good behavior, regard for others, and purpose in activity are outraged, and feelings of disapproval, displeasure, and even anxiety are aroused by the child's hostile and provocative acting out. This is particularly understandable when the child continues in his uncontrolled, destructive, diffuse behavior for prolonged periods. A sense of failure, ineffectualness, and futility is then added to the other feelings. Therapists feel frustrated by a child-patient who alters neither his manners nor his personality and confess to even anger when the pattern of behavior continues with seemingly no end in view.

[7] I was once accused that my high standards for psychotherapists and others who work with children demand that they be supermen. My answer was: "They need not be supermen, but rather superior men."

There are also patients who by their physical set-up, appearance, and mannerisms arouse dislike and even hostility in others, to which the therapist, being human, is no exception.

These and similar feelings are unavoidable. The therapist is not extra-human and is subject to emotional infection as is everyone. A personal psychoanalysis fortifies one against much of this and makes possible self-examination, objective introspection, and control over these dislikes and irritations. He can understand and accept the fact that what annoys him in the patient are characteristics that he has possessed or that he still possesses, which he would like to eliminate from his own personality. He can recognize that the irritation with the child's defiance is similar to that of his own parent when he, the therapist, was a child, or that the feeling of abhorrence is a reaction to or a defense against his own latent impulses. The analyzed psychotherapist can eliminate almost entirely negative feelings toward patients. There are, of course, the comparatively few fortunate individuals who by virtue of their constitutions or particularly favorable home conditions, or both, are free from strong emotivity. They are what may be termed *constitutionally tolerant* persons, whose emotions are not readily activated. They may react with even better equanimity and detachment than do those who have undergone psychoanalysis.

Negative countertransference can stem from a basic lack of psychological contact (perhaps identification) with children. This in itself may be the result of the therapist's deep-rooted rejection of his childhood, as in cases of difficult Oedipal conflict, accelerated maturity, eroginization of intellect, or other causes of self-rejection or self-hatred. There may also be constitutional and hereditary elements in this psychologic complex.

Positive countertransference is activated by qualities in the child's personality that please the psychotherapist because of conditioned preferences, memories of the past, or shortcomings in his own self-image. The young patient's "cuteness," attractive physique, good coloring, easy use of good language and manners may recall the therapist's desire to possess just such qualities.

Sometimes the patient resembles the therapist's own child or a favorite young relative or sibling.

The psychotherapist must withhold his pleasure at the patient's cooperation or with his improvement, if he feels such pleasure at all. If he finds it necessary, for therapeutic reasons, to express approval, he must do so objectively and couch it in terms of the patient's advantage. He may not, however, feel elated or convey his gratification because the patient is improving. Except in activity group psychotherapy, the burden of improvement is with the patient. The disadvantages of this form of positive countertransference are that (*a*) the patient will change his behavior just to please the therapist as a parent substitute—an act of submission rather than a result of inner growth; (*b*) in periods of negative transference the patient will cling to his problems and conduct from spite or because of hostility against the psychotherapist.

The therapist must be aware of these and numerous other pitfalls in his relations with his patients.

Another type of countertransference may be termed *aim attachment.* Therapists sometimes covertly set an aim for the patient—a specific objective toward which the therapist attempts to direct the patient's development. In such instances the therapist sets up a purpose of his own rather than the patient's direction and aims. The desire on the psychotherapist's part to effect improvement in the patient is still another pitfall in aim attachment. The therapist's wish for improvement may have the effect of destroying the patient's initiative—a reliving of earlier experiences in this area. This may result, as in the case of positive countertransference, either in his submission in order to please the therapist or in a negativistic frustration of the therapist by his unconscious shunning of all favorable change. Rather than attempt to influence such aims and wishes, the psychotherapist should help the patient progressively in developing his own purposes as they are related to or emerge from his own emotional growth. This the therapist must do, despite his awareness of the nuclear problem and the necessity of reaching it and working it through. The latter is the focus of treatment, rather than a psychologically self-derived aim. The two must be strictly differentiated. Self-confidence in the therapeutic situation that comes from good training, wide experience, and previous successes generally prevents aim attachment.

Of equal importance are objectivity and acceptance of the fact that one can do no more than his best, whatever the results. But this objectivity does not free one from moral responsibility toward his patients. One must be certain of his personal fitness for the practice of psychotherapy, the adequacy of his training, and that he really had exerted his best efforts and used his skills to their best advantage. Callous indifference is criminal; callousness is quite different from interested detachment.

EDUCATIONAL BACKGROUND

The psychotherapist must have a knowledge of the normal physiological processes of the human body and of its malformations and malfunctions. He needs to know the neurologic, endocrine, and other organic sources of maladjustment. Since the relation between the soma and the psyche is very close, it is necessary that the psychotherapist be thoroughly acquainted with both, so that he can recognize the etiological relation of the two in any given patient. If he himself does not possess such knowledge, there must be someone available for consultation who has this information, but the psychotherapist mut be prepared to understand the meaning of the findings.

A thorough knowledge of the natural laws and sequences that govern child development and the needs of childhood is essential in order to evaluate the extent of personality distortion. Knowledge of normal development gives one also the key to pathology. The therapist should be thoroughly acquainted with the various types of psychotherapy that have been evolved and are being currently employed and their probable efficacy for various personality problems. Therapy must suit the specific needs of each patient, his capacity to accept treatment, and his life situation; the therapist must not try to fit the patient to his own preferred method. Knowledge of many types of treatment [8]

[8] See pp. 250–55.

is essential for the therapist, and he should be prepared to employ these in accordance with indicated needs. Formal information is, therefore, not enough. The therapist should have good judgment and the ability to evaluate and to readapt techniques to suit the patient's requirements. This approach will be elaborated and illustrated in Chapter VIII, where planning treatment is described.

In addition to much specific professional information in general fields, the therapist's educational background should lead toward intellectual (as well as emotional) maturity. His personal qualifications should be further enriched by a store of general information, so as to answer questions which children may ask during interviews, and by manual skills of interest to them. Such facilities bring the therapist closer to the child's world; the transference is aided by them, and they enhance the therapist's significance as an object of identification and as an ego ideal.

Those who teach, train, and supervise future psychotherapists must, therefore, possess these skills, be themselves alert, perceptive, and quick in judgment so as to evoke these qualities in their students. Dull, restricted, and unimaginative teachers and supervisors limit the development and the effectiveness of trainees and indirectly harm their future patients. The choice of supervisors and teachers for medical schools, hospitals, and child-guidance clinics is pivotal for the future development of child psychotherapy. They must have a special flare and gift for the practice of therapy, and in addition they must be articulate and able to formulate and convey to others their knowledge and skills. The latter is extremely important. Education and even prolonged experience are in themselves inadequate qualifications for training others.

Only by in-service training is it possible to become an effective psychotherapist. The skills and judgments required cannot be learned from books or in the classroom. Psychotherapy is a craft, and like all crafts it must be acquired through practice guided by gifted persons who also possess teaching ability.

The psychotherapist's factual information should include genetic, experimnetal, dynamic, behavioristic, integrative, and depth psychologies so that he can visualize the whole psychological process in an individual. This, with knowledge about the nature and function of the organism, would give him an understanding and appreciation of the organism-as-a-whole. A background of zoology, especially laws governing individual and species survival and the expression of emotions and group behavior in animals, is of great value. Such knowledge helps one to view man in the setting of nature and as an animal who is activated by the same drives as are other animals. The knowledge of genetics helps one to have a more vivid understanding of the biologic and immutable factors of heredity that determine personality. Knowledge of embryology, gestation, and foetal growth further add to the vividness and deeper appreciation of man as a growing, functioning, striving, and struggling entity. Familiarity with physiology is essential equipment for the psychotherapist, for it gives him a perspective and an understanding of the nature of function in man. The study of neurology and endocrinology makes clear man's reactions to environmental stimuli, the genesis of personality, and its formation. Knowledge of these two subjects is essential not only for these reasons but also because they aid in the better understanding of emotional disturbances. Because the nerves and the ductless glands are so strongly involved in personality, neurology and endocrinology must be part of the curriculum for all psychotherapists. Whether physician or not, the psychotherapist should be able to recognize endocrine disturbances for which there are observable and obvious symptoms and enlist the help and advice of a specialist in that field when necessary.

The psychotherapist must have a thorough knowledge of the course of child development so that he may recognize the points at which development was interfered with and problems set in. To define the nuclear and peripheral problems for which the patient needs treatment it is necessary to trace in the child's history points at which pathogenic influences and experiences have occurred. This cannot be done without a complete knowledge of the requirements of normal development.

The psychotherapist should also be familiar with the well-formulated and well-described clinical material of psychopathology. However, this subject should not be studied statistically or in terms of classifications and diagnostic formulae alone. It should also be studied and understood dynamically, as a process.

Since the patient cannot be viewed as a current phenomenon only, his history must be analyzed and broken down so that in an interview one may select significant events from those that have no bearing on the immediate treatment situation. In training psychotherapists, history taking and the interpretation of events in the development of a patient are important considerations. Special skills are required in order to elicit pertinent information from the prospective patient and his relatives and to understand its significance for the presenting problem. Frequently a full anamnesis cannot be obtained in advance, and additional facts have to be garnered as treatment progresses, but the therapist must have in advance the facts most necessary for understanding the patient.

A thoroughgoing study of the nature and processes of psychotherapy is the next and final stage in the didactic training, to be followed by supervised practice.

SKILLS AND FUNCTIONS

In the transference situation we are dealing with three types of relations: unilateral, bilateral, and multilateral.

A unilateral relation exists when the emotional flow is in one direction, from one person to another, without reciprocal response. The best example of this is the relation between psychoanalyst and patient. In this treatment the emotional flow is only from the patient to the analyst. This unilateral relation is also characteristic of activity group therapy. The relation between the client and the group therapist is a unilateral one, for the therapist maintains a *neutral role.* Because of this neutrality, each child can view the therapist according to whatever symbol he may wish the adult to represent. It is important, also, that the therapist shall not give preference to any one member of the group, but rather shall meet the needs of each one objectively and on a warm and friendly basis. He cannot develop a relationship with any one of the children without disturbing the others. The child toward whom the therapist may have definite feelings becomes a preferred child or a rejected child, as the case may be, with a consequent activation of sibling rivalry, jealousy, and hostility.

A bilateral relation exists in less intense forms of psychotherapy than psychoanalysis. In these derivative and psychoanalytically oriented therapies the patient must feel the understanding and warmth of the therapist toward him if he is to overcome resistances and blockings, break through reservations, and establish a transference relation.

Group psychotherapy is founded upon the concept of *multilateral relations*. Individual relations are steps in growth to a point at which the patient can accept a group situation. He must be able to move freely from one person to another and to participate in relations in which more than two persons are involved. Multilateral relations are both the tools and the aims of all forms of group psychotherapy. In fact, the paramount qualification for selecting clients for group treatment is their capacity to face a situation in which multilateral relations exist. A child who fears multilateral relations needs a preliminary stage of individual treatment (bilateral relation) before he can face a group situation (multilateral relation).

The withdrawn and taciturn resort to bilateral and often unilateral relations even within the group as a transitional stage. However, to be accepted for group treatment a patient must have the capacity to develop multilateral relations. Lacking this he would not be accessible to group treatment, nor would he attend sessions.

Because of the bilateral relation in individual child psychotherapy, the therapist cannot remain as passive and impersonal as in the psychoanalysis of adults or in the practice of activity group therapy. The dependence, fear, and confusion of the child, that is, his lack of fully developed individuation, cause him to depend upon the therapist. He needs response and support, and what appears to the child as "coldness" may cause him to withdraw from treatment. But, as already indicated, too active participation interferes with free association. It is necessary to balance passivity and activity so that the child may still receive the necessary ego support without being diverted or frustrated.

Within the level of the child's understanding, the therapist has to interpret latent intent and meaning of overt acts. A child's disguises can be much more easily penetrated than can those of adult patients. In this the therapist is helped by his knowledge of the nuclear problem, and a well-placed and well-timed question not only aids free association but also demonstrates empathy and understanding, which cement the positive transference.

The therapist must be aware of periods when fear, anxiety, and resistance make their appearance and by reassurance must help the child to overcome them. Reassurance, however, should be used sparingly and only at periods of specific stress. The child must have permanent and continuous *assurance* in his relation with the therapist, derived from empathy and the feeling of being accepted and understood. When this relation exists, reassurance is not necessary. In fact, it may even be detrimental for the child, who is suspicious of all adults and may feel that it is a trap to get him to confess, or view it as hypocrisy, or become dependent on it.

Interpretation must be focused upon the specific problem or conflict the patient reveals or presents at the moment. These may be nuclear or secondary. The therapist, however, has to be aware of the nuclear difficulties, for they are often obscured. A child may talk of his resentments toward a sibling, which may assume a different meaning when it is known that behind it is resentment against the treatment he receives from his mother. A boy may rant against girls, but the therapist must recognize that this hostility is only an extension and displacement of the child's hatred for his sister, whom his father prefers. The patient who attacks all persons in authority must be led to recognize his behavior as a result of his own feelings of weakness and affect hunger.

In activity group therapy *action-interpretation* is employed instead of *direct* interpretation. The therapist's responses or reactions to the child's behavior assume special significance. They may have either an inhibitive or releasing effect upon him and upon his general development, as well as lead to derivative insight. When children in activity groups indulge in destructiveness, the neutral role of the therapist requires that he shall not look directly at what is going on. Watching without comment implies approval. It is essential that the therapist be aware of the course of such activity so as to prevent the increase of destructiveness and possible physical injury, but he must do this without direct observation. Aggression may take the form of hammering on a wall or table, attempts to break a chair, setting fire to pieces of wood or paper, painting on walls and furniture, throwing objects through the windows at passers-by, and similar acts.

Because the members of the group are accustomed to having their activities accepted and their achievements recognized in a positive manner in the past, denial of attention or withholding praise constitutes interpretation, for it reflects the therapist's attitude. When a child verbalizes hostility against or disapproval of another, the therapist does not react to it in any way. He is impassive and unresponsive. This conveys to the child that the therapist does not wish to be involved; also, that he does not accept negative feelings on the part of one child toward another. Occasionally children attempt to draw the therapist into a discussion of their relations to members of their families. To this the therapist does not respond, an indication that this is an area in the child's life into which he does not wish to enter. When at the refreshment table children conduct themselves in a disorderly, rowdy manner and eat sloppily, the therapist does not correct or admonish them, but his own deportment must be unimpeachable. He continues to eat so as to contrast his table manners with their own, thus conveying that the prevailing behavior is not approved by him.

When a habitually dependent, though actually capable, child seeks help with a project which it is believed he can do very well by himself, the therapist pretends that he does not hear the request. When the child repeats the query once or twice without eliciting a response, he usually proceeds by himself. Unless the request for help is insistent, the therapist remains impassive. This unresponsiveness serves to convey to the child the therapist's attitude toward his feigned helplessness. It is, of course, important that no error be made in judgment if the child is genuinely unable to proceed because of lack of skill, feeling of inadequacy, or general anxiety.

When a member of the group seeks the therapist's approval of an act in which the other members are involved, the therapist refers him to the group. When he asks permission to take some essential tools or materials home in the early stages of treatment, the therapist is always permissive and acquiescent. However, as the child's frustration tolerance is increased, the therapist refers him to the group, who may either allow or refuse the request.

These and similar strategies of action-interpretation are employed to stimulate the children's own growing powers to restrain impulses, regulate wishes, accept outer authority, build inner mastery, and particularly help them to become aware of their reactions. Throughout, the therapist does not deviate from his neutral role, for obviously he cannot discipline children unless they can react to his discipline and discuss it together, which cannot be done in activity groups.[9] Due to the fact that children's phantasies about adults—that they are unfriendly, negativistic, and rejecting persons—and because the therapist cannot work these feelings through with them in interviews, he must assume a neutral role.

In play-group psychotherapy for children under six years of age [10] interpretation is given by the therapist when it becomes relevant to the child's problem and he is ready to accept it. A few illustrations of this will suffice at this point.

In a group of six-year-olds conflict arose between two boys as to who asked the therapist first for help in making their model aeroplanes. Each insisted that he was ahead of the other, and when they could not come to an understanding, the therapist said that she thought that John was the first to ask her for help.

[9] See ch. x.

[10] See pp. 293–95.

Morris's reaction to this was to say that the therapist was "a dope." The therapist countered by saying: "You're angry because I am helping John first. I do this because he asked me first, but I really like you both the same." As soon as she had finished with John's project, she turned to Morris and helped him. The feeling of satisfaction Morris gained from this experience was revealed later, when he went to look at John's plane and said that it was "gorgeous."

At another time, Morris wanted to use up the materials belonging to a boy who was absent from the session. When the therapist called attention to this, Morris stated that because Charlie was not there he had a right to use his materials. The therapist said to Morris: "Morris, you want to have more than the others. You think that if you don't have more I don't like you as much. I like you as much as the others, even though I cannot let you have more things than the others have."

When the children in a five- to six-year-old group were told by the therapist that she was going to be married and would not see them for four weeks, one of the boys at once called her by her surname rather than her first name, which he had used before. The children asked a number of questions concerning her marriage. One of the boys then became very aggressive toward her and tried to jump down from a table onto her back. Distractibility in the group was noticeably increased. With one exception, the children were unable to concentrate on their work. They ran about the room, starting one occupation after another. A boy who had been particularly fond of the therapist, withdrew from her and did not address her for some time.

The therapist sensed the disturbance in the children and pointed out to them that their distractibility and hyperactivity had something to do with her telling them that she would be married; they must have feelings about it. What is it that they don't like about her getting married? The children did not respond to this.

At the subsequent two sessions the boy who had withdrawn from the therapist had again attempted to get close to her physically. There was an increased attempt on the part of one or two of the children to stand on a table and jump onto the therapist's back. One continued to avoid her, but displaced his mounting hostility on another member of the group. The therapist again attempted to elicit the children's feelings about her approaching marriage and the fact that she would not meet with them for four weeks. She stated that she understood their being angry about this. A few of the children said it was quite true that they did not like to have her marry and go away from them. The boy who was particularly fond of the therapist began to build a fire on one of the tables. Even though only little response was elicited, the therapist's verbalizing the children's feelings markedly reduced their anxiety. This interpretation cannot be given in activity therapy groups.

The therapist has to be able to recognize, ascertain, and help develop the positive assets of the child's personality and his resources that can effect improvement of the self-image and the ego-organization. Among these are special talents, latent capabilities, and personal or physical attributes and qualities. At the same time he must seek to eliminate the *pseudo-positive assets,* such as being good, obedient, orderly, dutiful, cooperative, which the child employs as means of placating the therapist as he did his parents and teachers. These patterns of behavior usually mask hostility and aggression and impede personal and social development.

The ego-supportive function of the therapist is not confined to relaxing inhibitions. He also strengthens and aids its integrative duties. In the case of the psychoneurotic child, it is important to dissolve the rigidities that the psyche has established as defenses against anxiety manifested in the repetition compulsion (Freud). This is accomplished by diminishing the superego pressures and the ego-strengthening inherent in the transference. But it must be kept in mind that the majority of prepubertal children present problems of behavior disorders and character deviations that require, not relaxation of the superego controls, but rather the buttressing of the inhibitive functions of the ego and its strengthening. The therapist, therefore, has to prohibit and restrain and thus become the external authority which, it is hoped, the child will internalize.

Because of the child's immaturity and his unreadiness to deal with id impulses, they have to be regulated and controlled by an outside source—parents, nurses, teachers, and therapists. We have seen how their self-control and self-discipline are incorporated by the child through imitation and identification and because of consistent authority that the therapist represents. Too often parents alternate between disapproval, annoyance, irritation, anger, praise, and maudlin sentimentality. Teachers are impersonal and impatient, too preoccupied and harassed to give individual attention to or permit the expression of pupil's vagaries. The therapist, because he has no special aim beyond correcting the child's difficulties, can be consistent. He does not yield to the child's efforts at cajoling, seduction, and ingratiation; nor does he react by punishment, aggression, or violence. This consistency and self-control are in themselves correctives for the child's impulsiveness and self-indulgence.

We have seen that in the treatment of children restraint by the psychotherapist is essential. Restraint can be *passive* or *active*. The most common form of the former genre, as described in relation to activity group therapy,[11] is not to respond or react to the child's aggressive statements or acts. Another technique of passive restraint is to prevent the child's undesirable behavior by removing in advance the stimuli in the setting or objects which he uses in acting out. The entire setting of the therapy room must be based upon that principle. The situational configuration must include elements in the environment that in themselves condition the childrens' behavior. This applies especially to those situations that may be dangerous or disturbing. Thus, an activity therapy room should have no doors except those for entrance to and exit from the room. If there are doors to closets or other rooms, those rooms must be accessible to the children so that no phantasies and curiosities would be aroused. All cupboards should be conspicuously within the room.

Windows must be so protected that there would be no danger

[11] See pp. 280 *et seq.*

of the children's falling against or through them. Thus, if low windows extend nearly to the floor, guards must be placed to prevent accidents. If window panes are so placed that they may be broken, when playing table tennis or ball, they should be protected with wire mesh. In one of our rooms the staircase from an upper floor leads directly to a door opening onto the street. The door has a large glass panel. Children are prone to run down the stairs and push the door impulsively, and they might cut their wrists if they should break a glass panel. To prevent this, we placed a stout, framed wire mesh against the glass pane. These precautions obviate the necessity on the part of the therapist of warning the children against danger or of restraining them in their activities. The therapist has to prevent confirming the phantasy children have that adults are prohibitive, dictatorial, and rejecting.

Another example of passive restraint is the following. In one of our nine- to ten-year-old boys' groups the work table which we found in the room had a tool cupboard underneath it. This could hold two children in cramped and close positions. Crawling into this enclosure and closing themselves in had become a regular pastime of the group. This was repeatedly instigated by a boy who, though young, had feminine identifications and probably homosexual tendencies. As this game was repeated a number of times, we tore out the cupboard, but the boys began to run into a large built-in closet where the materials and tools were stored. The shelves ran lengthwise along the wall providing a large space for playing in this dark enclosure. The boys preferred to play with the door closed, as other members of the group would lock the door on those inside. It was evident that this game was far from beneficial because of its phantasy-provoking nature and other implications. Therefore, we rebuilt the shelves crosswise in the front of the cupboard so that the boys could not go into the closet.

Another instance relates to food which plays an important part in the activity group therapeutic sessions. The early arrivals in a group of eleven-year-old boys had taken to consuming the food as soon as they came to the sessions, which aroused considerable consternation in those who came later. In phantasy this meant that they were being punished by the therapist, who rejected them and preferred the others. Considerable conflict, strife, and retaliation resulted. It was then decided that food be sent to the room about an hour after the time set for the session, when all the children were usually present.

A group of ten-year-old girls adopted the scheme of going to a near-by park weekly instead of holding sessions indoors. We felt that the therapeutic gains from these trips were minimal. They lacked the direct face-to-face interreactions characteristic of indoor sessions, which were at this stage more desirable for the girls. After three or four such excursions we sent a letter to the therapist indicating that there was a limit of 30 cents per person set to their expenditures. We said in the letter that in view of the fact that these trips had proven rather costly it was necessary to limit the expense. Since the fare to the park and back was 20 cents and only 10 cents were left for refreshments, the girls gave up the idea of going to the park. Excursions were later arranged at appropriate times.

A group of twelve-year-old girls took to painting pictures on the walls of the room in which they met. In view of the fact that the room was used by other groups, as well as for other clinic purposes, the paintings on the wall proved to be annoying. Instead of directly prohibiting this activity, the walls were repainted so as to eradicate the pictures before the next session. When the girls came into the room the following week, they said: "I guess they don't want us to paint on the walls," which they never did again.

In active restraint the therapist directly impedes, prohibits, or sets limits to the child's behavior and language. He may even end the interview session and send the child home when he challenges him or is extremely disobedient. The therapist has to exercise judgment as to the appropriate course to follow and must be certain of the transference relation before he takes any steps in active restraint. When infantile character traits are predominant, direct restraint is indicated, while in behavior disorders, indirect restraint has to be used at first. This is especially true when a neurotic trait or severe neurotic anxiety is also present. Frequently a child cannot establish a positive transference without direct control from the therapist, because his real need is met through it. In meeting this need the therapist lays the basis for positive feelings in the child.

Direct restraint should be employed with utmost caution. It must always be based on a thorough understanding of the child's mechanisms, the meaning of his acts, and his capacity to accept frustration and authority.

When development has been arrested, the therapist may have to assume for a time the role of educator. Earlier restrictions and limitations may have to be overcome by what is sometimes referred to as a "growth producing environment." Such an environment is characterized by permissiveness, encouragement of spontaneity, interesting and challenging occupations, free motility, and fluid relationships. A therapy group is such an environment, and when a group is not available other resources in the community that offer these opportunities to the child may have to be employed. When group relations are inadvisable or unavailable, the therapeutic interviews themselves have to provide these evocative and personality expanding occupations and relationships. Thus, working with the child in arts and crafts, writing stories, composing music, or play-acting may for a period comprise the treatment. Such means for enriching the personality, correcting the self-image, and reality testing are frequently important first steps, and in some instances, for very young children, they may be even the major or the sole therapeutic requirements.

I have elsewhere stated that the therapist's functions can be grouped under four categories: (1) directional, (2) stimulative, (3) extensional, and (4) interpretative.[12] This is an oversimplification of his roles, but it is useful for the purpose of emphasizing and summarizing the ideas already outlined.

[12] *Analytic Group Psychotherapy*, pp. 108 *et. seq.*

The therapist's function is *directional* when he helps the patient by questions or by returning to a previous point in catharsis to move toward his central or nuclear problem, but when this is not done appropriately the patient will resist by silence, diffusion, desultoriness, and irrelevancy. He may change topics frequently, speak in a confused manner, and becloud the issues. However, when in the therapist's judgment the patient is ready to pursue a special problem and his hesitancy is not too intense, he may safely suggest returning to the pertinent subject. The therapist thus focuses and directs the associations of the patient along indicated lines.

In some instances the therapist has to *stimulate* or help the patient to bring out content which he perceives is on the threshold of awareness (preconscious). Either because of resistance, unawareness, or distractibility, the child may indulge in much irrelevant talk about superficial and meaningless events, or he may come to the interviews with well-planned and well-prepared subjects for conversation. Understandably a child's daily life is filled with numerous matters that concern him. School, playmates, homework, clothes, and such topics, are all-important, but they do not yield significant or emotionally charged material for the interviews. The therapist's skill may be greatly tried to find an opportunity in such trivial talk for converting it into therapeutically valuable subject matter.

Frequently a therapist feels that the child is dealing only with surface aspects of his problems, being either afraid or unwilling to uncover his deeper feelings. This may be an indication of a weak transference; then the therapist has to turn his attention to solidifying it. When this has been accomplished and the child pursues his old course, the therapist may exercise his *extensional* function by probing or questioning to help the child deepen his emotional explorations to deeper levels. But he must be certain of the patient's readiness and the relevance of the ideas that he may be suggesting. The therapist must at all times follow the associative thinking and the free association of the patient and build upon it whatever further efforts he may wish to make.

The therapist's *interpretive* functions have been amply treated in preceding pages and require only mention here for completeness.

These descriptions of the therapist's functions and his role in therapy should not be taken to mean that he is required to be excessively active and to dominate the interviews. Most of his function is rather symbolic and has meaning to the child to accord with his specific problems and his evolving personality. Because of the intrapsychic changes in the patient, the therapist, both as a symbol and as a reality, changes. As the child becomes more comfortably adjusted, his suspiciousness of the therapist abates, and with more balanced libido distribution, the therapist becomes the recipient of less love as well as less hatred. The role of the therapist varies also in relation to the age of the patient. Because of the many psychological differences incidental to age, the therapist's functions also differ. The very young child, for example, who has repressed impulses and strivings and has not established taboos and social amenities directly acts out many of his primitive drives which require restraint and control by the therapist. The rule that the therapist should remain by and large passive and leave most of the activity to the patient should be adhered to as much as possible.

VIII

Planning Treatment

THE PATIENT IN HISTORIC PERSPECTIVE

IN ASSESSING THE PROBLEM OF A PATIENT, the psychotherapist must understand him in the context of his past history, as well as his current life situation. The patient's personality organization, state of health, special assets and liabilities, as well as his pathogenesis and psychopathology, have to be taken into consideration. The aim should be to derive a unified and dynamic picture of his personality and his relation to the total environment. Some therapists attach more significance to external and social conditions than do others. They believe that the current external conditions are more important than the background and the intrapsychic states of a patient. Furthermore, they assert that if one is to understand him one "should move from the outside inward" and that in studying him one should begin with a description of the environment and the patient's effort to adjust to it. Only secondarily should one consider "the fixed, intrapsychic determinents of behavior," which seem to be unaffected by environmental factors.

My own position is that the individual is not a product of his current environment, but rather a culmination of his history, and that he may be understood only in terms of that history. According to this view little can be achieved by limiting corrective efforts to current conditions only. If real damage has been done to the personality, it cannot be rectified by a change in his attitudes and thinking. In some instances, when the damage has not been too serious, behavior can probably be altered by altering external factors and relationships. But this has little application when serious character deviations, psychoneuroses, or other intense disturbances are present. In these conditions the individual continues inflexibly in his own patterns, even if the environment does change. Only in some mild reactive (primary behavior) disorders in children can one say that changes in environment would affect important changes in personality. The fact that the environment is involved in psychotherapy and in child guidance does not mean that the change in it is therapy. Rather it is a part of therapy, for especially in adults the intrapsychic damage must still be subjected to direct corrective processes.

It is clear from the preceding discussions in this volume, which will be further supported, that the individual cannot be completely dissociated from his environment and the group culture. This relation must always be preserved intact. Atomization and fragmentation only mislead, and one is likely to overemphasize some elements at the expense of others according to one's conscious and unconscious bias. This can only result in detriment to the patient. Recognition that environmental conditions are important in shaping personality should not blind one to the need for reorganizing his psychic forces through psychotherapy.

In order to convey a clearer picture of what is involved in understanding a patient and planning treatment for him, it will be necessary to delineate here its various component parts, leaving it to the student and practitioner to integrate them into a unitary whole in his thinking and work.

It has already become clear that persons who practice the healing art must be aware, among other things, of the basic biological needs of man, the requirements of his vaso-motor activity to be expressed in rhythmic and dynamic forms, the individual's instinctive urges, his acquired attitudes and values, the conditions of his life and of his micro- and macro-cultures. The child passes through many phases in his development; each having its specific place in the formation of the final product, the adult. But the wholesomeness of the adult is conditioned by the adequacy of the child's opportunities to bring his powers to fruition and to attain adequate gratifications of his primary and derivative needs. We have seen that in orderly growth the child passes through the phases of kyrokinesis, microkinesis, and macrokinesis. He goes through the cycles of manipulative-exploratory, practical-inventive, reflective-epistemonic, group association, and social-participatory phases. All of these leave their imprint on him. Inadequate fulfillment of any of them precludes the natural harmony of the body and the mind and prevents personality integration. To understand normal development dynamically the therapist should recognize the stages of nurture, discipline and education, incorporation, individuation, and reintegration in the development of the child.[1] With rare exceptions emotional problems and disturbances in any area of the personality are caused by the inappropriate treatment of the young child during the formative phases of his development. This historic and dynamic perspective of child development gives one a scientific base for psychotherapy.

One should also take cognizance of individual differences in people. While men are alike in gross physical and psychologic structure, they differ in many and important respects from one another. Temperament and congenital and hereditary variations are too great to demand from all persons similar or identical reactions or to expect that their capacities to achieve or to bear stress and frustration would be alike.

However, this knowledge, important in itself, must be considered only in the service of psychotherapy, not as an end in itself. The science of man and the knowledge of a process can only buttress the art of a practice. We have already emphasized that successful practice involves perceptiveness, skill, tact, and insights. Planning is a must for sound practice, and the therapist needs to have essential information about his patients as well as about psychotherapy as such.

NUCLEAR AND PERIPHERAL PROBLEMS

The foundation of planning treatment is the clinical diagnosis, but in the case of children, at least, the therapist cannot rely solely on clinical classifications and diagnostic categories. Rather, it is essential to know the intrapsychic dynamics and etiological and circumstantial factors involved in the personality disturbance. The *nuclear problem* of the patient should be determined

[1] See ch. i.

as soon as possible. I suggest the term "nuclear problem" to describe the major traumatic experience or condition in the past or current life of the patient and his basic conflicts and strivings. If possible, the nuclear, or central, problem should be ascertained before therapy begins; if not then, as early in the course of treatment as possible. It is not enough to know that a patient suffers from a psychoneurosis, for example, and that it always arises from the Oedipal conflict. One must know specifically whether the conflict and the anxiety have been induced by fears of castration because of an overbearing, harsh father, or whether it arose from the father's weakness and therefore inadequate protection against incestuous sexual impulses toward the mother, or from witnessing the primal scene, or from exposure to a seductive parent. The knowledge of such differences in etiology are important for focusing the psychotherapeutic effort.

Frequently much waste in the therapist's time and effort and distress for the patient result from flailing about in a mass of irrelevant or minor facts because the central pathogenesis and basic unconscious aims of the patient have not been ascertained or understood. A patient's real problems can easily be obscured in a maze of symptoms, conflicting psychodynamics, and circuitous background history that so confuse and complicate the picture that the therapy is forced into fortuitous channels rather than toward a clear-cut aim and direction. What we recommend here is that history taking shall have clearly defined elements which would reveal the main source of the patient's disturbance, wishes, and aims. It is these wishes, or intrapsychic constellations, that most concern the therapist. The nuclear problem of a girl may be her desire to be a boy because her brother was the preferred child. Out of this single wish a number of personal difficulties and social maladjustments may arise for which she is brought to a psychotherapist for treatment—being a tomboy, quarreling with girls and with her brother, contempt for boys, school problems, rebelliousness at home, truancy, stealing, running away, or sexual delinquency. The psychotherapist, however, sees these overt difficulties as of only secondary importance, resulting from the primary or nuclear problem, that is, penis envy.

The critical importance of this differentiation becomes clear when one considers the two possible approaches to the treatment of the girl. In one, she may be asked to talk about her conduct so that the therapist may "guide" her and suggest more desirable behavior. He may even explain her deep-rooted jealousy of her brother as the cause of her acts. But all this would be of little help unless the girl can change her primary identifications from the masculine to a feminine pattern, which can be achieved only through a transference relation with a woman psychotherapist or close relations with a group of girls her own age. Attempts at making her behave more acceptably or exposing her to the temptation of feminine games instead of ball-playing and acting the tomboy would be doomed to failure, because we should be dealing with only the external effects of an unconscious wish.

A child may come to a therapist for treatment with a complication of fears, anxieties, tensions, distractibility, and hypermotility. It would be futile to deal with these directly as though they were the basic problems. Though it may not be evident at once, the history may indicate that they are reactions to an overwhelming anxiety originating from his having overheard his parents at night or witnessing the primal scene. Under these circumstances it is necessary to direct therapy toward the child's feelings in relation to the traumatic situation rather than the resulting symptom. In fact, further understanding of the child's deep-rooted and repressed wishes may disclose that the nuclear problem is his wish to kill his father.

Another factor in child psychotherapy that contrasts with psychoanalysis is that its aim is very frequently not to resolve the original conflict, whence the symptoms flow, but rather to eliminate its *representatives in behavior or consciousness.* For example, in the case of the girl who wished to be like her brother, the actual conflict may arise from penis envy and her phantasy of having been castrated by her mother. These feelings and phantasies are scarcely ever actually worked out with young children. The change in ego-ideal and her acceptance of her biological destiny through identification with the therapist's personality and pattern of life may be sufficient. This is reinforced if she is helped to recognize that she had been envious of her brother because he had been preferred.

Similarly, the boy whose neurotic symptoms have been caused by his having slept in the same room with his parents may or may not actually talk about his nocturnal experiences, and he will certainly not reach the depths where he would become conscious of his homicidal drives toward his father. Nonetheless, numerous children with these problems have been greatly improved by analytically oriented child psychotherapy. The draining off through transference and catharsis of the psychic energies that had been hampered by anxiety reduces fears and normalizes the id-ego-superego relation. Guidance or treatment of parents [2] and changes in sleeping arrangements are necessary in such cases. The original conflict may not have been resolved, or it may not have been even touched upon, but its representative as expressed in behavior was eliminated because of the strengthened ego and better libido distribution.

In psychotherapy with adults as well we frequently aim at the representative in consciousness as against the primary conflict. A case in point is the young woman who suffered from agrophobia in the form of being afraid to walk on the street. In treatment it became clear that "walking the streets" was associated in her mind with "streetwalking," that is, prostitution. The immediate fear was that she would be accosted by men, which had as its background her incestuous wishes for her father. She was helped by psychotherapy to clear up the confusion between walking on the streets and streetwalking and to recognize the fact that men do not accost young women indiscriminately. As a result she resumed her job, reestablished her social contacts, and in every way behaved like a "normal" woman. The basic conflict around her incestuous urges had not been worked out in treatment, though it was undoubtedly diminished. What psycho-

[2] See ch. ix.

therapy had achieved in this case was to eliminate the immediate rather than the ultimate cause of the incapacity. The conflict itself may be termed the *nuerotic residue,* which in this case will unquestionably interfere with her adjustment in many areas, such as wife and mother, later in life. To achieve a complete change would probably require a thoroughgoing and prolonged psychoanalysis.

It must be called to the reader's attention that, at least in child psychotherapy, the term "nuclear problem" does not necessarily refer to the basic conflict as it does in adult cases, but to that part of the difficulty which exists as a wish, a striving, or a conflict in the patient. This is an important differentiation, for children can more readily accept and deal with the latter than with the deeper and more involved unconscious causations.

To further illustrate the concept of the nuclear problem and its relation to planning treatment, two cases of boys from our records will be briefly summarized.[3]

Jimmy, a twelve-year-old boy, diagnosis unclear, came from a very pathological family setting. The father ignored the child from birth, treated him cruelly, and beat him severely. When the boy was about seven years old the father abandoned the family. The mother had had many boy friends with whom she had had sexual relations in the home, which was small and crowded. When he was referred for treatment, Jimmy customarily could not fall asleep until late at night, ostensibly reading the funnies, but actually attempting to overhear what was going on in the bedroom where his mother and her lovers were. This room was connected to his by a door and a transom.

At the first interview the boy behaved in a very infantile manner, talked baby talk, played like a small child, and called the therapist "da-da." The therapist was "permissive," accepted the boy's behavior, and was very warm and friendly. After the first interview the boy gave up his infantile pattern and became rather antagonistic, calling the therapist names and refusing to talk to him about any of his problems. The only activity he

[3] See also case reported in ch. xi.

would indulge in was playing checkers, and he repeatedly asked the therapist for food and "treats." Because little progress was made in the case, it was reviewed. We found that the therapist had wrongly assumed that the boy craved a father substitute and, therefore, sought to play out the role of the "good father."

It was not difficult to show that the nuclear problem of this boy was the Oedipal involvement with his mother, to whom he of necessity had had to turn, and his disturbance at his mother's intimate association with men. The reason for the boy's regressive behavior in the first interview, which misled the therapist, was his phantasy that the therapist would be as cruel to him as his father had been. He therefore attempted to impress the therapist that he was very young and helpless, requiring love and protection. Just as soon as he discovered that the therapist was an accepting, friendly individual who would not be cruel to him, the boy no longer needed to employ the façade of infantilism and helplessness, and he acted out his hostility toward the men who usurped his mother.

It would seem that there was a combination of the beginning of a psychoneurosis and, quite definitely, an infantile character. Therapeutically, this child must be first treated for the latter, and his ego must be strengthened. The neurotic residue would require attention later. The role of the therapist should be quite the reverse from the one he assumed. Instead of being indulging and permissive, he should have from the very start conveyed to the boy that regressive behavior was not necessary or acceptable. Since the therapist did not define the child's nuclear problem correctly, his treatment focus was wrong as well. The boy's wheedling was a way of controlling the interviews. It was in the nature of resistance.

Another instance of a similar confusion as to the nuclear problem is the case of Simon, a twelve-year-old boy, diagnosed as primary behavior disorder, pre-Oedipal type, who lived with his mother and his grandmother, his father having left the home when the boy was very young. The mother, an efficient, enterprising woman, supported the family. Grandmother and grandson were antagonistic to one another and quarreled constantly, the grandmother reporting on the boy when the mother came home from work. This situation created considerable tension, and the problem having become intensified by the boy's increasingly poor adjustment, he was referred to a psychotherapist.

Since the diagnosis was primary behavior disorder, the therapist followed the rule and directed her attention toward working out the relation between the boy and his mother. Both were seen regularly, but the mother was preoccupied with financial matters and boy friends and saw the therapist infrequently. Simon, however, appeared for his interviews regularly, but very little progress was made in the case, which came up for consultation. I indicated to the therapist that she had overlooked the nuclear problem. In this instance the conflict between the grandmother and the child was the center of the difficulty, not the relation of the child to his mother. The relation between the child and his grandmother was one of sibling rivalry. The grandmother had always been a dependent person who now turned her dependency toward her daughter, as a mother substitute. She thus became a sibling to the boy, and they reacted to each other as real siblings would. Because this relation was not understood, the grandmother was never interviewed in the prolonged course of treatment, and it was not known to what extent her complaints had been founded in reality and the degree to which her desire to have her daughter all to herself played a part.

The procedure of ascertaining and defining the nuclear problem has proven to be very helpful in teaching and in training psychotherapists. Instead of keeping in mind the frequently confusing mass of symptoms and dynamics, discovering and defining the nuclear problem not only makes it simpler but also actually clarifies the whole picture to the neophyte and frequently also to the mature and experienced therapist. I recall a fairly experienced psychotherapist who was puzzled about a case, particularly about her own role in it. When she was told in a consultative interview that the child's nuclear problem was his identification with his dead mother, her spontaneous response was:

"This rings a bell." From that time she was able independently to understand traits of the child and much of his puzzling behavior that had previously baffled her in the interviews. What is more important, she herself recognized that she had assumed a role in relation to her patient that was the very opposite of what was required in the case. Recognition of the nuclear problem usually illuminates a case with startling clarity.

In addition to the nuclear problem which the therapist has to keep in mind and toward which therapy should be focused, there are always a number of *peripheral problems* present. These are the manifest and observable difficulties in behavior or attitude for which children are usually brought to a psychotherapist for treatment. Such difficulties may be behavior difficulties, habit disorders, symptoms such as tics, enuresis, fire-setting, stealing, social maladjustment, and numerous other symptoms, traits, and acts that annoy or disturb the adults involved in the child's life. These presenting difficulties, which are usually the major preoccupations of relatives and teachers, are used by the experienced psychotherapist only to reconstruct, together with the developmental history, the background and the dynamics that finally lead to the nuclear problem.

The plan of employing peripheral problems as a means for hunting down the nuclear problem and the basic conflict is particularly helpful in classroom teaching and seminars. It prevents confusion in the group from the inevitable diversity of opinion and misconceptions on the part of students by providing a base for the discussions of dynamics and treatment. It offers a common frame of reference for ideas and analyses. As a result the learning process is greatly facilitated.

The content of the verbal interviews and of the acting out by young patients is quite understandably drawn from the peripheral problems. Both the patient and his relatives are preoccupied with the immediate pressures and tensions. These form the *top reality,* and the psychotherapist has to encourage (associative) catharsis along these superficial lines at first, and frequently for a long period, in the treatment. Such concerns, in themselves, are not sufficient, even if there is improvement in overt behavior and adaptations. Dealing with the present *only* is not good psychotherapy. For more or less permanent improvement within the psychic structure of the personality, at least the representative in the conscious or in behavior must be reached, even if the basic conflict cannot be. Just changing behavior or sloughing off symptoms as a result of "self-control" or because of a "transference improvement" is not acceptable. Relatives and school teachers may be impressed and satisfied with such "startling" changes in the child, but not the therapist. He knows their ephemeral nature.

Even in activity group psychotherapy, where no explanations or interpretations are given, the treatment is in terms of the nuclear problem. The child's activity catharsis has to be understood in terms of that problem, and the action-interpretation must follow that line. In fact, children are accepted or rejected for activity groups on the basis of their nuclear problems. The consideration of the nuclear problem also enters into the plan and treatment by the other types of groups in which verbalization is the therapeutic means, such as play-group and activity-interview-group psychotherapy.

IDENTIFYING MAJOR FACTORS

In planning the line of treatment of a particular patient many factors have to be taken into consideration that may have contributed to his maladjustment and intrapsychic difficulties. Although in child guidance and child psychotherapy our aim is to correct the relationship and weighting of the psychic forces (cathexis) that affect attitudes and behavior, we cannot rely solely upon the psychologic restructuring of the personality in the treatment of children. Children are inherently part of their environment and draw upon it for their physical, emotional, and intellectual sustenance. They cannot detach themselves from and become independent of it; nor can they select or choose it according to their will to the same extent that adults and even adolescents do. They cannot change their life-setting, nor can they remove themselves from it. Therefore, in planning a child's treatment it is essential to survey as completely as possible the numerous elements in his living conditions that have forged the child's character in the past and that influence his adjustment and behavior in the present.

For the purpose of clarity, even if this may seem an oversimplification, we are going to divide these elements into six specific categories. The reader is asked, however, to keep in mind that these are not separate or distinct from one another, but are irrevocably fused and related; that they coincide, coalesce, interact, and counteract in the actual living situation. These factors are: (1) intrapersonal, (2) interpersonal, (3) the vicious circle, (4) situational, (5) cultural, and (6) the self-image.

1. *Intrapersonal factors.*—In considering the intrapersonal factors it is necessary to go beyond the psychological considerations which have been of major concern in the preceding pages of this volume and ascertain as far as possible constitutional and hereditary factors that may determine, delimit, or enhance the development of the child, particularly those that may be assets in his growth and treatment. Special abilities are particularly important. These can be gleaned from the developmental history, the preferences the child currently demonstrates, and projective tests that help to reveal such endowments and the limits to which they can be developed. Determination of optimal limits are particularly important, since it prevents setting aims too high for the rate of progress and outcome of treatment. One needs to consider in this regard constitutional and organic boundaries, as well as the psychological possibilities for success determined by native predispositions and situational opportunities. Awareness of the limitations is as essential in psychotherapy as it is in education as a preventive of failure and overstrain to both the therapist and the patient. At the same time, all the assets, both within the child and in his environment, must be utilized so as to carry forth his growth and development to maximal stages under all the given circumstances and conditions.

Psychometric and projective tests are among the main keys to these plans. When they are indicated, medical, endocrine, and neurological examinations should be instituted. Case histories and the psychotherapist's own judgment help in this connection, not only for the purpose of planning but also because peculiarities, deficiencies, and other suspicious traits and developmental manifestations come to light through them.

Emphasis should be given to special interests, such as scientific, artistic, mechanical, handicraft, literary, and the numerous other preoccupations that a child may display. They need to be utilized in the therapeutic process to strengthen the ego through the satisfactions they yield and the beneficial effect they have on the self-image.

A Negro girl under treatment by group psychotherapy displayed an interest in music, and through her singing at the group sessions the therapist recognized a special musical talent in this girl. Through the therapist's effort a scholarship was secured for this eleven-year-old patient with a leading teacher of operatic stars who found that she possessed an inordinately good voice, on a par with or better than some of the maestro's world-renown former pupils. Not only did this child make progress in her musical education, but her total demeanor changed. She grew more poised, more secure, and more assertive toward a particularly domineering and oppressive grandmother with whom she lived.

The girl lived in a very difficult and pathologic home setting. Her mother had died in childbirth, and, abandoned by her father, she was reared by her near-psychotic, obsessional paternal grandmother who, with her aged husband, conducted a tiny, poverty-stricken business in a slum section of a large metropolitan city. The grandmother was, in addition, a religious fanatic whose tenets prohibited play and pleasure of any sort and required its adherents to attend church services four times a week. The grandmother had disliked intensely her deceased daughter-in-law for her worldliness and pleasurable indulgences, and she identified her grandchild with the latter's dead mother, wreaking all her hatred on the child. In addition to these restrictions, the child had to endure merciless beatings on the slightest provacation.

Efforts at "softening" the grandmother toward the girl were

entirely futile, as were also suggestions that she allow the child more freedom. But interestingly enough, as the music lessons proceeded and the girl grew more secure and more self-reliant, the grandmother's rejection and hostility abated. She became less exacting, less restricting, and less domineering. Once she even visited the therapist, voluntarily stating, among other things, that she had observed the change in her granddaughter and was pleased with the progress she was making in her music. As a result the aged woman became more accessible to suggestions the therapist had made.

Boys who were referred to "science clubs" conducted by special organizations and museums and to arts and crafts groups in neighborhood centers and schools as part of the treatment plan have gained a great deal from carrying through their special interests and have participated better in the treatment process.

Among the liabilities frequently present are the various physical defects and inadequacies among which visible stigma are the most harassing. Smallness, lameness, deafness, poor eyesight, and other infirmities that limit the child or render him incapable of participating in play and activities with his contemporaries frequently present a real problem. One case that comes to mind is that of a boy who suffered from undetected extreme congenital myopia, which was at the root of his school and social maladjustments, because he was unable to see the writing on the blackboard or the ball in baseball and basketball games. When his marked withdrawal was called to the attention of a psychotherapist and traced to the eye defect, correction of the vision with glasses was the beginning of a successful child-guidance program, without which all efforts had been futile in the past.[4]

2. *Interpersonal factors.*—In view of the rather lengthy discussion of interpersonal relations and their part in pathogenesis contained in Chapter II and their less extensive treatment at a number of other points in this volume, they need only brief mention at this juncture. The major factors that require scrutiny are the intra- and extra-familial relations: the presence of

[4] See also ch. xi.

grandparents, uncles, and aunts within and outside the home who influence the emotional equilibrium in the family, school adjustment, relations with schoolmates, and other associations within and outside of school.

3. *The vicious circle.*—The analysis of the total intra- and extra-familial setting of the patient and the relationships in it expose the nature of the vicious circle in which the child lives. By the "vicious circle" is meant the total human environment in which centers of infection or pathogenic activation occur with succeeding chain reactions that have a deleterious effect upon the patient. These pathogenic centers may be the patient himself, another member of the family, and even persons outside the home, such as teachers. Perhaps this point should be illustrated because of its significance to the therapeutic planning and process.

A mother, unable to accept her feminine role and envious of her son's maleness, dominates and restricts him. As a reaction to this, he nags, annoys, and beats his younger sister, who, he perceives, is more welcome in the family circle than he is. The mother reports to her husband the boy's infractions. He punishes and beats his son. The latter, being resentful, not only intensifies his attacks on his sister, but increases his disobedience to his mother and as further retaliation carries over his aggressions to the school. Now the teacher and the school authorities become involved. He is punished, and complaints are lodged with his mother, who, in turn, upbraids and punishes the boy and again involves the father in her punitive efforts.

We see here how the vicious circle operates. The mother is the center of infection that activates a whole series of pathogenic reactions in a number of people who are part of the child's biosphere. Obviously little can be done therapeutically for a young child until the threat and pressure of these many adults upon him are alleviated. But because they are directly and indirectly activated by the mother, she would require treatment or prolonged psychologic guidance so that she can at least reduce her pressure on the boy, even if she cannot be reconciled to her biological destiny. Depending upon the degree and nature of the content of the mother's disturbance and her accessibility, intensive treatment or psychologic or administrative guidance[5] may have to be instituted before therapy with the child can be rendered effective.

The social diagnosis is not always so easy, nor is the center of activation so apparent and discernible as in the case cited. Sometimes prolonged treatment and intensive, as well as astute, study is necessary before the facts are revealed, but in child psychotherapy these measures are essential, and auxiliary therapy, that is, therapy of the relatives—relational therapy—must be instituted to buttress the work with the child. Sometimes cultural and religious conflicts are the sources of the difficulty or that the father is in subtle rivalry with his son or the mother with her daughter. There are instances in which the center of activation is the physical situation within and outside the home, such as overcrowding, sexual overstimulation, unwholesome sleeping arrangements, neighborhood forces, as in cases of cultural and religious minority groups, and numerous such factors in our excessively complex urban life.

Some cases in child guidance clinics show that the child, despite his difficulties, is not the major subject for treatment. Rather treatment for the *effective persons* in his life—parents, relatives, siblings, teachers—is indicated or changes in the physical setting in the home, in the school, or in the neighborhood are necessary to give the child's self-repairing processes a chance.

The person who is the center of infection or activation is sometimes inaccessible, and the situation is so involved with psychopathological, psychosocial, and economic elements as to be insoluble. In such instances the child has to be the focus of the psychotherapeutic effort and carry the entire burden. But as already exemplified by the girl with the good singing voice, referred to above, improvement in the patient may effect improvement in persons responsible for her condition. In my own experience there were hundreds of instances in which improvement in the child was reflected in the relatives and a calmer atmosphere in the home. In some of these instances the child was the true center of activation, and when irritation or aggression on his part ceased,

[5] See p. 255, "Managerial Therapy."

the other members of the family were kept under control. I recall a telephone conversation with an assistant principal about a boy treated in activity group therapy exclusively who had been particularly difficult in her school and had brought the wrath of the officials down upon his head. During the conversation she said: "I don't know what you did to him, but it is a miracle." The favorable change in the pupil wrought like improvement in the teachers' attitudes. In extreme cases of family dislocation removal of the child from the home is indicated.

4. *Situational factors.*—The interpersonal relations which we have discussed are part and parcel of the total life situation to which the child has to adjust. However, material and unpersonal elements in the environment contribute in many instances considerably to the stress. Among these is the general atmosphere in the home. The child is affected by the home when it is permeated by depression and gloom resulting from economic or social insecurity and underlying emotional tensions. Physical congestion in apartments having no exit into a back yard is a source of constant irritation. It exposes their occupants to various kinds of overstimulation that give rise to irrascibility, open quarreling, and conflicts.

Sleeping arrangements that force the child to share the bedroom with the parents or to sleep in the same bed with one or both parents or with a sibling, of the same or opposite sex, contribute greatly to and are not infrequently the source of the presenting problem. In preparing the history of a case a detailed account of these arrangements, the periods when a child shared a room or bed with other persons, and their ages is essential. This information may throw much light on a difficulty that would otherwise remain obscure. We have found, for example, that forced proximity during sleep with a sibling toward whom a child is antagonistic produced neurotic reactions and sleeplessness. Sharing a room or a bed with senile grandparents, which is a frequent occurrence in families in the low-income group, stirs up fears and tensions in children and many concomitant disorders and anxieties. Poverty and material deprivation, with accompanying guilt on the part of parents and resentment by the children, generate much disharmony, recrimination, and conflict and are additional elements requiring scrutiny and evaluation in relation to the problem and in planning treatment.

5. *Cultural factors.*—The general culture, with its emphasis upon definite values, manner of behavior, quality of attitudes, and the total value system, is absorbed by the individual, who makes it a part of himself by a process that can be justifiably described as *psychological osmosis* through the imponderable and intangible atmosphere a culture creates. Some of these influences are identifications which begin at the family level and later radiate out into the world beyond it in expanding cocentric circles that later include groups, ideas, and ideals. One can identify with saints or sinners, gangsters or reformers. Association with individuals and groups has a telling effect upon the emerging personality. Religion, the minister, the politicians, political parties, teachers, and schools—all have their share in conditioning the growing individual. The subtler and less easily identifiable atmosphere of peace or strife, quiet or tension, cooperation or competition that a community creates gives tone to each individual who comes under its influence and begets a common psychological complexion that is sometimes referred to as the socially determined basic personality.

Tradition—the ties to the past, a token of security and certainty—is a major conditioning factor which may or may not be an irritant to a given individual. When traditions conflict with primary and native traits and predilections or newly evolving patterns and values, they may set off serious strains within the individuals and between them and their environment. The attitudes toward self, or the self-image, is to a considerable degree fashioned by the perceptions of the individual in relation to others around him, as well as by his awareness of strength and adequacy. In fact, adequacy itself is perceived in relation to others. In the genesis of intrapsychic problems and social maladaptations tradition plays an important role. Cases in point are children who are in conflict with parents adhering to values and traditions at variance with those prevailing in the child's world. Traditions also conflict with and frustrate the child's own strivings and predilections, and what the community expects from him may conflict with his own desires.

Minority and majority status are also important elements in the emergence of values and attitudes. Minority status produces an awareness of being different and results in feelings of insecurity and inadequacy. Plant has rightly stated that once racial insecurity has been experienced, it never disappears.[6] It is experienced as a stigma, as rejection and humiliation, and becomes a barrier between the individual and his environment.

6. *Self-image.*—The product of the innumerable forces and conditions that impinge upon the child during his formative years, of which only a bare indication has been given in the preceding pages of this book, is the structure, color and quality of the personality. To a considerable extent the self-image is both a reflection and a summation of multifarious influences. Whether the child comes to us with feelings of weakness or strength, of worthlessness or self-esteem, of capability or incompetence, of potency or impotency, or the numerous admixtures of these and ambivalence concerning them, he is the resultant of the forces that operated in his life. To understand the child's attitudes toward himself, it is essential for the therapist to understand the depth of his hopelessness, dejection, and guilt in order to steer the course of the interviews to the best advantage and to decide on the quality and content of interpretation. A therapist would be hard pressed to discharge his functions appropriately in the individual treatment interviews or therapy-group sessions did he not understand his patient's basic problem, which is in many respects the keystone to his personality and to the therapeutic plan.

Whether the therapist will praise and encourage, help or withhold help, interpret or not will rest upon his knowledge as to each patient's thoughts and feelings about himself as much as upon the nuclear and peripheral problems. The ego is usually greatly strained in patients who come to a psychotherapist. It is called upon to bear up under the feelings that arise from a de-

[6] James S. Plant, *The Envelope*, New York, The Commonwealth Fund, 1950, p. 15.

structive self-image, feelings of inadequacy, unworthiness, weakness, and guilt. The therapeutic interviews would fall far short of their name were they to add further to these burdens. It has already been stressed that the defenses built up against becoming aware of these defects or exposing them to view must not be commented upon before the ego is strengthened. Knowledge of a patient's self-image is a reliable guide in this situation. It must be kept in mind that the self-image is not revealed at once or *in toto*. It takes many interviews and skill in piecing together the fragments before a full picture of it can be constructed. The psychotherapist has to exercise special care not to be misled by the defensive façade presented by patients: the most boastful are often the weakest, and the seemingly diffident may actually be towers of strength: hostility may hide a craving for love, and amenability may shield aggression.

The following, taken from a fifth interview with a boy nine-and-one-half years old, clearly indicates what the self-image in a patient may be.

"There are a lot of things about myself I don't like," said the boy. "I can talk about them here because this is that kind of place [referring to the child guidance clinic]. Here you help people with such things." With very serious mien and in a childish voice he proceeded: "It just can't make any sense. I don't like New York people. I'd like to go back to Maine, where my mother and sisters are. Then I stutter a lot. I wish I didn't stutter. . . . Boys don't like me very much. I don't fight back when they bother me. Well, I guess I don't like them either; they are too tough. I would like to be handsome, not as ugly as I am. Look at the size of my lips. Don't they look awful?" He stopped for a moment, then added: "I know why, but it sounds kind of girlish. Well, I guess I am not much like a boy, sort of girlish. . . . Girls are better treated than boys, they are not spanked, they are not juvenile delinquents. I use big words just like girls do." He then returned to the subject of his appearance saying: "I would like to have dark hair and a little thinner lips, like a boy in my class. I would like to look like him; at least then I would look more normal. I am not normal. Can you help me become more normal?"

OUTLINE OF PERSONALITY HISTORY

In summary of the preceding comments on the elements involved in planning the treatment for children, we are reproducing an outline for a case history that was evolved at the Jewish Board of Guardians in New York City by a staff committee of which the present writer was a member. The committee deliberated more than three years in preparing the outline and the various revisions, which were found necessary when it was applied. This outline might be considered far too detailed, and certainly the information required cannot be obtained in advance. Much of it would be derived from the interviews, and some of it deduced by the therapist. However, its very detailed nature offers the advantage of completeness which suggests that if it is used at all, it should be used discriminately and flexibly. Any effort to gather information for all the items in the outline would prove not only burdensome but also confusing. Understandably, only certain pertinent portions would be used.

A) GENERAL APPEARANCE AND BEHAVIOR

Give a brief description of the patient as a living person; his attitudes, conduct, and general demeanor; also, when significant, his attitude toward his life situation and illness.

B) SYMPTOMS

Enumerate the emotional disabilities, including a statement of the structured and unstructured symptoms, as well as the psychosomatic disorder, if any.

C) THE ENVIRONMENT OF THE PATIENT

A concise statement of the significant environmental factors; the social, religious, and economic status, leading to a characterization of the cultural identity of the patient; in addition, a brief descriptive evaluation of the family configuration—the more significant relationships and the values which the family represents.

D) REALITY ADAPTATION

Delineate the components of behavior which represent the patient's effort to adapt to his actual life situation. In what respects is the effort successful, and in what respects does it fail? Bear in mind the patient's aspirations and goals, and if possible indicate their relative adequacy. What forms of reality are accepted? Are some forms of reality avoided, denied, or passively resisted? What forms of reality are distorted; by what means? (Correlate this with the later statement concerning defenses.)

E) INTERPERSONAL RELATIONS

I. Attitude toward others

a) Capacity for personal relationships

1. Minimal capacity (infantile personality and extreme narcissism)
2. Limited capacity (immature, "pregenital")
    a. Dependent tendency
        i. Passive dependence strivings—passive aggression ("moral character")
        ii. Tendency to deny dependent needs resulting in emotional detachment
    b. Possession and control of other persons ("anal character")
    Character of the ambivalence in the above levels of relationship
3. Mature capacity (object relationships)
    a. With anxiety
    Identification with parents
    Excessive submission
    Excessive rebellion
    Fear of punishment
    b. Without anxiety
    Full achievement of individuality
    Normal assertiveness

II. Attitude toward self
- *a*) The degree of self-absorption (ego-centricity); the degree of narcissism.
- *b*) The patient's concept of self; his idea of self as a person; his inner image of his own identity. Is the patient's image of his identity clear, unified, or dissociated and confused, etc.? (Use whatever descriptive terms seem to fit the patient's concept of self.)
- *c*) The idealized image of self and the patient's attempts to build and reach toward it.
- *d*) What discrepancy is there between the real concept of self and the idealized image?
- *e*) What patterns of inferiority exist?
- *f*) What trends toward compensatory self-aggrandizement?
- *g*) What is the basis of the patient's self-esteem and confidence and his unique specific areas of failure?
- *h*) What are the patient's goals and his actual achievements? To what degree do they coincide and to what degree is there a discrepancy?
  Insight: What degree of real understanding does the patient have of his own function?

F) QUALITY OF AFFECTS

a) Spontaneity
b) Stability
c) Depth; richness
d) Appropriateness
e) Flexibility

(a–e: Their relation to activity patterns)

f) Capacity for rapport
g) Range of emotional interests
Broad or constricted
Genuine or pretended
Lasting or temporary and fickle

G) ANXIETY

1. Quantity
2. Quality
3. Localization (diffuse or bound in symptom formation)
4. Control (stable or unstable)
5. Panic reactions; adequacy of defenses

H) CONTROL PATTERNS

1. General integration: adequate or deficient
2. Degree of impulsivity
Conscious
Unconscious
3. Control of impulses at periphery of personality (i.e., suppression of action)
4. Control of inner impulses: unconscious control (repression)
Normal
Deficient
Excessive
5. Capacity for pleasure and spontaneous self-expression
Adequate
Deficient
Conscience function excessive in quantity; deviant in quality
Guilt tendency and guilt equivalents
6. Depression
7. Suicidal tendency
8. Other self-destructive patterns

I) DEFENSE PATTERNS

1. Quality
Range of defenses (narrow or wide)
Rigid or changeable (shift from one defense to another)
Reliability of defenses
Panic reaction followed by emotional disorganization

2. Types of defense used mainly
Avoidance
Opposition
Substitution of aggression for anxiety
Denial of external reality
Denial of psychic reality; denial of elements of personal identity
Repression
Projection
Introjection
Displacement
Condensation
Compensation
Reaction formation
Sublimation

J) **CENTRAL CONFLICTS**
Formulate the salient unconscious conflicts of the patient, as exemplified in the patient's symptoms and in the disturbance in his relations with other persons. Correlate these conflicts with the type of anxiety and the main defenses which the patient uses to control his anxiety. Correlate these conflicts with the genetic patterns which represent their origin.

TYPES OF THERAPY

Before we proceed with the brief outline of the various types of therapy, it ought to be restated that the considerable diversity in theory and practice extant in the field reflect personal predilections of practitioners more than they do contrasts in essential dynamics. Every effective psychotherapy, no matter what the semantic confusion may be, is based upon the six basic elements: transference, catharsis, insight, ego-strengthening, reality testing, and sublimation. The fact that each is modified in its details because of circumstance or preference or that they are understood somewhat differently by different "schools" of psychotherapy or individual therapists does not alter this basic law. *If psychotherapy is to produce results, it must be rooted in these no matter how disguised or denied.*

From a full study of a case the type and intensity of the required therapy should be revealed. The nature of the presenting symptoms, the psychodynamic causatives, the depth and severity of the pathology, the clinical categories, and the centers of activation are among the numerous factors that point to the direction, scope and depth of therapy indicated. A partial or complete anamnesis should determine whether the child's problem can be resolved by a thoroughgoing analytic psychotherapy or can be corrected through one or another of the many derivative therapies or a combination of them. During the course of treatment of nearly all children the therapist finds that he has to employ different approaches as the child's personality changes and as different problems are unearthed. Thus, direct-interview therapy may give way to play or acting out, evoking of self-generated insight may be superseded at some periods by explanation, education, and the giving of information. Stages are reached when release and abreaction are predominant needs of the moment rather than the revelation of repressed feelings, and painting and sculpture may be more suitable means for communication than is language. The therapist may find that siblings, parents, and other relatives have to be involved in treatment and that guidance should be given to teachers, nurses, club leaders, and recreational workers or changes be made in the child's physical environment and emotional relations.

This fluidity and flexibility are the very core of effective professional functioning. Rigid adherence to a set technique in child psychotherapy, even if the therapist has basic convictions and believes in a specific theory or philosophy, is bound to defeat his efforts. The human personality is not so consistently uniform. Particularly is it essential for children that their spontaneous needs be gratified. Children are vagarious and impulsive; their needs unpredictable and changeable. These characteristics have to form the basis of education and treatment. Not only does this policy encourage free catharsis, but it also cements the transference.

Some therapies currently employed are in my opinion actually similar in their basic elements, but they emphasize one type of procedure or parts of other more complete techniques. No effort will be made here to describe them in detail. Only concise and general statements will suffice.

Insight therapy identifies the type of therapy with which the largest part of this volume has been concerned. The term aims to describe the special characteristic of psychotherapy in which insight into one's psychological processes and problems is attained. This is achieved either through the patient's inner growth or through the therapist's interpretation, based largely upon the dreams that the patient discloses. Insight therapy is actually a segment of *psychoanalytic therapy,* in which transference, catharsis, and insight form the core of treatment. Psychoanalytic therapy is short-term *psychoanalysis,* which is intimately based upon the latter, but the process is much briefer, and in most of its applications the couch is not used. The equipment of the psychoanalytic therapist should be the same as that of a psychoanalyst. Sometimes the term *interpretive therapy* is employed to convey the idea that the therapy is not conducted on a superficial level, such as support, training and education. *Affect therapy* is a term used to convey the fact that the therapy does not address itself to the patient's intellect, but that a reeducation of emotions is sought. Obviously, this is a part of all good psychotherapy, and the use of the term confirms the assertion that some so-called psychotherapies are only segments of more complete forms.

Educational therapy consists of that phase of psychotherapy, especially with children, in which special and direct measures are taken with the child, to supply him with evocative and stimulating experiences to enhance his growth and activate extravertive activities leading to personality development and social adjustment. *Training therapy* is that procedure in which the therapist or the parents under his guidance sanction or prohibit and direct the behavior and activities of the child so as to produce a corrective effect. This technique is closely related to, but less strict than, *authoritative therapy,* in which the therapist asserts his authority to help the child to bring himself under control and to strengthen his ego. This form is usually necessary in the treatment of psychotics and very young children and in institutions.

In *habit therapy* the child is subjected to repeated training in habit formation, either by the therapist or, most often, by the parents and nurses under his supervision. Here are utilized the psychologic understandings necessary to facilitate the child's acceptance of this training which had been either neglected or improperly applied in the past. *Suggestion therapy* is what the name implies, and undoubtedly it is effective in positive transference, but as is the case with some of the other "therapies," it does not lead to self-directed functioning. It is most often used in "guidance." *Tutorial therapy* becomes necessary when the child is handicapped in learning equipment and is backward in school achievement. Because this effects the self-image and induces feelings of inadequacy, it may often be considered the most important part of the total treatment plan. Remedial work in school subjects, athletics, and leisure-time occupations are considered and supplied when indicated.

Interpersonal therapy, sometimes also referred to as *social therapy,* though the latter has broader implications, consists of utilizing group and other types of human relations as part of the treatment plan. Obviously, this can be employed only as already described. Activity group psychotherapy (once referred to as "sociatric therapy") utilizes entirely this type. But it must be pointed out that it is employable with children in latency and that on a basis of careful selection.[7] We have found that many restricted and even constricted children overcome their maladjustments through an appropriately planned and conducted interpersonal therapy. It is doubtful that such results can be achieved with adults. The term "social therapy" includes interpersonal relations, but has wider implications, for it attempts to effect changes in the wider environment of the patient, and some therapists extend it to include basic changes in the whole structure of society. *Impromptu therapy* is a term suggested by J. L. Moreno for the procedure in which the patient expresses his feelings and thoughts in playing a role in a dramatic situation set by the therapist. In this method two patients, or one patient and an "auxiliary ego," are assigned roles that are replicas of their problems in actual life and are instructed to create their own situations and dialogues without previous rehearsal.

Closely analagous to this technique is one created by David M. Levy, which he termed *release therapy*. This type of brief therapy

[7] S. R. Slavson, *Introduction to Group Therapy*, ch. iv.

is suitable for young children only and consists of allowing the child to abreact without any constraint or control to a recent traumatic experience. A physical setting is provided in which this can be done without risk. The furniture, for example, is made up entirely of packing boxes, so that the young patient can break it or chop it up. It is expected that the walls will not be spared either. This catharsis resembles that of activity group therapy, but in the latter its violence never reaches quite the same intensity because of the selection of patients and the restraining effect of the other members of the group.

Compensatory therapy is that in which the therapist seeks to supply to the child, through the transference relationship, special advantages and privileges to compensate for some of the lacks and deprivations suffered by him in earlier years. Of the same genre is *substitutive therapy,* sometimes referred to as "substitute gratifications." In *attitude therapy* the emphasis is laid upon feelings and attitudes the patient has concerning current situations and persons involved in his life and toward himself. It differs from psychoanalysis and the psychoanalytically derived therapists in that it considers the present situations and concerns and either ignores or underplays the past. It has some elements in common with *will therapy,* outlined by Otto Rank, and the *functional approach* in casework.

By *supportive therapy* is meant various types of techniques employed with the aim of helping the patient to bear up under stress, through direct encouragement, a positive relationship, and compensatory and substitutive devices. These strategies would seem to be part of all psychotherapy and obviously must be employed not only with children but also in varying degrees and at critical points during the treatment of older persons. It is particularly valuable if the parents of the child are rigid and rejecting and are the center of the difficulty, but are inaccessible or not available for treatment or guidance. Psychotherapy with a child in such instances, if undertaken at all, fortifies the child against them by a satisfying and empathetic relation with a substitute parental figure. In some instances supportive therapy is essential for parents of particularly difficult children until the latter can be brought under control through treatment. By this method feelings of disappointment, dejection, and futility can be dissipated in some parents, and the rabid, punitive, and vengeful can be kept under control. I have suggested the term *managerial therapy* for parents who because of resistance or intellectual backwardness are inaccessible to any degree of probing or uncovering. Many of these parents, especially mothers, actually do not know how to arrange even simple routines of living in the home and how to deal with their children's behavior or to answer their questions. The treatment of the child, however, requires that these essential, though simple, needs be met, otherwise the therapist's work may be negated. Parents can be interviewed at irregular intervals so that they may be given suggestions about dealing with these practical matters. Frequently it becomes necessary, also, to instruct parents how to handle the child in the home consistently with the psychotherapist's treatment plan and thus to aid its progress.

John Levy has given the name *relationship therapy* to both individual and group psychotherapy in which the relation between the therapist and patient is the prime and paramount factor. The actual techniques beyond that requirement are the usual probing, uncovering, and interpreting. This differs in no sense from "insight therapy," "transference therapy," and other types based on or derived from psychoanalysis. *Relational therapy* refers to the concurrent treatment of the patient's relatives. Chapter IX is devoted to this type of therapy, and Chapter X describes *group psychotherapy*.

I have suggested the terms *situational therapy* and *experiential therapy* in connection with activity group psychotherapy.[8] These terms seem advisable in order to emphasize the importance of the setting in this type of treatment in particular, although it is equally true for all treatment of children. "Experiential therapy" is also intended to emphasize the personal interactions of members in a therapy group and their adaptations to each other as persons and to the physical setting provided.

It is advisable to state again that with the exception of psycho-

[8] *Ibid.*, p. 16.

analysis and group psychotherapy the therapies enumerated are actually techniques only. By this we mean that each alone cannot be counted on to effect intrapsychic changes. Rather, some or all of them are used at different times as part of complete therapy.

IX

Psychotherapy and Therapeutic Guidance of Parents

IT IS CLEAR from what has already been said that in most treatment situations of prepubertal children the environmental factors must be considered an integral part of the treatment process. It is equally clear that the parents, and for obvious reasons the mother in particular, must be involved in various ways and degrees. There are psychotherapists especially psychoanalysts, who are convinced that little can be done therapeutically for young children without basically altering the personality of the mother. There is ample foundation for this belief. For many years the human child has no life apart from his mother. Negativism, disobedience, and rebellion are only reflections of this parasitic dependence. Thus, it is understandable that feelings, attitudes, and acts of the parents are reflected in the life and acts of the child and that disturbances in his personality and the malpatterning of his behavior proceed from and reflect direct and indirect parental influences. Any improvement in the personality structure or behavioral responses that may be affected by psychotherapy cannot be sustained by the child against the impact of parental countereffects or other contiguous cultural pressures, such as the school and the neighborhood. The fact that successes in this direction are achieved in practice is a rather interesting phenomenon and needs to be understood.

In instances in which the child is the center of infection or activation in the home or the school setting, the improvement in his behavior relaxes the total atmosphere. By his improved behavior he precludes counteraggression and attacks from others around him. However, in instances in which the parent and school are the sources of activation, they must relent if the child is to sustain his improvement achieved by psychotherapy. Of particular importance in this regard is the attitude of the mother and the treatment the child receives at her hands.

THERAPEUTIC GUIDANCE

As the title of this chapter implies, this may be achieved on different levels of intensity. The mother and the father may be treated either "as patients" or "as parents." In the first case the basic conflicts or their representatives in the conscious are eliminated, and fundamental changes in the personality are effected. In the other, only those feelings and attitudes that bear directly upon parenthood are relieved and corrected, and knowledge about children is imparted. The aim of the latter is largely to facilitate and help the treatment of the child and to prevent the counteraction of whatever gain he may have made through psychotherapy. Although the extreme view may be that for the child to hold his improvement, lasting and fundamental changes are necessary in the parents, actual experience with thousands of patients shows that diminution of pressures at home and at school upon the child facilitates treatment. In most instances, however, the therapeutic process itself, once started, does not end on the behavioral level. Affect is always activated, and permanent reorganization of the psychic forces results in parents, even though through guidance the deeper conflicts may not be reached.

The chief factors operating in this process are the transference toward the therapist or guidance worker and his acceptance and toleration of negative and hostile feelings. This reduces feelings of guilt that oppress every parent, to which some react punitively and with hostility. The fact that the therapist accepts these feelings without criticism and reassures the parent that they are universal reduces or eliminates the oppressive and aggressive emotions which have their roots in guilt or are displaced from other persons, such as mates and grandparents. The understanding and sympathetic attitude of the therapist adds to the comfort and inner well-being that comes from the support of a loving and security-giving substitute parent. Speaking to someone who is understanding and empathetic also serves to reduce the load that the mother's and father's ego has to bear and relieves it of that weight. This is sometimes referred to as the process of *ventilation.* It is as though the lungs and blood streams were overweighted by carbon dioxide and ventilated by the introduction of oxygen-laden clean air. The physically oppressive feeling resulting from a lack of oxygen is in many respects analagous to emotional oppression. Patients frequently speak of a "light feeling" after interviews or that they feel as though "a load has been removed from my shoulders." These are literally correct characterizations.

Another important dynamic operating here is the element of *universalization.* The all-pervasive and depressive guilt feelings that are inevitably and irrevocably attached to parenthood and are intensified by failure in that function can be considerably dissipated by understanding that they are inevitable and universal. The awareness and acceptance of the fact that everyone entertains the same negative and ambivalent feelings, which require intelligent handling, is a boon and source of comfort to many a guilt-ridden parent. The function of the therapist is to supply sufficient motivation for controlling impulses and for sublimating them in actions beneficial to the child. This is a skill that is required in all therapists who deal with parents and in guidance workers, in whose work transference and "intellectuation" play an important role.

The chief function of the therapist is to demonstrate to the parent what a good parent really is by acting it out toward the father and the mother of the young patient. Ideas cannot be translated into experience; only experience is translatable into experience. Most parents are only reenacting with their children their own childhood, whether it be positive or negative, without recognizing the effect on them. Many. of course, work out traumatic and hostile feelings originating in their own frustrations and suffering. To some extent this is one of the criteria for choice of the type and the depth of treatment or guidance for a given parent. When the parent's behavior and attitudes result from habit and example, tinged lightly with affect and feeling, less deeply involved guidance and education may suffice. However, when the treatment of the child on the part of the parent is a resolution of his deeply rooted and intensely cathexized conflicts, deeper psychotherapy is indicated. Experience shows that even those in the latter group can modify their behavior and relax their pressures on the child through individual or group guidance.

The therapist's handling of the transference in relation to the parent is in a real sense an educational experience in addition to its psychologic implications. Frequently it is the parent's first experience with a person in a parental role who is calm, understanding, sympathetic, and kindly, though firm. The pattern thus set and the example supplied are of immense value in refashioning much of the habit-set behavior of parents. Repetition of a new pattern of behavior brings in its wake also appropriately related feeling-tones. This alteration is also aided by the therapist's feelings toward the parent. Thus, the transference and the manner in which it is employed is at least as important, if not more so, in the reeducation of parental attitudes as is the content of the interviews.

To recognize that parents' attitudes are laden with ambivalence and feelings of hostility and guilt is essential. It is impossible, however, for some adults to face these facts. Their defenses and codified moral precepts preclude the acceptance of these and other truisms. They must needs take refuge in the commonplace beliefs and anxiety-denying principles, which may not be treated too roughly by the therapist or guidance worker. Although he may not be able to deal with them directly, unless he wishes to become involved in deeper therapeutic procedures, the therapist's very awareness and his occasional questions, explanations, and interpretations are colored and determined by this understanding. Once he himself is aware of the elements involved and clearly visualizes their processes, he can convey them to his patients. However, most parents who are not too dull or too defensive can be helped to comprehend some of the facts involved. Many actually arrive at an independent understanding of them and formulate them spontaneously, in their own words, out of their growing perceptions and progressive emotional flexibility.

What has been said does not preclude dealing directly with some of these rather sensitive areas. Parents are either readied by the guidance to accept and face them, or are able to face them because of their antecedent experience and education. In guiding the parent the therapist must promote the understanding of children's needs, the meaning of their behavior in general, and specifically the meaning of the annoying or disturbing behavior of a specific child. Practice shows that the appalling lack of understanding of a child's needs and cravings as they are conveyed by his acts is the greatest source of conflict between him and his parents. The average parent applies adult criteria to child behavior. He measures purpose, efficiency, and control in terms of adult standards. Frequently parents expect more maturity from the child than they themselves have attained, and they become violently annoyed at the lack of it in their children. Another error parents make is to assume that children will retain the same characteristics that they present at any given time. Although they are right to believe that if the child should carry them over without modification into adulthood, he would, indeed, make a sorry member of society. But the fact is that through organic and psychologic maturation and the impact of social interactions they are sure to be changed and modified.

The fact that a child is an activistic organism is difficult for most parents to accept or tolerate. They expect his behavior to conform to their concepts of order and self-control. Too many parents assume that the child's and sometimes even the baby's motility and seeming hyperactivity is directed against them; that it is designed to annoy or to injure them. Parents in guidance have to be helped to understand and accept the fact that the language of infants and children is action; that they communicate their feelings, ideas, and needs and find self-expression and self-fulfillment through activity. Parents should also be helped to understand this language of action and to respond to it as appropriately as they do to spoken language. It is only when the response by parents is inappropriate or inadequate that the child adopts behavior as a weapon of revenge and hostility.

Of utmost importance in this work is to lead the parents to accept the fact that the child's acts are not intended as aggression or means of annoyance or hostility on the part of the child. The only channel through which the child can communicate his needs and wants, express his growing powers, and become acquainted with the world around him is through action. This natural motility may undoubtedly interfere with the convenience and comfort of adults, to which they only too frequently react with prohibition and punishment. Parents can be led to understand that it is as a result of their own aggression against the child that the latter uses his unpopular behavior as a conscious tool of counteraggression and retaliation. Once parents accept these facts and begin to understand the language of childhood, which is activity and motility, they react to it constructively. This can be said to be the major aim of parent education and parent guidance on the psychological level.

Parents should also understand the effect of frustration on behavior and the importance of spontaneity and how to canalize it. As a matter of course, adults are disturbed by spontaneity, and instead of helping the child to find constructive and creative directions for it, they stifle it. It is also necessary to understand that damned up spontaneity is like damned up water: both create tension and pressures. Parents, like all adults, should be helped to feel comfortable in the presence of spontaneity and imagination in their children and to find ways to harness them for the enrichment of life instead of repressing them because of their own uneasiness. Spontaneity and imagination themselves become subject to greater control and utility as the individual truly matures, for the real sign of maturity is controlled spontaneity, not dullness.

During the guidance sessions, facts of child needs and child growth have to be imparted, but it is more effective to activate the parent to do his own thinking and discovery by asking questions and encouraging him to find the answers. The mental effort and the thinking process stimulated by this procedure has a salutary effect by deepening his understanding and stimulating his participation. The questions should be simple and relevant and, above all, clearly understood by the questioner himself. It is equally important that they be focused on a specific aim, rather than diffuse or general. Nor should the therapist permit digression and deflection, unless it is a defense against emotionally charged revelation or recognition, and without nagging or being obviously inconsistent he should return to the subject again and again until it is clarified.

The technique of stimulating a self-acquired understanding enriches the activistic side of the parent, and unless it results in a sickly kind of introspection it widens the parent's power to understand the latent significance of his child's acts and gives him greater capacity for identification. Didactic instructions and barren conveyance of facts should be avoided. All growth and true learning require effort. Without effort and exertion nothing of value is ever achieved. Self-directed thought is like a stone upon a surface of water: it radiates into ever-expanding circles, begets receptivity to new ideas and phenomena, and increases the capacity to apply knowledge to new situations. In child rearing there is an endless chain of new events requiring flexible insight rather than rigid rules and procedures.

But not only the child has to be understood; the parent has to be helped to understand himself as well. Mechanisms such as projection and displacement so universally employed by parents in dealing with their children must be revealed (without using such technical terminology), or the parent will not be able to deal adequately with his feelings. However, imparting this information is a very risky procedure, for one may not invade the parent's self-deceptive mechanisms and defenses. Awareness must come because of the increased emotional flexibility and ego-strength that accrue from a good transference relation, the reduced guilt and ambivalence that even a superficial type of therapeutic guidance as suggested here educes. In our experience parents have come to recognize quite independently that when they become "upset" (guilty) they are "impatient" with their children (displacement). Others have actually verbalized the fact that when they are threatened or feel guilty they "take it out" on their children. It is customary to have parents, especially mothers, state that they dislike their children because they resemble some one in the family—husband, father, brother, sister, or mother. This conscious recognition of their displacement mechanism reduces irrational responses and, as we have already established, also reflects a strengthened ego.

There are many facts that the parent in guidance cannot discover or deduce, and education in the form of imparting relevant facts is quite in order. The therapist himself may not be the slave of rigidities which he seeks to eliminate in his patients. A variety of techniques must be employed in dealing with human beings whenever suitable and relevant. In guidance as in psychotherapy, the methods employed should reflect the presenting need. An inordinate number of parents do not possess the simplest information on diet and health care, child development, sex education, and similar facts essential for children of different ages. The therapist must give this information either directly or by supplying or recommending reading and reference sources. In some instances it is necessary to give a parent direct information on psychologic matters, marital and child-parent relations, but this should be done sparingly and with care.

It is, however, always better and more effective to stimulate the parent to talk freely in accordance with the principle of associative thinking [1] so that he may purge himself of oppressive feelings and thoughts; also that he may arrive at emotional and intellectual clarification through his own efforts. This process may take longer than would direct teaching and the giving of advice, but the results are always more basic and more lasting.

Some parents, particularly mothers, need help in finding interests outside the home to widen their horizons and enrich their lives. The overintense and exclusive preoccupation on the part of such mothers with family and home, especially with the child under treatment, always proves an impediment to his growth.

[1] See p. 177.

The parasitic or symbiotic relation [2] that results from such a setting limits the child's growth possibilities and perpetuates his psychologic disabilities. The expansion of the mother's horizons and her life-sphere also reduces the emotional load imposed upon the child and eliminates the mother's need to perpetuate the child's difficulties so as to serve perverse needs within herself. Community and other social resources may be used in this process. Local women's groups, religious and national organizations, volunteer social services, hobbies and leisure-time activities, part-time paid jobs, and in some instances therapy groups are some of the channels through which a mother may find self-fulfillment and extend her interests and preoccupations.

On the other hand, there are mothers who are annoyed by family duties and resent the responsibilities thrust upon them by wifehood and motherhood. They escape by excessive preoccupation with extradomestic concerns and neglect of the home responsibilities. This may take the form of intense and often unnecessary exertion and excessive time-allotment on their jobs, community work, friends, and hobbies. Such rejection of their part in the scheme of life requires thorough study and understanding, for the psychodynamics in this life-pattern are usually involved and deep-rooted. Therapeutic guidance with such mothers can have only limited results. In most instances psychotherapy, and probably psychoanalysis, would be required, for some of them are victims of rather serious psychologic distortions. In some cases deep-rooted masculine drives that make an increasing number of women in modern times incapable of functioning fully in a feminine role as wives, homemakers, and mothers would make it necessary to help and guide them to find suitable work and careers that would satisfy their cravings. Sometimes because of guilt or social codes women may resist—on the conscious level—entering such extradomestic occupations.

In practice one sometimes encounters mothers who are defiant and aggressive in an individual treatment or guidance relation. They countradict, argue, and try to disprove everything the therapist says or suggests. They are in a state of rebellion and re-

[2] See pp. 102–5.

sent not only the interviews but also the very fact that they are placed in a relation of patient to therapist. Among such women are the oral incorporative,[3] or oral aggressive, women; women with masculine strivings; those with strong guilt feelings and resultant ego defenses; women with strong antagonisms, hatred and defiance of their mothers, and other psychologic problems too numerous to mention. We have found that women of this kind gain much from free-sharing discussions in special groups in which other women with similar problems participate. The diluted transference, the secondary role played by the leader (mother person), the universalization, and the catalytic influence of the various members of the group remove or weaken the defenses and resistances.[4]

One of the difficulties in psychotherapy and guidance of parents is that they do not have a separate and specific treatment aim for themselves. Their guilt and ego-defenses lead them to attach the blame for the difficulties to their children. They either ignore or underplay their part in the genesis of these problems. In their own minds, as a defensive pattern, they consider their children the patients, not themselves. To lead parents to accept or at least to become aware of their role in the pathogenesis is one of the responsibilities of the psychotherapist, and it is difficult, indeed. Many a parent has withdrawn from treatment because of a tactless or careless remark by the therapist. Usually the idea of the parent's part or responsibility should not be formulated in words. Rather, it is advisable and effective to analyze the situations and how they had been handled by the parent. The analysis of function is much more tolerable than a direct statement that inevitably carries accusative implications. Any blanket statement of failure intensifies guilt and deflates one's self-esteem too much for most mortals to bear.

In guidance, particularly, this is unnecessary, since the best results in this procedure are achieved by release, support, and understanding. In the course of psychotherapy, guilt and fear can be aroused, for they are worked through as an integral part of the therapeutic process itself. This is not the case in guidance,

[3] See p. 41.

[4] See also pp. 183 *et seq.*

and all intense emotions of this nature should be avoided or subordinated. In fact, sometimes parents accuse themselves violently of inadequacies and misdeeds during the interviews. If these self-accusations are based on fact, the therapist need not deny them, but he should meliorate the parent's strong guilt feelings by universalization, explanation, and other means that would not leave him disturbed or dejected. This must be done for several reasons. Confession is, like acting out, a form of resistance. The patient anticipates by it the therapist's attack on him or avoids growth-producing regression through catharsis. It may be a masochistic, self-debasing pattern, a fatalistic outlook on life, a reliving of Oedipal relations. On the other hand, it may be an effort on the part of the patient to trap the therapist into agreeing, so that the resentment aroused will justify his withdrawal from treatment because of anger. This, too, is a form of resistance.

Whatever the patient's motive may be, his confession and his self-accusation should arouse caution on the part of the therapist. Though this may actually be the case, he must not assume that it represents emotional growth or an increased ability to face reality. It should always be suspected as resistance.

Fathers present therapeutic and guidance problems similar to those of mothers, except that according to our experience their basic feeling is guilt, while that of the mothers is resentment. There is, of course, a large range of variation in parents' feelings, and the preceding characterizes only the predominance of one emotion over the other, rather than the exclusiveness of either. However, our work with large numbers of parents of both sexes in groups and a careful study of the transcription of the interviews unmistakably reveals this interesting fact. Perhaps it may be of help to say that this impression was confirmed by others and can be supported on theoretic grounds as well.

Even though this may not be actually so, culturally the male, that is, the father, is the controlling and guiding person in the family. Any failure in the conduct and life of that group or its disruption is therefore automatically associated with the father's inadequacy. The problems in many homes are ultimately and sometimes erroneously traced to economic circumstances; equally as many are the result of the wife's attitudes and acts, while for some, relatives are responsible. These and similar conditions are within the province of the male's control and supervision. Any dislocation or malfunction in them engenders feelings of inadequacy in him. As a matter of fact, a study of children's unconscious attitudes toward tensions and disruption in the home shows that they blame the father, even though consciously they may ascribe the blame to others. It is as if they think that if the father had wanted things to be different, they would have been. This unconscious association of failure to the man of the family is also characteristic of society in general. The tacit understanding is that disruption in a family is the husband's fault and that in divorce it is the husband who proved himself too weak or inadequate to keep the relation intact. In all relations, social, professional, and business, the man whose family life attracts public attention is looked upon askance, more so than is the woman, even though she may be the real cause of the difficulties. In the business world the belief is extant that a man who cannot manage his personal affairs cannot be effective in directing the business of others.

The woman is let off much more easily in such circumstances, both by the children and by the outside world. Unconsciously she is viewed as the victim, even though the known facts indicate the contrary. It is as though she did not have the benefit of control and guidance by the stronger person, the husband, as a father substitute. As to the children's attitudes toward their parents, especially in separation, a multitude of psychodynamic forces are in operation. The sex of the children, their ages during their parents' separation, the quality of relationships, and the actual character of each parent play a role. However, in nearly all cases the father is blamed.

It is, therefore, understandable that tensions, malfunctions, and children's difficult and deviant development would increase the father's already existing feeling of guilt. The mother's complaints of overwork, her neglect of the children because she works outside the home, or any other unfavorable circumstance in the last analysis is tacitly or openly laid at the door of the father. This resulting fundamental feeling of guilt is reflected by the fathers in group discussions with unmistakable clarity.

Here we do not have the problem of extending the operational field in the lives of the fathers as we do with some mothers. Their daily work and associations provide for it. There are, of course, some exceptions, for particularly withdrawn or schizoid-like men require more detailed study to ascertain the cause and cure. Usually these are problems for deeper psychotherapy. Even if fathers do spend too much time at home, their presence is seldom as pathogenic as that of mothers, since they do not assume the responsibility for the conduct of the home or the nurture and education of the children.

It is really difficult to guide fathers who assume that their authoritarian and sometimes brutal treatment of the children is justified as the only way to deal with them. Under such circumstances the parents are hard to reach in the interest of their offspring. They are innured in their beliefs, cling to them tenaciously, and to change them requires inordinate patience and tolerance. In individual therapy these efforts frequently prove futile. Group guidance was found more effective in many instances.

Some fathers cannot assume their roles in the family constellation for various reasons, many of which do not fall within the scope of this discussion. The most common, and those that can be considered here with some profit, are basic homosexual identifications, feelings of inadequacy as husband and provider, Oedipal involvement with their mothers, rivalry with their own children and wives, infantile characters, and so forth. It is quite evident that these neurotic trends and character difficulties cannot be resolved in therapeutic guidance. They require deep psychotherapy or psychoanalysis, but through guidance, especially in groups, the man's behavior toward his wife and children can be modified. This can be achieved to some extent by reducing the feeling of guilt and inadequacy through universalization and stimulating some degree of self-control, even though the basic problems are not resolved.

We found that one of the difficulties in guidance is to hold the patients within the confines of that technique. Free association and the dynamic articulation of feelings and thoughts of patients during an interview frequently divulge their histories, important past experiences, feelings toward parents, siblings, and other persons, self-doubts, fears, insecurities, hostilities, preferences, marital conflicts, and sexual problems. Such communications, even if they cannot be dealt with in the interviews, serve as catharsis and ventilation, in themselves of great benefit because of the release from emotional pressures they afford. They signify trust in and identification with the therapist (positive transference), which diminish tension and serve to minimize the violence of reactions to annoyances in everyday living.

The therapist, however, has the unenviable task of limiting the therapeutic effort. If he is to accomplish this, he must not yield to the temptation to be drawn into an analysis of childhood traumata and interpretation of latent content. The communications should be limited as far as possible to current feelings and to past experiences only as a means of detensing emotions and releasing anxiety. Interpretation changes the nature of the transference.

The above should not be taken to mean that one may not pass from guidance to psychotherapy or combine the two when necessary. Judgment derived from experience indicates when this should be done, but in this respect the therapist, as in all other situations, must be very clear as to his aims and his own abilities and equipment.

PSYCHOTHERAPY VERSUS GUIDANCE FOR PARENTS

The chief differences between psychotherapy and guidance are that in the former more or less permanent basic changes in the personality of the patient are sought, while in the latter the patient is helped to deal more satisfactorily with the immediate problems in his life. In my opinion the confusion in theory and the vast variation in practices stem, at least in part, from the insufficient recognition of the difference between psychotherapy and guidance. Types of psychotherapy that emphasize the present and deal exclusively or predominantly with correcting behavior and superficial attitudes of adults cannot, by their very nature, affect deep and basic changes. They can, however, alter behavior, improve function, and detense the adult through the transference relation, support, ventilation, release, advice, managerial therapy, and better intellectual understanding. Whether the improvement will be permanent, however, is doubtful. The deep-rooted inadequacies and conflicts, lodged mainly in the unconscious, are neither revealed nor corrected by these means. We do not hold that this is necessary in all cases. In some situations and for some persons a less thorough change is sufficient. In fact, in practice one encounters patients who are basically so sick that any kind of uncovering or probing is counterindicated. Frequently the nature of the ego structure or latent pathology are deterents against unraveling the strongly repressed conflicts and unconscious urges. In some instances to do this is inadvisable because it would involve persons other than the patient or an alteration in the life pattern that would too profoundly affect him. In these cases whatever stability had been achieved should not be disturbed.

These considerations and the fact that sometimes immediate results are necessary rather than long-term improvement, should not blind the psychotherapist to the difference in the levels of his work. The term "psychotherapy" ought to be employed when more fundamental changes in personality are sought. The major differences between psychotherapy and therapeutic guidance are that in the first consideration is focused upon the past, while in the latter current events predominate; also, instead of unconscious conflicts and preoccupations, overt difficulties and conscious problems are discussed.

These very important differences affect the method and procedure, the content of the catharsis, and the function of the therapist. We have seen that probing, uncovering, and regression are parts of the psychotherapeutic process which are used sparingly or not at all in guidance. Transference, strongly charged with libidinal (sexual) strivings in psychotherapy, has a minimum of this element in guidance. The content of the interviews in psychotherapy must proceed from free association leading to the past (vertical direction) and effect regression in the patient. In guidance the interviews are predominantly of a free-association nature and deal with parallel or lateral matters and events. The past is dealt with perfunctorily, if at all. In guidance the therapist is much more active and directive than he is in true psychotherapy.

There is very little one can say about psychotherapy for parents that does not apply to psychotherapy in general. Once the parent is treated as a patient, in contrast to his treatment as a parent, all the techniques of psychotherapy described in this book apply. The emphasis is not upon the relations with children and mates, but upon overcoming traumata and conflicts that result in poor parenthood, as a secondary outcome. It is evident that a patient who is helped toward psychological reintegration and emotional normalcy will function better in the role of a parent as a matter of course. Much of what had been said in preceding chapters holds true for adult as well as child psychotherapy.

GROUP PSYCHOTHERAPY FOR PARENTS

Group psychotherapy has proven extraordinarily effective with parents. More of this work has so far been done with mothers, though groups of fathers have also been conducted. Impressive results are reported on the lessening of tensions in the home, more relaxed and normal behavior of the parents, and, particularly, better functioning in relation to mates and children.

In my own work in child guidance clinics, group therapy and group guidance with mothers and fathers, separately, have been of immeasurable help in normalizing the home atmosphere and reducing pressures on children, in addition to changing the parents' intrapsychic organization. The parents have helped each other understand their problems and those of their children and have afforded guidance and suggestion to one another as to ways of dealing with these difficulties. Of no little value in such groups is the additional interest injected into their otherwise not-too-variagated lives, the reduction of guilt through universalization, mutual identification, ego-strengthening, and the support the parents offered one another. Each helped the others correct unfavorable preconceived notions on child rearing and discipline and examined traditional and habit-conditioned patterns of parental behavior and attitudes.

It is singularly significant that all mothers have talked, among other things, about their parents, their siblings, their sexual experiences, and their sufferings as children. Records of the group interviews are replete with narrations of traumatic situations, of hostilities toward mothers and fathers, complaints against them for preferring their other children and for being neglected. They also shared their current difficulties not only with regard to their children but also in relation to their mates, their neighbors, their siblings, and their parents. Positive attitudes are reinforced through these discussions, while the negatives are examined and their effects evaluated by the group and suggestions for better methods for dealing with such situations evolved. Such unreserved sharing alone, even if there were no other benefits, is of inestimable value for normalizing feelings and actions, for it reduces the load of guilt, ambivalence, and uncertainty under which nearly every parent labors and by which nearly every ego is sorely tried.

The function of the psychotherapist in analytic therapy groups is in all major respects the same as in individual psychotherapy. In addition, he gives the group stability, balance, and seeks to prevent excessive acting out of aggression toward any one of the members. He has to steer clear of serious emotional disturbances and prevent reactions from going beyond what any one of the members can bear emotionally. He must keep in mind the limitations of each member's fitness for exposure to psychologic and social pressures. Deep-seated problems are often revealed in the group discussions, and much tension is created as a result. As would be expected, there is considerable interpatient therapy, as each functions as an instigator, a neutralizer, or a supportive ego.[5]

In true group psychotherapy, where patients may become

[5] S. R. Slavson, *Introduction to Group Therapy*, pp. 119, 153.

seriously disturbed by exposure and censure by fellow patients, individual interviews may be necessary in addition to the group sessions. As in individual treatment, timing of interpretation, exploration, and disclosure is of utmost importance. Receptivity and readiness are the criteria here as well. Interpretation must be specific and offered as a basis for elaboration by the group, to release feelings and to help the patients understand and formulate their problems and concepts. The group psychotherapist has to exercise tact in order to avoid conflict with the patients; direct and immediate satisfactions are often essential.

At later stages in the process each member of the group, whether therapy or guidance group, must recognize his part in the genesis and perpetuation of his child's problems. Each must be helped to face his aggressions and to discover through the group experience that friendliness, frankness, and affection are more satisfactory tools in human relations. The well-conducted group leads the members to discover, sometimes for the first time, the pleasures of mutual acceptance and tolerance, which they then apply in their relations with their children and mates and the family as a group.

Less focused conversation than in individual treatment and dilution of content are advantages of group treatment of parents, since they provide escapes from anxiety, but random and unfocused conversation may irritate some. In some of our groups, for example, the members complained that the "meetings" were too diffuse and that no problems were settled. They came for a specific purpose, they said, and wanted to concentrate on their problems.

The types of mother that gain more from group therapy than from any other type of treatment or guidance are:

1. Mothers who have a desire for social communication and group belonging, but because of some personality difficulty are unable to participate in ordinary social groups.

2. Women who are too preoccupied with their families and overprotect their children to the exclusion of interests outside the home. These women need avenues of self-fulfillment and interests outside the family circle. As the mothers' involvement

with home and children is diminished, the children are freed to grow more freely and normally. Treatment and guidance groups are useful as transitions to wider social participation.

3. Mothers whose interests outside the home, either as an escape or as a means for self-expression, result in their neglect of their homes and their children are helped by the discussions in the groups to face their situation more realistically or to accept their role with less conflict.

4. Women who for many reasons need a less intensive therapeutic experience than individual treatment imposes gain relief in sharing with others, and their problems appear less pressing and burdensome because of universalization. For the intellectually limited and the emotionally blocked this type of experience is real and meaningful.

5. Many men and women who are resistive to individual treatment can communicate their problems when supported by others with similar difficulties.

6. Adults who for various reasons cannot enter into a transference relation with a therapist find the transference dilution in groups helpful in establishing such a relation.

7. Some parents who suffer from a pathology so severe that it should not be disturbed may be included in groups as long as they have the capacity to relate to people. They may benefit in dealing with their children from the others in the group.

In order to gain the maximum results, especially from groups, the intelligence of the members should be as far as possible on a par, so that all may understand the contents of the discussions. Similarity in age and sex of the children under treatment is also helpful, since the immediate problems they face in everyday living are then similar, and they can help one another with them. It is also an advantage because boys and girls present different types of difficulty. Quite understandably, these criteria need not be applied in true psychotherapy groups, where the members are treated as patients regardless of their immediate situation or function.[6]

[6] For further information on group therapy and guidance with parents see Fannie Amster, "Collective Psychotherapy of Mothers of Emotionally Disturbed

The topic of group psychotherapy in its various applications has been described by me in a series of papers in various publications.[7] For the reader who may be interested in this subject my *Analytic Group Psychotherapy*,[8] especially Chapters VII and XII of that volume, is recommended. Many of the suggestions as to the functions of the psychotherapist made in an earlier part of the present volume are applicable to group psychotherapy (not guidance) with parents as well.[9]

GROUP GUIDANCE FOR PARENTS

Our experience has convinced us that group guidance of parents with lesser interpersonal disturbances is in every respect more effective, as well as more efficient, than is individual guidance. As is the latter, group guidance is confined to (1) understanding the meaning and intent of children's behavior generally and their specific acts and (2) finding satisfactory and practical means of dealing with them. In these groups, as is also the case in individual guidance, described in an earlier part of this chapter, the guidance worker, who should be a trained therapist, prevents the members from entering into discussions of their intrapsychic conflicts and anxieties. He discourages revelations of intimate matters relating to sexual adjustment, early traumatic experiences, relations with parents and mates, and hostilities toward their children. We have found that unless the parents are highly psychoneurotic and use their families in their

---

Children," *American Journal of Orthopsychiatry*, Vol. XIV, No. 1, January, 1944; Helen E. Durkin, Henrietta Glatzer, and Jeannette S. Hirsch, "Therapy of Mothers in Groups," *American Journal of Orthopsychiatry*, Etta Kolodney, "Treatment of Mothers in Groups as a Supplement to Child Psychotherapy," *Mental Hygiene*, Vol. XXVIII, No. 3, July, 1944; Lawson G. Lowrey, "Group Therapy for Mothers at the Brooklyn Child Guidance Center," *News Letter of the American Association of Psychiatric Social Workers*, winter, 1943, and "Group Treatment for Mothers," *American Journal of Orthopsychiatry*, Vol. XIV, No. 4, October, 1944; S. R. Slavson, "Group Therapy," in *Progress in Neurology and Psychiatry*, ed. by Ernst Spiegel, New York, Grune and Stratton, 1946, and "Current Practices in Group Therapy," *Mental Hygiene*, Vol. XXVIII, No. 3, July, 1944.

[7] See *Bibliography on Group Psychotherapy*, published by the American Group Psychotherapy Association, New York, 1950.

[8] Published by Columbia University Press, New York, 1950.

[9] See ch. vii.

neurotic constellation, more or less educationally oriented discussions are of a surprising value.

As a result of several weekly discussions, in some instances mothers have gained not only better understanding of and empathy with their children's vagaries but also actually have independently devised techniques for coping with conflict-situations with startling effectiveness. Whereas in the past certain of the children's demands or behavior had caused serious strife and family dislocation, when dealt with by the mothers more pliably and understandingly difficulties were avoided, and after a brief time children gave up their disturbing conduct. Instead of reacting to some particularly annoying act on the part of the child, some of the mothers withheld their response until they could "talk it over with the group." Others have reported that as a result of the deliberative group discussions, they have discovered that "things can be talked over" and that there is "no reason for giving people orders and expecting them to obey you." They even went so far as to not only discuss matters with their children that concerned them and their husbands but also to hold family councils on matters that involved them all.

As already indicated, it is rather important (1) that the group discussions be limited to promoting the understanding by the parents of their children's behavior and (2) that the members actively participate in them. The guidance worker should avoid instructing, lecturing, or in any other way dominating the conversations. The principle of self-directed, active groping for solutions and full interchange of ideas among the members must prevail. The group guidance worker may supplement, amplify, and give information when the group members apparently need them or when the participants seem unable to come to their own conclusions.

There are practitioners of group treatment of parents who go considerably deeper than we do in the plan outlined here. Whereas they do not enter the precincts of the unconscious or deal with deep traumata, they analyze the motivation, feelings, and unconscious reasons for the childrens' and the parents' conduct and the complexities of their relations to each other. In these groups also relationships with and attitudes of the parents toward their own parents are dissected and interpreted. Such group work falls between group psychotherapy and the guidance groups as we have outlined them.

It is obvious that the selection of parents to be treated in guidance groups has to be made with great care and on the basis of considerable experience. Only parents whose undesirable behavior toward their children stems from lack of knowledge of a child's needs, habits, the traditionally determined patterns, divergence of cultural patterns and values from those of their children and who misunderstand the role of parents in child development can profit from guidance groups. Parents whose drives are intense, who are motivated by unconscious conflicts, and who work out their neurotic needs through their children, are compulsively stubborn or determined and uncontrollably hostile and destructive would obviously gain little if anything from these groups. Only persons who have good self-control, are able to participate with others in a cooperative venture, and are receptive to new attitudes and values should be included in guidance groups.

DIVISION OF CASES

Whether parents should be involved in treatment or not and the type of treatment they are to receive must be decided on the basis of the case history, the current conditions in the family, and the part the parents play in the child's problem. By and large, guidance or therapy with parents is necessary where prepubertal children are involved. The symbiotic, or parasitic, relation existing between young children and their mothers requires correction of the latters' attitudes. Treatment can scarcely proceed and improvement be retained if the mother offsets its effects. Analysis of the vicious circle [10] usually reveals the intensity of the parents' contribution to the problem and therefore the intensity of treatment indicated for them. It has been our practice to interview at least the mothers of children under treatment, whether individually or in groups. Sometimes only occasional interviews

[10] See p. 241.

are sufficient for general advice or guidance in specific matters relating to the child. Such interviews also help the therapist assess progress and learn of new developments that may be relevant to the treatment plan and effort. In many cases prolonged individual or group guidance or psychotherapy are indicated for either father or mother or both.

Children's cases may be divided into four categories in relation to the treatment of their parents: (1) exclusive, (2) cooperative, (3) divided, (4) cooperative-divided.

The *exclusive cases* are those for which the treatment is concentrated on the child and the same psychotherapist sees the parents also. *Cooperative cases* are those in which more than one therapist is involved in the treatment of the child himself, for example, when he is a member of a therapy group concurrently with individual treatment. The term *divided cases* is applied when different psychotherapists treat the child and the parent, and *cooperative-divided* when the child is a cooperative case and the parents are seen by a third therapist.

Whether the case should remain exclusive or be divided is decided on the basis of the relation between the child and his parent. When the child is hostile, distrustful, and rejecting of the parent, division of the case is essential. Because of his suspiciousness and antagonism the child would not confide in the therapist, partly because of resentment, but more often due to the fear that the therapist might pass on information to the parent. Due to his emotional deprivation, the child cannot share the therapist with anyone, especially one whom he distrusts and dislikes, in this case the parent. Errors in child guidance agencies occur with astonishing frequency on this score. Therapists are sometimes at a loss to understand the unrelenting resistance and finally termination of treatment by some child-patients, only to discover that their contact with the "hated" parent is the source of the difficulty. When a therapist plans to see a parent for any reason, the child's permission must be obtained, and he should be told of the purpose of the interview. This step, however, must not be taken before a sound and positive transference has been established and the child fully trusts the therapist.

X

Group Psychotherapy with Children

GROUP PSYCHOTHERAPY WITH PREPUBERTAL CHILDREN as practiced at the present time falls into four different categories: (1) activity group psychotherapy, (2) transitional groups, (3) play group psychotherapy, and (4) activity-interview group psychotherapy. We are omitting interview (analytic) groups, because they are designed for postpubertal patients.

ACTIVITY GROUP PSYCHOTHERAPY

The general pattern of activity group therapy for small groups of no more than eight children, is free acting out in a specially designed physical setting and carefully planned group milieu. The setting must be simple so that the children can feel free to display their aggressions against the physical environment, and the group must be so planned that they are equally free to behave in a like manner toward each other. The only person the young patients are not permitted directly to harass or attack is the therapist, nor can they invade his personality in any other manner. Hostility and aggression that children inevitably feel toward him as a substitute for parents and teachers may be displaced upon the materials, the walls, and the furniture of the treatment room and upon each other. The therapist is aware of the true intent of such behavior, but he does not call attention to it, nor does he react to it in any way. The therapist plays a *neutral role*. By this is meant that he does not assume any specific characteristics or set criteria for behavior. Unilateral transference, that is, transference from the patient to the therapist only, is necessary in this type of therapy for a number of reasons. Chief among them are the presence of more than one patient and the fact that interpretation is not employed. Each child assigns a role to the therapist most appropriate to his particular emotional state or stage of development, and he can act out his feelings in the group setting.

In order to maintain a neutral role, the therapist is as passive as the children will allow. This predominantly passive role is confined to both his physical and his emotional activity, which leaves the children free to utilize him in whatever capacity they desire at a given time. Children whose basic attitudes are hostile may act them out; those who need a good and indulgent parent substitute may find one in him; while those who need restraint and control may expect that at appropriate times he will exert them if the other group members fail to do so. This variety of roles can be assumed by an adult only when he remains neutral so that he can meet the unconscious needs of each. Because of this role, the therapist can be always positive and encouraging. He neither criticizes, prohibits, nor in any way expresses disapproval, but his failure to respond serves as action interpretation.

The free atmosphere in the groups and the interactions of the children automatically places them in specific, though fluid, relations to each other. Some become the dominant individuals; others the submissive. There are some whose contributions to the group are almost nil; the group is not affected by either their presence or their absence. There are those who by various and devious means isolate themselves from relations with others. They are similar to spectators. In order to describe the various roles assumed by different children, we have designated them respectively as instigators, neutralizers, social neuters, and isolates.

The *instigators* are rather important in all forms of group psychotherapy, because they set up the emotional and social dynamics essential for the creation of situations similar to those in the outer social reality. When there are no instigators present to activate the others either emotionally or in physical activity, the groups stagnate and have very little therapeutic effect, for in these groups the therapy results from the active contacts of the individuals in them. The action level must be rather high at the early stages of treatment, but should subside when personality integration is attained and the ego of each is strengthened by freeing impulses from repression or bringing them under control when necessary. However, when the instigators are weak and infantile, the hyperactivity they arouse in the group may become too uncontrollable for the group to tolerate. The aggression tolerance of any given group has definite limits, and when they are exceeded, disorganization is likely to follow, accompanied by anxiety in the individual members. Children who are selected for the role of instigator in groups must possess at least a minimal degree of ego and superego development. If they are lacking, the therapeutic effect of the group on all who are involved in it is negligible.

The *neutralizers* are the more integrated individuals whose superego development is on a higher level and whose ego strengths are sufficient to keep impulses in check and to regulate behavior. Therefore, they possess the strength to influence other children and the course of the members' behavior and acts. Thus, when a stage of excessive hilarity is reached, the neutralizer can reduce the high level of hyperactivity and inaugurate a state of comparative quiet. This transition is essential, for the actual improvement in the young patients occurs at the point of transition from the high peak of hyperactivity, which we term "nodal behavior," to the low level of activity, or "anti-nodal behavior." [1] It is during this transition, when the individuals in the group bring themselves under control that the regulative forces of the personality are brought to the fore and are developed and strengthened.

The *social neuters,* as the name implies, are the ineffectual persons who do not influence the atmosphere or the behavior of the group by themselves and fall in with the current activities, games, and play instigated by stronger group members. As treatment proceeds, however, they often blossom out into leaders and even instigators.

The *isolates* are the individuals who because of specific personality difficulties, such as neurotic anxieties and fears or other

[1] S. R. Slavson, "Some Elements in Activity Group Therapy," *American Journal of Orthopsychiatry,* October, 1944.

constrictions of character, are actually afraid of close association and direct contacts. They must have an opportunity to overcome their emotional encapsulation by slow stages and therefore should at first be allowed to remain by themselves until they gather enough security to join the group.

Despite the definiteness of these characterizations of the patients in groups, actually the roles of the children are fluid and changeable. Often an isolate ultimately becomes an active participant in the group. He may even assume the part of an instigator, while an instigator on the other hand, may level off and become a neutralizer. The reversibility of roles and relations is one of the major aspects of the therapeutic dynamics in activity group therapy and is made possible only by the fact that the group has no specific plan of organization, no program or objectives and that the therapist is nondirective and neutral. The absence of these external rigidities makes it possible for the children to work out their inner difficulties and social barriers so that they can alter their roles in relation to one another and to the group as a whole. This fluidity in groups I term *group motility,* in contrast to the structure of ordinary clubs or recreational groups, which are planned so that each has a specific function or part in them. This pattern I have described as *group fixity,* which is inevitable and desirable in working with persons for whom the aim is not therapy.

The arts and crafts materials and tools supplied to such groups have a unique place in the therapeutic process, which is quite different from their function in an educational setting, such as arts and crafts, shopwork or in a special-interest group. The materials are used here to direct the children's libido and attendant aggressions from their companions and onto inanimate objects. Because the personality problems of children accepted for group therapy are such that the children are unable to utilize personal relations constructively and are not mature enough or resourceful enough to create for themselves a meaningful environment, idleness could lead only to extreme disorganization, hilarity, and uncontrolled aggression.

The function of the materials and tools is to *fix* the libido—

in this case the nonsexual, but sometimes the sexual libido as well—upon the materials first. This is intended to be only a temporary step. The underlying intention is that activities and interests which are at first directed toward objects will eventually be transferred to the other members of the group and the therapist and that the materials will be gradually relegated to the background. This happens in all groups. One of the reasons for this, in addition to personality growth and increased security, is the fact that the materials and the tools are always the same. No matter how long the group may meet, the equipment is not changed. This is intended to invoke the law of diminishing returns through monotony and the loss of interest and the transfer of interest by the group members to each other. Additional materials and tools and greater opportunities for creative work would isolate them from each other and prevent emotional interaction. Constancy and the uniformity of the physical environment accelerate social contacts in each in accordance with his state of readiness.

An important part of the therapy sessions is the refreshment period. Sharing a simple repast in an atmosphere different in every respect from that to which the children have been accustomed in their homes in the company of an understanding and tolerant adult is an experience that leaves indelible memories. The standard of conduct here, as in other respects at the "meetings," is left entirely to the participants. They can either eat the food, throw it at each other, stuff it in their pockets, give it away, or take it home. No one except, perhaps, one of their own number, expects them to behave well or to display any decorum. Only the therapist displays perfect table manners and retains his equanimity, no matter how intense is the hilarity or annoying the provocation. At refreshment time the children find themselves together face-to-face and in a physical setting quite different from that of the play and occupational part of the session. In the latter they may remain apart or form small subgroups of two or three for work, conversation, or emotional support, but not at the refreshment table. Here eight or more of them, with the therapist nearby, must find some *modus operandi* for this common experience.[2] Because all young animals, human children not excluded, are stimulated by food and become hyperactive, we must expect and accept such behavior by these children.

In addition, many of the problems of feeding, the unpleasant conflicts of family living that had occurred at the home dining table (dawdling, food aversions, tensions, screaming, and recriminations) may be reactivated. The therapist makes careful note of the exacerbations of former patterns and tolerates them until new modes of reactions appear and behavior is normalized. Because of unhappy home experiences and generally weak personality development, some children may still be unable to face the impact of the apparently inescapable proximity and may leave the group before refreshments are served, consume their food in lonely isolation in a corner of the room, or assuage their hunger while continuing their arts and crafts occupations. Such escape from human intercourse, however, usually gives way later to free and friendly participation.

As deference, fear, caution, and timidity subside, the group is offered the chance to indulge in self-selected trips and excursions. These may include visits to baseball games, industrial plants, exhibits, museums, theaters, movies, the circus, and picnics and participation in games appropriate to sex and age. The repetition of such experiences serves to expand the children's living sphere and their knowledge of their world and tests them against the wider and more imposing realities. They further decrease the monotony of the sessions and help give the participants a larger and more difficult testing ground. Such educational and widening experiences must be part of the expanding and maturing process in the treatment of children.

Therapy groups provide for the child tangible social reality, and the conditions under which they are conducted help to improve the self-image and strengthen the ego. Because the therapist always praises appropriately, encourages, and helps, attaining one's ends serves these and other aims of psychotherapy. The

[2] This is well demonstrated in the film "Activity Group Therapy," distributed by Columbia University Educational Films, Columbia University, New York.

therapist's calm, tolerant, and kindly behavior makes him a suitable object of identification, and the children unconsciously assume his manners and attitudes. The therapist, however, is not the sole object of identification, for other children, as well, serve in the same capacity, and because of this it is essential that children who would have a too-negative influence on their fellow members shall not be included in these groups. Corrective identifications, the therapist's action interpretation, and restraint by fellow members cause each to regulate and to restrain himself in return for group acceptance. Continuous exposure to the need for such adaptation and the repetition of self-control and selective judgment result in a strengthened ego. The reader has probably already become aware of the fact that activity group therapy is predominantly an ego therapy, and children who have suffered intensive libido distortion and disorganization cannot be helped by activity group therapy exclusively. In many instances it is employed as supplementary to individual treatment.

Children with inadequately developed superegos can also be benefited by activity groups, beause criteria for and standards of behavior and concepts of right and wrong inevitably emerge from the compresence and interaction of the members in an important and realistic setting. The group also supplies sublimations for the numerous infantile impulses with which the child may come to the group. Play with water, clay, and fire, hammering, shouting, and other activities are provided for, so that the disturbing tensions and drives are sublimated in phantasy, in creative expression, and in real activity. The groups supply direct release from tension through aggressive acts against others, through attack on the physical environment, and through constructive effort with tools and materials.

Successful achievement, acceptance by the therapist and by the group, and praise by parents and relatives of the often inordinately impressive pieces of art work and art objects made by the children in the group contribute toward correcting the self-image and raising self-esteem. In some instances it is essential that parents be helped to react favorably to the child's efforts at self-expression and creative achievement, and they must be encouraged to praise and sustain their children. As the child's self-image and self-esteem are improved, he is better able to accept himself, which always is a precondition to his acceptance of others. This new attitude prevents counteraggression and rejection from persons in his environment—the school, the home, and the street—and better social adjustment results.

Appropriate and meaningful identifications and participation with others correct the sexual confusion from which many children who come for treatment suffer. Boys who because of a solely or predominantly feminine environment or an unsuccessful sibling rivalry with sisters reject a masculine role, or are ambivalent or confused about it,[3] establish male identifications by participating without fear or conflict in masculine activities. They perceptibly assume boys' attitudes and characteristics, and those who had been isolated, lonely, or stigmatized as a result soon find friends and playmates and become better adjusted in their social environment. Similarly, girls whose home environment was equally unfavorable, can accept their feminine role with greater equanimity because of such intimate group association.

The infantilized child finds in these groups an educational and maturing environment. Here protection and controls that he habitually sought and expected from his parents are not forthcoming. He must learn to stand on his own feet. His dependence trends are not nurtured or encouraged, and the operational field for his life is appropriate for his age and increased powers. Such a child may at first play like a baby, lie on the floor or a table on his abdomen, read the funnies, or suck his thumb, but he soon gives up these anachronistic acts because of the examples set by the others in the group, who act more maturely and more responsibly. The immature child may attach himself briefly to another on whom he leans for support in his upward climb, and having received this sustenance, he may soon begin to work and act on his own more appropriately. This is the phenomenon of the *supportive ego*. In the beginning such a child may demand

[3] See interview with boy, p. 246. This boy's mother preferred his sister and retained custody of her, while he was turned over to his paternal grandparents.

the therapist's exclusive attention and seek out physical proximity with him, but action interpretation or direct dealing when advisable with his feigned or assumed helplessness and dependence soon wean him.

For the infantile child, active restraint[4] is recommended. His ego organization is too weak to make even the first steps toward self-control and self-reliance, and he must be helped to continue on his upward path. Permitting him to remain in his habitually dependent way of life only furthers his weakness. At first such a child has to draw parasitically on the strength and power of adults and children who are stronger than he. He must incorporate restraints and controls from others before he can make them his own. The group supplies him with this basic and essential sustenance. For infantile children and for children with constricted and restricted personalities therapy groups, with their attenuated reality and low social pressures, serve as a growth-producing environment and have in addition significant educational as well as therapeutic values.

For all children the ultimate outcome of such an experience within a group is that their frustration tolerance is greatly enhanced, which is the essence of maturity. The unruly narcissistic cravings for power and the feelings of omnipotence are overcome by the fact that the child has realistically come to grips with an environment that, though limiting and proscriptive in some respects, was not antagonistic or repressive, but rather friendly. He has discovered the inevitable limitations and inexorable controls in the external world and because the hostile element was absent and his resentments had not been aroused he is willing to bring himself under control. He has come to accept without violent reaction the limitations imposed on his anarchic impulses and narcissistic drives. Increased tolerance for limitation and frustration is one of the chief objectives in psychotherapy with children. Many of the difficulties in the way of their adjustment arise from their violent, and sometimes unnecessarily intense reactions to essential controls and frustrations. Enhanced tolerance is the foundation for future adjustment and is auto-

[4] See p. 221.

matically a result of the strengthened ego which accrues from this type of therapy.

Children without any brothers or sisters, and therefore lacking the opportunities for sharing an intimate communion, find in these groups the first opportunities to acquire the disposition and skill for doing so. When there is only one child in a family, the problem of sharing—in the first instance, the parents—the inevitable self-preoccupation, and the need to possess may become sources of real difficulties in later life. Activity groups are definitely advantageous for such children.

Children who have not had siblings of the same sex find it difficult to adapt themselves to playmates during latency, and some of them become unable to do so because of additional pathogenic conditions in the home and elsewhere. In activity groups an opportunity is found to relate to substitute siblings and to make the outer and inner adaptations necessary for a more satisfactory functioning in one's peer culture.

Activity group therapy is suitable only for children during the latency period, especially between the ages of eight and twelve. In this period the sexual libido remains in a stage of comparative dormancy, and ego development attains its maximum acceleration; also centripetal interests [5] and identifications are at their height. Group associations are, therefore, most important and most meaningful at this stage in the child's development. At the height of genital development or during the first and second Oedipal periods [6] activity therapy groups alone cannot be considered adequate, because they inherently deal with libido redistribution problems only indirectly.

In the clinical categories the children who have gained most from activity group therapy are the primary behavior disorders, Oedipal type; primary behavior disorders, pre-Oedipal type, if the hyperactivity and aggressiveness are not so intense as to disturb the group beyond a permissible degree; character disorders, particularly those involving constriction and restriction or faulty identifications and a distorted self-image and low self-esteem; children with neurotic traits and mild psychoneuroses. Children

[5] See p. 29.

[6] See p. 120.

to be excluded from activity groups are psychopathic personalities, psychotics, extreme schizoid characters, though mild schizoid children can gain a great deal from activity group psychotherapy, confirmed delinquents, and severe psychoneurotics. Thus, from a clinical point of view the children who can gain from this type of therapy fall within the middle group between psychopathy and severe psychoneurosis. Among the nonclinical indications for assignment to activity group therapy are inaccessibility to individual treatment, uncommunicativeness, infantilization, rivalry with or dependence upon siblings, emotional exploitation by parents, tapering off individual treatment, and the need for "socialization."

Of necessity the discussion on group psychotherapy in a general work of this kind has to be brief. The student who is interested further in activity group psychotherapy is advised to read the following: S. R. Slavson, *An Introduction to Group Therapy,* New York, International Universities Press, 1943; Nathan W. Ackerman, "Dynamics Patterns in Group Psychotherapy," *Psychiatry,* November, 1944; Mildred Becker, "The Effects of Activity Group Therapy on Sibling Rivalry," *Journal of Social Casework,* June, 1948; Helen M. Glauber, "Group Therapy from the Viewpoint of a Psychiatric Caseworker," *American Journal of Orthopsychiatry,* October, 1943; George Holland, and others, "Treatment of a Case of Behavior Disorder through Activity Group Therapy," in *The Practice of Group Therapy,* ed. by S. R. Slavson, New York, International Universities Press, 1947; Leon Lucas, "Treatment of Young Children in a Group," *The News Letter of the American Association of Psychiatric Social Workers,* Winter Issue, 1943–44; Lillian Margolis, "Criteria for Selection of Children for Activity Group Therapy," *Smith College Studies in Social Work,* September, 1946; Geraldine Pederson-Krag, "Unconscious Factors in Group Therapy," *The Psychoanalytic Quarterly,* April, 1946; Saul Scheidlinger, "Activity Group Therapy with Primary Behavior Disorders in Children," in *The Practice of Group Therapy, loc. cit.;* Saul Scheidlinger, "Group Therapy—Its Place in Psychotherapy," *Journal of Social Casework,* October, 1948; Mortimer Schiffer, "Activity Group

Therapy with Exceptional Children," in *The Practice of Group Therapy, loc. cit.;* Oscar Sternbach, "The Dynamics of Psychotherapy in the Group," *Journal of Child Psychiatry,* I (1947), 91.

S. R. Slavson, "Group Therapy," *Mental Hygiene,* January, 1940; "Treatment of Aggression through Group Therapy," *American Journal of Orthopsychiatry,* July, 1943; "Principles and Dynamics of Group Therapy," *American Journal of Orthopsychiatry,* October, 1943; "Some Elements in Activity Group Therapy," *American Journal of Orthopsychiatry,* October, 1944; "Group Therapy with Children," in *Modern Trends in Child Psychiatry,* ed. by Nolan D. C. Lewis and Bernard L. Pacella, The International Universities Press, 1945; "Differential Methods of Group Therapy in Relation to Age Levels," *The Nervous Child,* April, 1945; "Treatment of Withdrawal through Group Therapy," *American Journal of Orthopsychiatry,* October, 1945; "Group Psychotherapy Today," in *Current Psychiatric Treatment of Personality Disorders,* ed. by Bernard Glueck, New York, Grune & Stratton, Inc., 1946; "Activity Group Psychotherapy with Character Deviations in Children," in *The Practice of Group Therapy, loc. cit.;* "Contra-Indications of Group Therapy for Patients with Psychopathic Personalities," *ibid.;* S. R. Slavson and Charles Miller, "Integration of Individual and Group Therapy in the Treatment of a Problem Boy," *American Journal of Orthopsychiatry,* October, 1939; S. R. Slavson, Henry Wiener, and Saul Scheidlinger, "Activity Group Therapy with a Delinquent, Dull Boy of Eleven," *The Nervous Child,* April, 1945.

TRANSITIONAL GROUPS

Transitional groups are so termed because they serve as a bridge between therapy groups or individual psychotherapy, whence patients are chosen, and the social realities of their world. Children who are not ready to take part in group activities or regular social clubs need a more protected social environment and are assigned to such groups. Their members are carefully selected, and the "leader" is a trained psychotherapist. These groups, unlike therapy groups, follow a program of organized activities and have a plan. The group elects officers, keeps minutes of proceedings, and has a treasurer. Various facilities, such as tools, materials, food, and a field for uninhibited acting out, are not provided here. Under the leadership and stimulation of the "leader," the members censor, punish, and control the acts of their fellow members, and the group as a whole planfully takes action and makes decisions on all matters relating to its work and plans.

The difference between these groups and ordinary clubs lies in the fact that their members are selected because, though almost ready for realistic social participation, they are as yet unable to enter into the competitive relations and high social pressures of the latter. Another difference is that the leader, who is really a therapist, is aware of the needs of the members as individuals, which is not always the case in social clubs. He prevents conflicts and dissensions that may prove too difficult for the members to resolve. Also, participation in intergroup activities is carefully graded, even though transitional groups meet in a neighborhood center or a settlement house. Transitional groups also provide an attenuated reality, but here the social demands are much greater than in therapy groups. Programing, planning, and carrying out projects make demands upon the members which are strictly avoided in the latter. But caution is exercised that too great responsibilities are not thrust upon the children or demands made upon them for which they may not be ready.

Instead of a specially designed setting and an isolated environment, the transitional groups meet in ordinary meeting rooms in a neighborhood center at the same time that other groups meet. The members are, therefore, exposed to contact with other children in the community. The leader makes a conscious, though cautious, effort to bring them into contact with the other members of the center and to involve them in its activities. This is done by visiting clubs, special activity rooms, gymnasiums, and to different parts of the building. The children meet staff members and are encouraged to join the various activities of the center. Some of the members of the transitional groups may be interested in art, some in athletics, others in dramatics, still others in music, science, or arts and crafts shops. Gradually the programing and planning of the group is directed toward the general activities in the building, which may include individuals outside the group itself and other clubs. These widened social contacts bring in their wake real and increased demands, which must occur with graded intensity. Each child needs to be helped to fit into them. Usually the transitional groups finally pattern themselves after other clubs in the center, join them in their activities, and are included in the roster of the regular clubs under the direction of a regular leader. Our experience shows that these clubs do not survive long because of the absence of a true social and interest homogeneity. They always disband, each member joining a group best suited to his needs and special interests.[7]

PLAY GROUP PSYCHOTHERAPY

Play group psychotherapy is employed for children of preschool age whose maladjustments are severe and who suffer from deep psychoneuroses, as well as behavior disorders. The conduct of these groups conforms in every respect to the same principles and techniques as are used in individual play therapy, except that when three to five children are present they interact with one another and activate each other's catharsis. The meaning and significance of the play is greatly enhanced when it occurs in the presence of other children and is stimulated and shared by them. The materials employed are the same as those used in individual play therapy. Their basic characteristics are that they are *libido-revealing* and *libido-activating*, in contrast to those recommended for activity groups, where the materials are rather *libido-fixating*. Activation of the libido is necessary in treating children chosen for these groups, since it is in this area that their difficulties usually lie. Therefore, they have to act out their oral, anal, urethral, and sexual phantasies and preoccupations in play, as well as their hostilities and resentments. They must have opportunities to abreact to and to reenact traumatic

[7] For further reading on transitional groups see S. R. Slavson, *Introduction to Group Therapy*, pp. 326 *et seq.*

and disturbing situations in their homes, rid themselves of the emotional pressures, and attain insight into their feelings and actions on their own level through interpretation by the other patients and by the psychotherapist.

The materials must, therefore, be adjusted to meet these needs. Water, clay, plasticene, water-color paints, a doll's house, with toy figures of males, females, and children, bedroom furnishings, bathroom equipment, rubber tubing, sponges, toy guns, soldiers, animals, masks, dolls of various kinds with which the children can identify and play out their phantasies. Refreshments are served in play psychotherapy groups, where the therapist reenacts the maternal role as she does in activity groups and where the children can behave as they do at home. The children are permitted to act out freely their aggressions and to abreact to frustrations and hostilities and recreate situations that disturb them. The therapist in these groups should be preferably a woman.

In play group psychotherapy the therapist is active. As in individual play therapy, she participates with the children, interprets behavior both to individual children and to the group as a whole, encourages their attempts to uncover the motivating feelings behind action, and relates current feelings to the trauma to which the children attempt vaguely to react. Background facts and events are elicited from the young patients in so far as they are capable of supplying and understanding them. Thus, this therapy proceeds in precisely the same manner as does individual psychotherapy. Libido distribution and the changing of the self-image as much as is possible for little children are its goals. The children in these groups (unlike those in the activity groups) are allowed to attack the therapist physically, and the reasons are interpreted to them. Because of the youth of the children and their limited ego development and controls, hyperactivity is regulated by the psychotherapist, for she uses both passive and active restraint. The passive restraint is practiced, as it is in activity group therapy, by the physical setting and action interpretation. Direct restraint is exercised when the therapist feels that the anxiety generated by the behavior may disturb the young patients or lead to intense disorganization of the group.

The children chosen for these groups may include serious cases of psychoneurosis, primary behavior disorders, and character disorders, as well as schizoid personalities who would not be frightened by the other children. For these groups selection need not be as rigid as for activity group therapy. However, children who disturb the group climate seriously enough to arouse anxiety in fellow members are eliminated here as well. Transference in these groups is bi-lateral; the therapist is active and utilizes the transference in a therapeutic process as in interpretation. The age range of children in these groups should not be more than six months, in contrast to two years in activity groups.[8]

ACTIVITY-INTERVIEW GROUP PSYCHOTHERAPY

In activity-interview group psychotherapy we also treat children in the latency period, but this procedure differs from activity group therapy in the choice of patients and in the function of the therapist. Activity-interview group psychotherapy is actually a combination of activity group therapy and individual interview psychotherapy and has many elements in common with both as well as with play group psychotherapy. The term has been chosen because of the commonness of these elements.

The setting in activity-interview therapy is the same as that in activity group therapy, with the addition of some of the libido activating materials, as in play group psychotherapy, but suitable for older children. The catharsis is both active and verbal. The children are free to act out, as in activity groups, but their acts are interpreted by the therapist, who also encourages the young patients to communicate to each other and to the therapist their problems, difficulties, preoccupations, fears, and anxieties. These are openly discussed, either with one child or with the group as

[8] For further reading on play group psychotherapy see Susan Burlingham, "Therapeutic Effects of a Play Group for Pre-school Children," *American Journal of Orthopsychiatry*, Vol. VIII, No. 4, Oct., 1938; S. R. Slavson, "Play Group Therapy for Young Children," *The Nervous Child*, Vol. VII, No. 3, July, 1948; "Current Practices of Group Therapy," *Mental Hygiene*, Vol. XXVIII, No. 3, July, 1948; *Analytic Group Psychotherapy*, especially ch. viii; "Differential Methods of Group Therapy in Relation to Age Levels," *The Nervous Child*, Vol. IV, No. 3, April, 1945.

a whole, depending upon the situation and the need. The aims here are libido distribution, ego-strengthening, and changing the self-image. Severely psychoneurotic children may therefore be included in these groups. The function of the therapist is the same as it is in individual psychotherapy, but instead of working with one patient, in these groups he may work sometimes with one, at other times with several children, and, again, with the whole group. The similarity between play group psychotherapy and activity-interview psychotherapy is apparent. The difference is that the latter has a wider scope of activities and there is less control over the behavior of the children. The benefits to the child from this treatment are the same as listed under activity group psychotherapy [9] because both are of the same age. To these must be added the correction in libido distribution, reduction of traumatic foci, and acquisition of insight.[10]

[9] See pp. 285–89.

[10] For further reading on activity-interview groups see Helen E. Durkin, "Dr. John Levy's Relationship Therapy As Applied to a Play Group," *American Journal of Orthopsychiatry*, July, 1939; Betty Gabriel, "An Experiment in Group Treatment," *American Journal of Orthopsychiatry*, July, 1939; Slavson, *Analytic Group Psychotherapy*, especially ch. ix, and "Differential Dynamics of Activity and Interview Group Therapy," *American Journal of Orthopsychiatry*, April, 1947.

XI

Treatment of a Neurotic Nine-Year-Old Boy with Organic Deficiency

WE HAVE CHOSEN the case of Harry for the concluding chapter because it illustrates many of the theoretic formulations and suggestions for the practice of psychotherapy in other parts of this volume. Here we have illustrated the results of an inadequate, dependent mother and an indifferent father, and the disturbing effect of an older, domineering, and more successful sibling. The positive value of a relative living in the home—an affectionate grandfather—is also well demonstrated. The case reveals clearly a variety of relations in a family group and interpersonal tensions inherent in such a setting which emanate primarily from one center of infection, the mother.

The resulting castration anxieties, bizarre body-image, defective self-image, and ego deficiencies cause the boy's social maladjustment, his isolation from human relations, escape into phantasy, and school failure. As the treatment is described, unavoidably in a telescoped fashion, we see how the transference upon the psychotherapist develops through her supportive and constructive attitudes. By following the boy's emotional and intellectual unfoldment and well-placed interpretation the therapist aids catharsis and the emergence of a limited level of insight. When the boy is ready a field of social experimentation and reality testing in the forms of a therapy group and camp life are introduced. These growth-producing and strengthening experiences aid the child's ego-organization and correct his self-image and self-awareness, a process for which the foundation was laid by individual treatment. He develops a transference toward the male group therapist, who is also an adequate model of identification, and he identifies with the other boys in the group. Harry utilizes "supportive egos" in a constructive way. This case summary also shows how important it is to decrease the pressure on the patient at the source and how treatment of the mother has benefited the therapy of the child.

These dynamics and others in preceding pages, too numerous to mention here, are illustrated in this brief summary of the treatment history. The reader should be aware that Harry's case does not present as serious pathology as could be found in many cases under treatment privately or in clinics. It was chosen only because of the many facets it reveals in psycho-social and psychosexual dynamics and in the use of a number of coordinated treatment resources. It is also noteworthy that the fundamental or basic unconscious conflict had not been brought out nor interpreted. Rather, therapy was limited to representatives in the conscious and in behavior, with impressive results. This, as the reader will recall, is sufficient in most cases of prepubertal children and to a much lesser extent also for older patients.

In the interest of economy of space we have refrained from including a more extensive interpretation of the latent content of the patient's communications and his treatment career in the group.

Harry Peters[1] was referred to the clinic at the age of eight and one half years by his mother, because of severe stuttering, difficulty in expressing his personal feelings, and fear of the dark, of animals, and of being hurt. He had difficulty in chewing his food, and in the past had refused entirely to masticate. The onset of most of these symptoms dated from the age of two and a half years, at which time a kettle of boiling water was overturned which scalded Harry on the chest. At approximately the same time there occurred marked disturbances in his sleep. He would

1 Muriel Chaves, psychiatric caseworker, summarized her treatment of Harry for this chapter, and William Phillips, the therapist of the activity group of which Harry was a member, supplied the material dealing with that phase in Harry's treatment. Doris Hallowitz reported on her work with Harry's mother. Dr. Sidney Green was the psychiatric consultant on this case. The psychological testing was carried out by Leah Levinger. The case was taken from the files of the Child Guidance Institute of the Jewish Board of Guardians, New York.

scream, had nightmares, and frequently walked in his sleep.

In school his performance was extremely poor. Although he seemed to strive to conform, he was unable to take his place with his contemporaries either in school work or in social relations. Though he desired companionship, he was withdrawn and usually alone and isolated. Harry complained of burning sensations on the back of his neck, which he frequently experienced before he went to sleep, usually when he felt "nervous." He had periods of temporary "blindness," from several minutes to an hour in duration. He maintained that the attacks of blindness occurred usually in school, when he could not read. As a result, the teacher did not call on him to recite.

Harry was a well-built, chubby, but not obese, youngster with a pleasant, gentle expression and fair, curly hair. He was always neatly dressed. His entire manner was characterized by a sort of tentativeness, infantile mannerisms, and a sense of weakness. He gave the impression that he had poor muscular coordination, which was visible in his gait, as well as in his bodily movements. The clinical diagnosis was indefinite.

Before treatment was initiated, a psychological test was administered, as well as a complete neurological examination, including an electro-encephalogram. The presence of "diffuse organicity" was revealed. These findings were confirmed by the consulting psychiatrist, who also felt that the total picture indicated some organic disturbance which retarded the child's maturation and contributed toward his diffuse, poorly motivated, impulsive behavior and poor perceptions. It was also suspected that superimposed upon this condition were many defenses mobilized by the youngster in an attempt to cope with his very difficult environment. It seemed likely that much of his passivity was a result of the absence of a positive identification with an adult male figure. His phantasies and dreams revealed an inhibited, fearful little boy, who saw the world as a threatening menace.

The family consisted of his father, his mother, his maternal grandfather, his brother, Paul, ten years older than Harry, and Harry. His mother was a rigid, repressed, guilt-ridden, though not hostile, person. She had lavished attention upon Paul, who had also been in treatment at the clinic. She expected from her older son the satisfactions that she felt had been denied her by her father and her husband. She had given little attention to Harry, partly because she had wished to have a daughter and partly because she no longer expected any satisfactions from any male. The mother was now disappointed in Paul as well.

The father was a more accepting, friendly person, who gave equal attention to both his children, often played with Harry, and had taken him to various places of interest. The most constructive relation in the family set-up for Harry was his grandfather, who was very fond of the boy.

Individual treatment by a woman psychiatric caseworker was conducted on a weekly basis. The mother was assigned to another psychiatric caseworker, whom she visited during the same period, though less frequently. At appropriate intervals in the treatment summer camp life and activity group therapy were introduced.

During the first fourteen interviews Harry talked about superficial matters, being careful not to reveal his feelings or to become emotionally involved. Indeed, in the very first interview he spoke in babyish English, but he evidenced no fear. He was brought by his mother to the clinic and did not object to coming into the interviewing room alone. He confided that he had a speech difficulty and stressed his dislike of the speech teacher, who was punitive and "treated the children like babies." At first he said that his only difficulty was in pronouncing the word "yesterday," but later he said that he can now say that correctly. He appeared restless, rejected an invitation to explore the play materials, and complained of a burning sensation on the back of his neck. In response to a question, he maintained that he once had friends, but that they had all moved away from the neighborhood, because "their mothers got jobs." He denied that he felt lonely and quite obviously fabricated a friend, whom he called "Melvin," and half-heartedly attempted to be humorous in illustrating a game they played together. He then spoke of his activities in a neighborhood "Y," but stressed how big and tough the fellows were there. His teacher "is just as big as a speech teacher, and the speech teacher is almost as big as you [the caseworker, who was of medium height]." The boys in the club at the "Y" were "fat and tough." They brought colored fellows to the club and applied a lighted match to his coat. The preceding day he was standing in front of a store, and when he turned around a fellow had a knife at his back. He complained that the policemen stationed near his school "don't do any good." When he returned to his mother in the waiting room at the end of the first session, she fussed over him, while he stood beside her very impassively.

In the second interview he made sure that the door was closed so that there were no interruptions, and it should be noted that he came upstairs alone; his mother remained downstairs. The caseworker said to him that he seemed to want to grow up. In the second interview he was at first timid, whispered, was constrained, and moved about the room warily. Before doing or touching anything, he would ask for permission. He asked for some clay and commented that his brother was a "big fellow," even bigger than his mother, and that his father was even bigger than his brother. He did not use the clay, but asked if he could draw a picture. He abandoned this and returned to the clay. Again he asked whether he could paint a house, and finally ventured to do so. His drawing was very undifferentiated and infantile for his age. He then said that his paints at home had been ruined. He turned to the finger paints and asked how to use them. The therapist told him that he might use either his fingers or a brush. He decided to try a brush, but soon rejected the finger paints entirely, saying: "It's no good, it's too dirty." Again he returned to the clay and decided to make a "man on skiis."

When asked what had given him this idea, he said he had read about it in a geography book. The clay figure consisted of a head and two legs coming out of the head. When asked whether or not he wanted to make anything else on the man, he said he guessed that the man should have some other parts, stuck some clay in the front, called it a stomach and said, "Now he has everything." This was followed by a phantasy of a snowball fight, in which everyone involved in the fight was afraid to come out of doors.

In the third interview Harry told of a drunken Negro who had come to the school and told the teacher that he would kill all the children if she did not lock the doors. The therapist commented that Harry thought it was up to the teacher to protect the children against danger. Harry nodded and said she kept the doors shut real tight. When asked if he had seen this Negro man, he abruptly dropped the subject and asked permission to draw a cowboy, which was as primitive as the clay man. The figure was small and utterly isolated on an otherwise empty sheet of paper. He then said that he had found a big brass gun. He used to have a small plastic gun, but now he has a big brassy one. Until now, the cops in the neighborhood arrested children who had guns, and therefore he had not been able to play with his plastic one. However, the cops are not doing this any more.

During the fourth interview he initiated a project that seemed very ambitious. He continued to work on this project during many interviews, but in an unsustained manner. His activity consisted essentially of painting over and over again the cheese box he had brought with him. He never really completed his undertaking. In the fifth interview he spoke about his fancied friend "Herman," who, he phantasied, lived in a very crowded house, where two families have to share the facilities. Herman is very much afraid of the dark and wants a light at night, he said. Harry spoke very energetically about this; he seemed to be released by the narration. Herman is also very much afraid of the bogeyman. Harry then switched and told how on the Milton Berle television show a man jumped out of the window. He will miss Herman, since the latter had moved from the neighborhood. The caseworker inquired about Harry's own home situation. He said that he slept in "a big, big bed" in a room which he shared with his brother, the latter sleeping in a very small bed. His mother does not know this, but Harry keeps all sorts of things in his bed, like pieces of wood and a toy typewriter, which he plays with under the covers.

In the sixth interview the therapist arrived several minutes late for the appointment. Harry said he had been very busy with other things in the waiting room, implying that he had not missed her, thus expressing his resentment. During this interview he was asked about his plans for the summer, and he said he does not like to go away, neither does he enjoy swimming in a neighborhood public swimming pool, because "the cops stand around."

In the ninth session he phantasied a fight with his older brother in which the latter tried to scare him with a blanket, but he hit his brother hard over the head and hurt him more than he had been hurt. He then said that sometimes he does not sleep well at night. The therapist casually suggested that sometimes fellows have dreams at night in which they may do some of the things that they would really like to do during the day. He then said that he often dreams of killings and fights, and he made a snorting sound. When asked what it meant, Harry explained that he always restrains his sneezes because he does not like "to let it out." He then said that a very funny thing happened in school, and when the teacher yelled at the kids for laughing: "I laughed and laughed and laughed and never could stop laughing." What was so funny? The teacher told a boy to go to the window, and while doing so the boy's pants slipped down. Did the boy also laugh? Yes, the boy also laughed. The therapist then commented that perhaps even though the boy to whom this happened laughed, inside he may have felt badly. Harry began to mutter, and when the therapist asked what he was doing, he said he always mutters this way when someone does something to him that he does not like. What happens when he mutters? Harry said that the person who said or did the thing that he does not like just then has to go away.

In the tenth interview he again pretended that he had come to the therapist alone. The therapist said that perhaps this was something he still wished to do, but was not quite ready for it. Harry said he preferred going out with his parents without his older brother. He then banged with the hammer, drove nails into the paint box, and for the first time painted his name on the box, which he then placed on the shelf. Some time later he told that his "girl friend" had given him a toy jumping frog; that she was nice, but she has "a very fat brother." He himself weighs 99 pounds, and soon he will weigh 100, and "I am a big boy." After playing with "the doctor set," he said that he used to have a doctor set at home when he was little. What happened to that doctor set? His mother threw it away because he was too big to play with such things. Again he announced that he would come by himself the following week. However, following this he spoke of his periods of blindness in school, which he himself associated with the fact that when he cannot see the teacher cannot call on him to read.

At the next interview, the eleventh, the therapist had a book of Gilbert and Sullivan operettas, Harry having mentioned his interest in them. He was extremely surprised and delighted that she knew about these operettas and showed elation that both listened to the same radio program. He commented that no one in his family knows these operettas, and it seemed that for the first time, through this mutual interest, he was able to identify with another person (therapist). He then phantasied about teaching his "girl friend" these operettas and stated his aspiration to be an opera star. He was disappointed to find that the Metropolitan Opera House was so old and dirty. He hoped that some day there would be a nice shiny bright opera house. He then complained about his mother's refusal to give him bubble gum, but said that it was really his father who told him that one can get a disease by chewing the gum.

During the twelfth interview he referred to his brother as "a big shot" and to himself as "a little shot." The therapist said it must be tough to be in such rivalry with a much older brother. Harry admitted that they do not get along, but immediately phantasied that he broke his brother's finger because the brother had hit him. At the thirteenth interview Harry complained about the dearth of play material available in the interviewing room, and the therapist suggested that Harry help prepare a list of things he would like to have. He then asked for the clay man he had made some weeks earlier and was delighted to learn that it had been kept for him. Harry commented that the man had no arms and laughed as though to poke fun at his earlier attempt. He then played with this clay man, insisting that the clay man sit absolutely still in a little chair. When the therapist asked why the clay man had to do this, Harry said because he, Harry, never leaves his front porch unless something very important is happening such as his trip to see the caseworker. This was the first real step toward recognizing that he was an isolate.

At the fourteenth interview he said that the strongest kid on the block sneaked up on him; then he corrected this description by saying, "we [that is, the other kid and Harry] are the strongest kids on the block." After this attempt at identification with an aggressive act, it was followed by a very enthusiastic report of an accident which he had watched, and he told how much he enjoyed watching accidents. However, immediately afterward he complained that "the kids" played with firecrackers on his block and then expressed concern that they might shoot off his whole porch (the place from which Harry "never moved"). At this point he began to hammer, rather timidly at first and then making a terrific racket. Harry was told that the therapist was leaving for her vacation, but rather than discuss it he began to speak of a friend of his who had gone to Baltimore, and he asked how far away Baltimore was. The therapist said she thought maybe he was asking her how far away she was going and whether she would be sure to come back. He then said he did wonder where she was going, and he was told very specifically where and how far away she would be that summer and when she would return.

At the fifteenth interview, the first after the summer vacation, he greeted the therapist by saying: "I guess there are many things I know that you don't know." He proceeded to explain how movies are made, and although his description was unrealistic, he concluded his recitation by saying: "I am very smart." During the course of this session he had difficulty in opening some of the paint jars, and when he was otherwise engaged, the therapist managed to loosen them enough so that when he returned to them later he succeeded in opening them. His reaction to being able to open the jars was: "My mother calls me now when she needs a job done. My brother is a sissy." The therapist commented that she knew that Harry wanted to be strong, but there were times when he, perhaps, did not feel that way. At the end of this session he picked up a baby bottle. After fondling it, he asked what it was for, and when told that sometimes children use it to feed the baby (doll), he decided to fill the bottle and take a drink from it himself.

In the next interview he at once picked up the baby bottle, filled it, and drank from it frequently throughout the hour, sitting back, sucking on the bottle, closing his eyes in gratification, much as an infant does. He would intermittently open his eyes, gaze at the therapist, who was sitting quietly by, and then close his eyes and return to sucking. After some time of this he said he really disliked playing with guns, then told about his having jumped from the window. He characteristically seemed to relate personal strength to injury and destruction. He knew of another little boy who was very much afraid to jump because it is too dangerous, and then he told of another auto accident which he had witnessed. With much relish he explained that "I had a front row place."

During following interviews Harry spoke of a man who returned from work and found his child, his wife, and his maternal grandmother killed. When asked about the age of the child, his reply was: "Nine years old, like me." He also spoke of boys who had had all their fingers and arms below the elbow cut off at a school and that the "colored fellows" even hang their teachers in the basement. During these communications Harry would suck at the baby bottle with great vehemence. At times his speech was blurred, and he often spoke in an almost inaudible whisper. His behavior seemed even more aimless and markedly disorganized, and he manifested increasing anxiety.

On one occasion he asked to leave the interview early. During this period he kept his mouth wide open or continued to suck on the bottle, refusing to play with guns or even to phantasy about aggression. All interest in any of his work projects disappeared. During this period the therapist was extremely quiet and gentle with Harry, and she would speak quietly to him about whatever seemed to interest him at the time. Her aim was essentially to lull the boy into a state of peace through her attitude and voice, rather than her words. He gave the impression of a very small baby seeking contact with and warmth from an adult.

After about six or seven such sessions Harry suddenly announced that he no longer needed his bottle for drinking: "It tastes better out of a glass." He commented about the pictures on the wall and decided to draw something. Rather feebly he copied a fish from one of the books. It was apparent that in this attempt there was the beginning of competition on a realistic level. For the first time he asked the therapist to play checkers with him. He followed arbitrary rules that he set up, which helped him win the games. The therapist went along with whatever rules Harry set up.

In the following session, the twenty-sixth, he told a phantasy about Texas Rangers in a shooting scene. He had only half of his gun. The therapist asked what had happened to the other half, and Harry explained that the other half "just seemed to be missing." He then took from the toy shelf the largest gun and illustrated what happened to the Texas Ranger's gun by pretending to chop this gun in half. The therapist asked what the Ranger did in this difficult spot, and Harry said that he went to the sheriff, and the sheriff gave him a new gun with all of the parts and that the Ranger was able to shoot successfully. The therapist expressed delight that the Ranger was able to go to the sheriff, who helped him to have a strong gun, and she asked what kind of sheriff Harry thought he was. Harry said the sheriff "was strong like a king and was a big shot." He, too, was delighted that the sheriff helped the Ranger.

Later in this interview he spoke derogatorily of cops as "rookies" and told that he had been made a monitor for a fire drill at school (which was true). For the first time he asked if he could stay a little longer than his usual time, gazed at the baby bottle, rejected it, and shot off a few of the guns before leaving.

During the next thirty interviews Harry utilized symbolic material, through which he expressed his feelings and needs. There was also more acting out and living through roles from which he gained gratification, enlisting the therapist in support of these programs. When this period was half over, Harry began to travel by himself and asked to be sent to a summer camp. Thus, he voluntarily substituted real gratifications for his phantasy life. Also, mutilation phantasies were subordinated to phantasies of becoming a hero.

During an early interview in this period Harry began to use his own pencil and repeatedly sharpened the point; the therapist remarked that he seemed very fond of his pencil. He told how the pencil used to be a pen, until "somebody shot the insides out of it." The lead, he felt, came out of the pencil with difficulty, and so he put a nail on the top with which he could push the lead out. He said he would trust the therapist to examine the inside of his pencil, which she proceeded to do with care. In another interview he began to explore new possibilities of his environment. Although at first somewhat timid about using the dictaphone, he now used it freely as a substitute for a radio. Once, when the therapist introduced Harry somewhat bombastically, he looked at her affectionately and said: "Don't overdo it."

Harry became generally freer and more relaxed and read freely from books into the dictaphone. Inquiries at his school revealed that Harry tended to adjust by passivity and conformity. Upon the urgent request from the psychotherapist, he was removed from the speech class. His response to this was: "I sure won that!" His manner was more secure, he initiated contact with other staff members in the clinic, would go to the store to buy materials, telling the therapist that she could wait in the office now. His mother reported improvement in the home and cessation of nightmares and phantasies of mutilation. He was rather domineering over and assertive toward the therapist, but he told his mother once that he often watched the therapist while she was doing things for him and that he thinks she has a "very lovely face."

In the spring Harry recalled the therapist's casual comment about summer camp and said he thought it might be nice to go to a camp. When encouraged to elaborate on his idea of camp, it was, indeed, phantastic, for he believed that real Indians would be there. The therapist tried to convey to Harry what actually occurs at camp through role playing and acting out a typical camp day with him. He finally decided to go, saying: "I need a change—get away from the family." His play with pencils and pens continued, until finally, at the thirty-sixth interview, Harry placed a pen on the desk, commenting that the eraser on his pencil was missing. He was given an eraser from an old pencil. He very diligently worked to attach the eraser to his pencil. After he succeeded in doing this, he commented that he now had "a wonderful pencil," and looked appreciatively at the therapist. In this interview, also, he called the therapist by name for the first time, and said: "I want to talk with you." He then expressed his apprehension that he might have to miss interviews if his teacher kept him after school. The therapist reassured him in this regard.

In the thirty-seventh interview he placed a new automatic pencil on the therapist's desk and asked her to teach him how to shoot a bow and arrow. He showed disappointment when he did not succeed in killing the bear on the paper target.

A number of sessions were devoted to preparation for summer camp and elimination of his fears and phantasies concerning this new experience. He now began to talk about playing baseball and being a captain of a baseball team. Prior to leaving for camp, Harry presented to the caseworker a large box of candy, and his mother reported that he told her: "If I were older, I would like to marry Miss Chaves." Harry got along well in camp and participated freely in the activities there.

Because of his desire to be a baseball player and the successful camp experience, it was suggested to Harry that he might join a club (therapy group) conducted by the clinic. He was very reluctant to do this, but he began to play ball in the interviewing room and to explain the various plays to the therapist. In doing this he referred several times to the possibility of physical injury, and when this was called to his attention, he stated that he "guessed" most of the fellows on the team were his friends. The therapist related this to Harry's pleasant experiences in camp and indicated the possibility of continuing them in a club. He ignored this, and continued to ask the therapist's help with archery. At later sessions Harry voluntarily brought up the question of joining a group.

The general plan was to discourage Harry from returning to his rationalizations and phantasies and to encourage him to test reality. In playing checkers, for example, he was told that one simple, but meaningful, rule be followed. Harry, though at first he resisted this, finally acquiesced, won the game, and gleefully said: "This is the first time I have won a *real* checker game." He was returned to the speech class in school, but unlike his previous reaction, Harry decided that he did not mind it and that "the teacher is not as mean; and I like it." He no longer phantasied horrors in the new school to which he was to be transferred, and said he was not afraid of it. "Now I can take care of myself," he added.

When Harry was invited to a club (therapy group), he ignored the first invitation, ostensibly because he had to attend a class in a parochial school. The therapist did not urge him, but formulated some of his past fears of children and agreed to accompany him to the clubroom so that with her he could explore the setting of the club. After attending a few sessions, he complained of the other boys' aggressiveness and stopped coming. His diffidence and his feelings about this new situation were discussed with the group therapist, who recognized that Harry feared the situation would become acutely dangerous for him if the leader did not curb the aggressiveness of the other boys. His earlier feeling that "cops" are ineffectual and punitive rather than protective was recalled, and Harry was reassured that the "club leader" would intervene should there be real danger. Harry did not return to the group at this time, however.

During this period his older brother left home and joined the army of occupation in Japan. It is likely that because of the older brother's absence Harry now had more status at home. This brother was now the focus of Harry's interviews. He expressed his hostility toward his older brother and his family because of the latter's hostility toward himself. The therapist indicated that other boys had similar feelings of aggression and that the club is a place where they may express it, always, however, reassuring him that should the situation really become dangerous, the leader would intervene. After another summer in camp, Harry agreed to join the therapy group.

The meaning of his group experience is, perhaps, best symbolized by a comment, in one of the interviews, that he had attempted to make a drawing in the "club." It was the first time he had tried to draw since his early, very feeble effort. In contrast to that attempt, this drawing was remarkably well organized. It consisted of a lamp post on the left side of the paper and the figure of a man, who is saying: "I give light in dark corners." In the middle of the paper was a fairly well-constructed house, with a door, a doorknob, windows, and other details, and a tall chimney out of which poured smoke. At the right of the house was drawn a rather masculine looking man, complete with extremities, including five fingers on each hand, who was saying: "Ah, at last, a light!" After he finished drawing this man Harry spontaneously, but emphatically, added a pipe out of which smoke was coming. At approximately this time Harry stopped playing with crayons, pencils, and pens, all of which had symbolic significance (penis and castration phantasies).

Harry was now able to say how delighted he was that his brother was out of the home, and he began to participate in some of the activities in the neighborhood, such as playing baseball and the harmonica, which were his brother's pastimes. He expressed anger at the inequality between himself and his much older brother. At the same time, he said that now that he can do things during the day, he does not have to do things in his sleep any more, such as sleepwalking. He once confessed that he had thrown "a lot of junk" onto his brother's bed.

The school reported improvement in Harry's capacity to cope with his environment; also he was no longer on the periphery of the therapy group, but participated as a full-fledged member. There were also indications that his reading was not merely on a rote basis. He now read more accurately and with greater emphasis on content. Both in school and at home he began to relinquish his infantile patterns.

It was during this time that Harry was able to speak more specifically about his intellectual and other limitations, and he related them to the fact that when he was very little he had had an accident (the scalding) and that if this had not happened to him, he would be as smart as the other fellows, without any doubt. This rationalization was allowed to stand, but his admission that he felt different from others made it possible to indicate that there was still a great deal that he could do within his own capacities, to which he agreed. He was reassured when he was reminded that he was able to deal with a difficult school situation, about which he had had phantasies of mutilation (children's fingers and arms being cut off and boys hanging their teachers). He was also able to take his problems to the school guidance director, who helped Harry to cope realistically with some of the difficulties in school, rather than to escape them. His attendance at the "club" also revealed his strength.

Harry became absorbed in a chemistry set, which in addition to other values, gave him the opportunity to experiment with materials which he himself deemed dangerous. Harry, now almost eleven years old, suggested that the number of interviews be reduced. He felt that he was old enough now and that he did not have as many difficulties. This did not mean that he liked the therapist any less, he quickly added.

When his brother returned from Japan sooner than expected, there was some exacerbation of Harry's difficulties, including the recurrence of diarrhea. Of his own accord, he asked to resume more frequent contacts with the therapist. Harry was helped to see that not only does he not have to be afraid of his brother but also he is an entity apart from his brother and it is not necessary for him to obliterate himself as a person in his own right. He was able to see that just as his brother had broken away from his mother and had gone off to Japan independently, he, Harry, had developed to the point where he, too, can do things on his own. Although he again hesitated about going to summer camp (largely because of his sibling rivalry), after the above interview he said: "Now that I got that all out of my system, I can't wait to get to camp."

Harry spent a very happy third summer at camp, where it was reported that he again was a fully accepted member of the group and evidenced a real sense of belonging. Termination of individual therapy was discussed with Harry shortly after his return from camp. He was told, however, that he could continue in the "club." He had been in a group for about nine months, with good attendance. Harry accepted this plan, but called occasionally on the caseworker for a friendly brief chat, gradually discontinuing contact altogether.

As indicated in the foregoing summary of the individual treatment, Harry was placed in an activity therapy group, to which he was rather resistive at first. He came to eight sessions out of twenty. When sessions were resumed in the fall, Harry was encouraged by his caseworker to try the group once more. He did so and continued to attend regularly.

In the beginning he sought out the group therapist exclusively, calling at his office and walking with him to the "club room." He was very compliant, assisted the therapist in cleaning up, and sought to please him in other ways. Harry stuttered a great deal and was much frightened by the other boys' aggressive acts, especially toward himself. At first he worked with arts and crafts, but after two months he indulged in playful activities with the others, seeking to hold their attention. Later he began to make passes at other boys, lunged at them, and occasionally lost his temper and displayed anger.

Still being insecure, Harry would ally himself with the stronger faction in the group. In one instance he entered into an alliance with the group's bully, but when several boys joined forces to resist this domination and bring him under control, Harry transferred his allegiance to them. At one point, however, when this strongest member was treated too roughly, Harry's guilts seemed to have been aroused, and he protected him. Harry became so incensed by the injustice that he was ready to fight single-handed the strongest boy of the cabal. Harry's action eradicated the factionalism in the group. Whenever dissension flared up, Harry acted as the mediator and neutralizer between the two opposing cliques. This he did partly because of his fear of his and the other boys' aggression. This could be considered a self-protective mechanism.

Harry came into his own when the threatening bully was finally removed from the group. He began to act out much more freely, frequently getting into fights. Though he was slow to anger and seldom lost control of his temper, his eyes would flash with hatred (and perhaps fear). When he became more secure and self-reliant, he would wrestle with all the boys in the group. He prided himself that he was the "second strongest in the club."

Harry was now able to mobilize enough of his latent aggressions to test himself against other members, having gained sufficient strength to express openly his repressed hostilities. At this period he grew much more vocal, freely stating his opinions and feelings about decisions made in the group. He no longer stuttered. Since he saw himself as the next-to-the-strongest boy in the group, he was compensated for his feelings of inadequacy at home. Here he was the successful sibling, in contrast to his inferior status in relation to his older brother.

Harry's successful self-assertion improved his self-image, since the group tolerated his aggressiveness and did not punish him for his boastfulness. Neither the boys nor the therapist forced him into the position of inferiority which had been the pattern of his life.

At this point Harry's solicitousness toward the therapist greatly decreased. He helped the latter with the chores only occasionally. He no longer helped clean up and keep the room in order, and being preoccupied with the other boys in the group he clung to the therapist much less.

The change in Harry that altered his behavior reflected itself in his bearing and his facial expression. He now withdrew into immobility only rarely. During play and conversation he actually looked animated and acted with spontaneous liveliness. Whereas when he came to the group his eyes looked as though he were attempting to withdraw from contact with the world, they were now expressive and luminous, and he seemed to communicate with the outside world.

In the spring of his first year in the group Harry began to initiate suggestions for outings and other activities that were accepted by the boys. He even attempted to ride a bicycle, but after three or four attempts, decided to abandon this effort. Apparently his coordination, because of "some organic disfunction," made this occupation impossible for him.

Harry told his caseworker that he thought "in some ways" he "was different from other children." This he did voluntarily and with impressive objectivity. There was no feeling of helplessness or evidence of inferiority. He accepted this as a fact and indicated that he was ready to deal with his inadequacy. The caseworker then told him of some of the positive contributions he had made both in the therapy group and at camp. She emphasized in that interview that he was able to get along with children and that they accepted and liked him.

At about this period Harry associated the group with his home. He brought his turtles for the boys to see. He again began to call for the group therapist on the day of the sessions. This fact was construed as a hint that it was time for individual treatment to be terminated because of his association with males. Individual interviews were reduced from weekly to bi-weekly visits. At one of these sessions a boy who knew the group therapist's wife said she was pretty. Harry, with the other boys, began to make remarks among themselves about a baby having been started. Harry walked over to the therapist and said: "I know where a baby comes from. My teacher told me. The mother eats and eats so much that part of it goes down into a separate pocket and the baby starts from that pocket." The therapist quietly asked: "Why don't men have babies?" Harry was nonplused. When the therapist went to the washroom, Harry followed him and asked: "Why don't men have babies?" Worker suggested he ask his caseworker about it. The next day, when Harry happened to meet the group therapist at the clinic, he said he was going to ask her. When Harry attended the next group session, he raised his arms and exclaimed several times: "Oh! what a horrible mess! Oh, what a horrible mess!"

Danny, one of the duller boys in the group, called on Harry about once a week to see if he were coming to the sessions. Occasionally Harry would call on Danny. A third, the strongest in the group, was later included in this friendship. When either one did not appear, Harry expressed concern, but he did not seem disturbed and would say that he would call them up to see whether they were coming to the club or not. By this time Harry had stopped working with materials and tools. At the earlier sessions Harry concentrated on work with materials, which isolated him from the others. His work with materials consisted largely of simple projects, such as hammering ashtrays. He had never made anything that required extensive planning or great exertion or skill. Then the focus of his interest was on the therapist, which later was transfered to the other boys, with whom he had developed free and easy relationships. By the end of the group year his mask-like expression and withdrawal had completely disappeared, but in camp it reappeared fleetingly when he was faced with a new situation, only to be replaced immediately by a normal animated expression. He had attended twenty-nine out of the possible thirty-two sessions that year. At the termination of the season's work the group therapist summarized Harry's progress as follows.

Harry's progress has been characterized by less attention-getting behavior, such as giggling in his peculiar sort of way or shouting when the lights were flicked off, and exaggerating his fears. Instead there appeared an increased self-assertion, which sometimes appeared as negativism. For example, when most of the group members were in opposition to the twins and were plotting against them, Harry let it be known in no uncertain terms that he no longer would share in such conspiracy and that henceforth he would be on the side of the twins. When Michael, one of the stronger boys, demurred, Harry reiterated decisively that he would not participate in such activities and stated that he would always be on the side of the twins, who were treated unfairly by the others.

Furthermore, Harry no longer feels the need to clean up the club room and is less submissive and ingratiating in his manner. He has maintained a telephone contact each week with Danny, but the two boys have engaged in friendly combat at a number of recent sessions. Harry is no longer frightened by Danny's verbiage and occasionally engages him in wrestling. He expresses his rebellion against Danny, to whom he has been submissive in the past, by yelling and shrieking at him, even though the latter is much taller and stronger. He has also asserted himself by a definite decision against returning to camp again. The year before, he said, the "stupid nurse sent me home for an appendicitis attack even before there was any danger." Harry stands up against the other boys when they attempt to dominate him, and he told the group therapist once that he is no longer frightened by "the filthy boys at school."

When Harry's older brother, Paul, had been in treatment at the clinic, his mother was interviewed occasionally by the caseworker in an effort to enlist her help. When Harry was referred for treatment, it was felt that his mother would require consistent guidance to work through some of her own difficulties. She was found to be an intelligent, alert woman, interested in cooperating with the clinic's treatment efforts. Her behavior during the interviews, however, was marked by extreme restlessness, moodiness, and anxiety. She often tore her handkerchiefs and shredded the blotter on the caseworker's desk. The interviews revealed that the feelings she harbored toward men were intensly negative, deep-rooted, and involved and required some resolution before her children could be helped.

Because of her negative relation with her father, she felt that both her husband and her sons had failed her. During the first months the mother scarcely mentioned Harry and concentrated on Paul, who had insisted on leaving home and joining the army. He was subsequently sent overseas to the Pacific with the armed forces. When the mother became increasingly aware of the fact that she displaced her feeling against her father on Paul and of the unrealistic nature of her expectations from her husband and her sons, she was enabled to cope more adequately with her father, who lived in her house. Her letters to Paul grew more understanding and supportive.

She now talked about men more freely and began to abreact in the interviews. Once, because of her fury against her father, she attacked the caseworker. The latter pointed out to Mrs. Peters what she was doing and told her that she was not her father. Mrs. Peters soon stopped displacing her feelings against her father onto other males in her environment and, instead, dealt directly with him. As Mrs. Peters discharged her intense pent-up feelings of hostility and guilt, the therapist was able to point out to her that neither she nor Mr. Peters nor the boys really caused her feelings.

She was now able to recognize that Harry had needs of his own beyond meeting her demands and expectations. As Mrs. Peters became more communicative and emotionally less confused, she was able to indicate to the therapist, sometimes by implication only, that in Paul, her first-born, she had seen a man who would have "redeemed" her and compensated for the ill-treatment she had received at the hands of men, namely, her father, her brother, and her husband. Having been disappointed in Paul, the birth of another male child seemed to have left her "cold," so that Harry became unimportant to her.

Between the birth of the two boys, which was ten years, a brother whom she had practically raised had died, and in a sense Harry was a substitute for this brother. She had accepted responsibility for the new-born baby, as she had done for her brother after her mother's untimely death. Unconsciously, however, she harbored the hope that Harry would satisfy the cravings and drives that she had expected her father, her brother, her husband, and her older son to gratify. However, he, too, had failed her. She saw that because of Harry's constitution he, too, would defeat her. As a self-protective mechanism, she divested herself of these expectations, resigned herself, and accepted him as a "responsibility which I must bear." This was similar to the responsibility imposed upon her by her mother's death and indirectly by her father, whom she unconsciously blamed.

The caseworker helped Mrs. Peters unravel this confusion of attitudes toward the various males. She was then able to accept Harry as an individual with needs of his own; as an independent person. When she recognized that her demands were unrealistic and unfair, she was able to derive real pleasure from some of the positive characteristics her sons and her husband really did possess. She must have conveyed this in her correspondence to Paul, for he once wrote her a touching letter full of understanding. He spoke of the better relationship they would have when he returned home. She brought this letter to the caseworker.

Her frustrations having been decreased through a more realistic understanding of her life's possibilities, her guilts also diminished, and she was now able to accept her status with greater equanimity and to give up her self-punishing and self-defeating mechanisms.

As a result of his strengthened ego, Harry was then able to verbalize his feelings to his mother. He once said to her: "When you look at me this way sometimes, I think you must hate me more than anyone you know." Mrs. Peters, instead of being resentful and punitive as she would have been in the past, told him calmly that there are times when, rightly or wrongly, she felt upset and when he came upon her at such moments, she unintentionally released her feelings upon him, but this did not mean that she did not love him. After this episode, Harry went out of the room, but returned a few minutes later to say that there was something he wanted to tell her. His mother encouraged him, and he said that many weeks earlier he had been playing Paul's gramaphone records and had broken some of them. Mrs. Peters asked why he had not told her about it before, and he said he was afraid of her reaction. She said she was sorry he had felt that way, but that at least she was glad he could tell her about it now. She explained that everybody had accidents and that she would help him replace the broken disks. Harry said he now felt much better, and when she went to tuck him into bed that night, he threw his arms around her neck and said that he had the "best mother and father in the world." This was the first time Harry had expressed such positive feelings about his parents which revealed his growing capacity for object relations.

In a sense Harry had contributed toward his mother's improvement. His changed attitude toward her, decreased fear of people, and his generally strengthened personality had made her feel more comfortable and more hopeful. Mrs. Peters had weekly sessions with the caseworker for a period of two years, being absent only occasionally.

After the case had been closed for more than a year so far as individual treatment was concerned, Harry called the caseworker on the telephone and expressed a desire to visit her and talk over some matters. Although he had never before traveled much, he was now able to go to another borough by himself, since the caseworker had in the interim moved to a different location. He was certain that with directions from his father he could manage the trip.

Harry arrived at the appointed time beaming, lacking his customary self-consciousness, and extended his hand in a warm and firm handshake. He had grown at least a head taller since last seen and had acquired a rather deep masculine voice. A slight stutter was noticeable.

Harry spoke spontaneously and freely about himself and family matters, announcing that his older brother had recently been married. He described the ceremony, the number of drinks he had had, the excitement of having so much company and stated that he is pleased to have the bedroom to himself again. Harry commented in passing that his own girl friend has been away for the summer, and when the caseworker suggested that he probably missed her, he explained that after all a fellow of his age does not really have "regular girl friends." He likes this particular girl, but knows he will like many more as he grows older. This seemed like a realistic appraisal of the difference between himself and his older brother, at the same time revealing some positive identification.

Harry narrated his plans to complete junior high school and to continue in a trade school with a major emphasis upon radio and television. In answer to the caseworker's question, he stated that this was the consensus of himself, his parents, and his teachers and that he knew he would do better at this than in academic subjects. He grinned and said that his present junior high school proved to be "not half as bad" as he had feared, that the colored fellows are still around, but they do not bother him, and added: "I still have some problems, but they are cut in half."

Harry expressed interest in the caseworker and her work, as well as in their common interest, music. In the following order, he asked: "Is there an 'automat' around here? Do they serve egg salad sandwiches?" When informed affirmatively, Harry said: "Then will you come to lunch with me?" The caseworker and Harry went to lunch, and though the restaurant was extremely noisy and crowded, Harry managed to get the food for both of them with proper decorum. He wished to extend his visit for a longer period, but when informed that the caseworker needed to return to work, he accepted her excuses with appreciative understanding. He politely walked back to the office with her and departed after a friendly leave-taking.

A year and a half after the case was closed, when Harry was about thirteen-and-a-half years old, a follow-up study was made which included a psychological examination and a Rorshach test. The psychologist found again diffuse organicity of an irreversible nature. Harry's intelligence, however, remained intact, and he was holding his own in this regard. The Rorshach test also demonstrated that nearly all the earlier anxieties and fears have disappeared and that he adjusted well to reality. He appeared much happier and more integrated as a person. His social adjustment was still good. He continued to have friends in the neighborhood, and he was free in his relationships with the boys on the street and in school. The earlier anxiety concerning school, Negroes, and policemen had disappeared. Harry's parents reported that in every respect his behavior was like that of any ordinary boy. In the opinion of the psychologist and the follow-up caseworker Harry is now a well-adjusted individual within the limits of his organic and constitutional limitations.

Index

Bei Fragen zur Produktsicherheit wenden Sie sich bitte an:
If you have any questions regarding product safety,
please contact:

Walter de Gruyter GmbH
Genthiner Straße 13
10785 Berlin
productsafety@degruyterbrill.com